Aircraft

Aircraft

Contents

Introduction

The dream of flying

Man's dream of flying exists in the myths and legends of every culture. Our ancestors in earliest times undoubtedly gazed longingly at the birds, envying them their freedom and their ability to move through the third dimension – and wishing they could float through the air with the same lightness. Remaining resolutely down to earth themselves, our ancestors were very well aware that the ability to fly was something particularly special.

The flying gods

It is little wonder that early humans gave their gods and heroes the ability to break free from the bonds of earth and move freely through the air. In 3000 BCE Etana, the Babylonian god of war, was depicted in flight in numerous artworks. In the pantheon of ancient Egypt the god Isis, Horus, the god of the sky, and Re, the sun god, could all fly. Hermes, the Greek messenger of the gods, was winged – as too was Nike, the goddess of victory. The ancient Indians depicted beings with feathered wings gazing across the Trans-Himalaya into Shiva's kingdom. The Indians had a seagull made of wood that had allegedly been used by human to fly. In 5000 BCE a ruling Chinese dynasty had a heavenly chariot in its possession. The Kalevala, the Finnish national epic, tells of the smith Ilmarinen, who built an iron eagle; and Weyland, the smith in the German fable, was captured but managed to fly away using an iron cloak he had crafted himself. Loki, the cunning Norse god, borrowed a feather cloak from the goddess Freya to retrieve the hammer that was stolen from Thor and hidden in the giants' mountain.

A myth becomes reality

From the Renaissance to modern times Daedalus and Icarus have often been used as motifs in the visual arts. Icarus ignored his father's warnings not to fly too close to the sun, and as a result its heat caused the wax used to secure the feathers to his wings to melt. Icarus fell to the earth (see illustration left). What was once intended as a parable for the punishment of disobedience is also often used today as an example that illustrates the association between air travel and flight safety.

The idea of flying remained in the world of myths and legends until the Renaissance. Leonardo da Vinci, undoubtedly the greatest artist, architect, technician and natural scientist of all time, carried out the first serious scientific investigations into the possibility of humans flying. His physical research and observations of birds in flight resulted in numerous designs for beating wings, helicopter calculations and construction of parachutes. However, despite the genius of his approaches, practical success was to elude him. It was still not known that humans' lack of muscular strength and the design of the cardiovascular system would make it impossible for them ever to achieve 'flapping' flight.

But the search for ways to conquer air space now spread all over Europe. In 1627 the bibliothecary Hermann Flayder of Tübingen published the first book on the subject of aviation. It appeared that the time had finally come for one of man's oldest dreams to come true. Invariably the first attempts resulted in failure – but still, we were gradually coming closer to solving the problem.

Lighter than air

The Montgolfier brothers won the competition for thoughts and ideas. Both had studied mathematics and physics. Their observations of scraps of paper rising up from their fireplace became their equivalent of Newton's apple – and led to further investigations into this phenomenon. They began to experiment with paper bags filled with hot air.

In the summer of 1783 one of their bags rose to a height of more than 1000 m. They then suspended animals under a hot-air balloon.

Finally, on 11 November 1783, their dream came true. In front of a vast crowd of people, the Director of the Pilâtre de Rozier Museum of Paris and the Marquis d'Arlandes ascended into the air in a captive balloon and remained there for five minutes before landing, without complication, to tumultuous applause from the enthusiastic crowd. The 'lighter-than-air' aircraft had been invented.

During their experiments the Montgolfier brothers realised that it was heated air that gave their balloon the required lift (see illustration left) and not, as they had earlier assumed, an unknown gas that was lighter than air. Consequently they developed a heating grid that, once in operation, considerably extended the duration of the balloon's flight.

There now followed a veritable explosion of developments. The physicist Jacques Charles was the first to fill the balloon with hydrogen gas, which is lighter than the ambient air and so caused the balloon to rise. Shortly after the Montgolfiers' first flight, Jacques Charles and two others became the first to fly for longer than two hours, covering a distance of 27 miles. In 1785 the Frenchman Jean-Pierre Blanchard and American Dr John Jeffries became the first people to cross the English Channel in a hot-air balloon.

As yet, though, the problem of guided flight remained unsolved. The Italian Count Zambeccari had already realised that a balloon could be controlled only if it had a drive that would enable the balloon to fly into the wind. The balloons soon came into practical use.

There has been something of a renaissance in hot-air flight in recent years. The production of hot air is today somewhat more user friendly than in the Montgolfiers' day.

Napoleon used them to follow the movements of his opponents' troops. However all attempts to drop bombs from balloons failed. During the German siege of Paris in 1870–1871, 67 balloons were used to break the blockades and transport both the mail and the injured. But the limitations of balloon flight soon became obvious.

Heavier than air

They were overcome by the German engineer and aviation pioneer Otto Lilienthal. Like Leonardo da Vinci he and his brother watched storks to observe birds in flight. He published his findings in his book *Birdflight as the Basis of Aviation*. One of the most important was that the movement of air along the top of a bird's wing created drag. Now we now that the upward movement of a wing is produced by around two-thirds drag along the top and one-third pressure on the underside.

From 1890 Lilienthal carried out numerous attempts with his flying machines, starting with a modest range of 5 m and ending with a height of 20 m and distances of 500 m. The craft were steered simply by the keen experimenter shifting his weight.

On 9 August 1896 he crashed while trying out new control devices, and died a day later in hospital. His theoretical and practical findings played an important role in the development of aviation.

In America the brothers Wilbur and Orville Wright studied Lilienthal's findings and practical experience. They realised that the main problems were solving stability and control issues, and the search for a strong yet light engine. They achieved both. On 17 December 1903 the first 'heavier-than-air' aircraft took off under its own power. The first flight lasted 12 seconds and covered a distance of 53 m. This was the dawning of a new age. The aircraft was on its way to victory.

Now progress really speeded up. Record followed record. There was a never-ending flow of new creations by talented and successful designers. Names of designers and pilots such as Santos-Dumont, Farman, Grade, Blériot, Etrich, Nieuport, Breguet and many others were soon well known.

Ignaz Etrich's Dove (our picture shows a replica) was one of the most famous aircraft from the pioneering days of aviation; a few were still used at the outbreak of WWI for reconnaissance purposes.

In 2003 100 years of motorised flight were celebrated with a replica of the first-ever flying machine by the Wright brothers.

In 1909 Blériot crossed the English Channel. There was an impressive increase in flight performances. In 1913 the course record was 1291 miles, the greatest height achieved was 6120 m, and the longest flying time was 13 hours 22 minutes. The very brave went along as passengers. The first air-mail services were started and developments in passenger aviation commenced.

The heyday of the airship

Let us not, however, lose sight of 'lighter-than-air' aviation. Here, too, there had been impressive achievements. At last it was possible to motorise the balloon, which meant it could be steered. Thus began the development of the fixed airship. The most famous constructor of fixed airships and dirigibles was Count Zeppelin. By 1914 there had been some 2000 airship flights carrying an impressive 37,000 passengers.

Because of their performance the Zeppelins were also of interest to the military – they meant that useful payloads could be transported long distances. It was gas that kept them airborne: hydrogen – easily flammable not only in the event of damage, but also under enemy fire.

World War I

At this time the outbreak of WWI created a break in the development of aviation. Military personnel in major countries closely followed its progress. The General Staff saw the airship and aircraft as important instruments of war which, as well as being useful for reconnaissance purposes, could also be used for bomb attacks.

The 'Hindenburg' airship LZ 129 offered its passengers a high level of comfort in salon-like public and dining rooms and on the promenade deck (see illustration top right). The fact that it was fuelled by hydrogen was eventually to be the cause of its destruction in an accident at Lakehurst in 1937, when it burnt out completely. The remaining German Zeppelins were then gradually scrapped.

In August 1914 the main warring countries had the following stocks:

	Aircraft	Airships
Germany	232	8
Austria-Hungary	48	1
France	165	10
Great Britain	63	–
Russia	263	4

Initially aircraft were used only for reconnaissance and courier tasks. From October 1914 artillery was fired from inside the aircraft. The observers in two-seater aircraft were given lightweight machine guns, but to little effect.

The invention of a synchroniser that made it possible to fire through a revolving propeller without damaging it and so fit the ammunition parallel to the aircraft's longitudinal axis was a tremendous leap forward in airborne fighting.

The tactics of aircraft use soon developed. Aircraft technology kept pace with the increase in requirements. The production figures for aircraft in the main warring countries increased dramatically.

However the development in aerial warfare not only improved quality, but also led to various specialisations among the aviators. Whereas fighter pilots were originally used only to protect scouts against enemy aircraft, tactical and operational thinking altered dramatically from 1916. The aim then was to disable the actions of all enemy aircraft types. Thus began the battle for superiority and supremacy in the skies.

The following summarises the development of aviators after WWI:

- Organisation, technology and operations changed completely during the course of the war, and matched the increased technical abilities of the aircraft;

- Strong operational flying associations – some already independent structural elements of the armed forces – were created;

- Reconnaissance, fighter, bomber and combat aviators had developed. The foundations for almost every single type of modern aircraft had been laid.

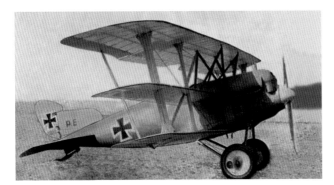

AEG C.VIII was constructed first as a biplane and then as a triplane at the beginning of WWI (illustration above).

World War II

After WWI the speed of development in military aviation slowed down again. A large number of prototypes from WWI remained in the inventory of many air forces. Germany was banned from building fighter aircraft and maintaining its own air force by the Treaty of Versailles. The wave of innovations did not resume until the mid-1930s.

New fighter aircraft with speeds of up to 370–435 mph were included in the armoury, and medium and heavy bombers were developed. WWII cast its shadow. When it broke out in 1939, the air forces played an extremely important role in warfare. The bomb war became the main strategic task. Germany had no strategic bomber potential. The leaders of its air force believed it would be possible to achieve all the aims of a Blitzkrieg with fast tactical blows. Many English towns and cities fell victim to the bombing terror in the aerial battle over England. But the longer the war dragged on, the stronger were the effects of the Allies' material superiority. Vast fleets of bombers were created to attack Germany and Germany's wartime economy was gradually paralysed. The bomb attacks were not just aimed at industry. The strategic aerial warfare became a bombing nightmare against the civilian population. The head of British Bomber Command, Air Marshal 'Bomber' Harris, appeared to share the theory of Italy's General Douhet, explained in his book *Air Supremacy*, which was published in 1921. The core idea was this: 'defence on land and at sea – mass attack from the air'.

This claim became Harris's creed, and Churchill gave him the green light for it. While the Americans attacked by day, the British did so

The Junkers Ju 52 remains a legend to this day, and is a symbol of passenger aviation in the 1930s.

The Supermarine Spitfire was one of the best-known and most-built fighter aircraft of WWII.

the 1990s and two wars with Iraq again showed the tremendous fighting potential of various air forces. It is a fact that these wars could not have been planned – or carried out in this form – without aerial superiority and supremacy.

Civil aviation

Civil aviation came into being shortly after the end of WWI. The research and production capacities that had been tied up with the war were now free, and could be used to benefit civilians. First of

On 14 October 1947 Charles Yeager broke the sound barrier for the first time in the Bell X-1, a single-jet experimental aircraft that in 1949 set the world altitude record of 22,250 m.

by night. By the end of 1944 almost all of Germany's major cities had been destroyed. Dresden did not burn until 13 February 1945, and to this day it is not known how many perished there. There was no longer any strategic requirement for the destruction of this city and Churchill distanced himself from Harris after the obliteration of Dresden.

The devastating end to the bomb war in WWII was the dropping of atomic bombs on Hiroshima and Nagasaki. The destructive forces of the use of bombs reached an unimaginable dimension.

The post-war period

After WWII the world froze in two blocks. This was the beginning of the Cold War. The unbridled competition in armaments was matched by an enormous increase in the air forces' combat abilities. Supersonic fighter and bomber aircraft joined the armouries. Strategic missiles could be sent to any corner of the earth with incredible precision. Atomic warheads – both on bombs and on missiles – with the explosive equivalent of mega-tons of TNT reached levels of destruction that went far beyond anything we had ever envisaged before.

But modern warfare was far from simply being a theoretical possibility. From the Korean War to Arab-Israeli conflicts and to the Vietnam War, the full range of missions by various air forces was experienced in practice – with the exception of nuclear weapons. The vicious circle of the competition for armaments was not broken until the dissolution of the military alliance of the Warsaw Agreement and the end of the Soviet Union. But the Balkan conflict of

all military aircraft were converted for civilian use. This was soon followed by the first passenger aircraft, with room for six to eight passengers and the pilot. The Junkers F 13 is a prime example. Its maiden flight was in 1919, and it was the first aircraft ever to have been designed and built exclusively for passengers. Low-wing aircraft, cantilevered wing unit, all-metal construction and a closed cabin were combined for the first time ever in this aircraft, which – in a sense the first modern aircraft – also offered its passengers a certain level of comfort.

In total there were more than 60 versions of the F 13 – 350 of them built between 1919 and 1930. The aircraft flew to many European countries, and it was exported to North and South America, Asia and Africa.

New types of passenger aircraft were created in every country that was involved in aviation. The first airlines were set up. The mid-1920s saw the creation of the first major airlines; Deutsche Luft Hansa, founded in 1926, is now Lufthansa. The first large passenger aircraft appeared at the end of the 1920s. The Junkers G 38 held 42 passengers, and flew to London, Amsterdam, Copenhagen, Malmö, Venice, Rome and Stockholm. With regard to capacity, these aircraft – like the gigantic passenger airship Do X – were years ahead of requirement, which is why only two or three were ever built.

The standard aircraft of the 1930s was the Ju 52, of which more than 5000 were constructed. It was used by 30 airlines in 25 countries on every continent. Several Ju 52 were still in use in 1979 and Deutsche Lufthansa operates a Ju 52 as a traditional aircraft today (illustration p. 12), using it in summer for round trips from various German airports..

Transatlantic flights

There was one problem that simply had to be solved if international air travel was to progress: crossing the oceans. A lurid film was even dedicated to this problem: *F.P.1 antwortet nicht (F.P.1 Doesn't Answer)* is about the construction of a floating aircraft platform in the middle of the Atlantic, which was intended for refuelling aircraft on the transatlantic route. Pure science fiction – but the reality soon made even these fantastic imaginings look old.

First the leap across the ocean was made from the north Atlantic and south Atlantic routes. In June 1919 the British aviators Alcock and Brown flew non-stop across the Atlantic from west to east. However the first solo flight was not until 20 May 1927, when the 25-year-old Charles Lindbergh took off in New York and landed 33 hours 30 minutes later, to the indescribable jubilation of vast crowds at Le Bourget.

In April of the following year German aviators Hermann Köhl and Günther Freiherr von Hünefeld crossed the Atlantic in the opposite direction. This was the beginning. In order to make the transatlantic lines suitable for passengers, the next step was to develop navigation and on-board instruments to make flying in bad weather conditions as safe as possible, and create the necessary logistics.

International air transport developed quickly after WWII. Civil aviation benefited greatly from the experience acquired in the construction of military aircraft, especially bombers. Scheduled services

The Lockheed Super Constellation flew the Atlantic for various airlines, including Deutsche Lufthansa, between 1956 and 1966.

The Airbus A380 is currently the world's biggest passenger aircraft. It is planned to be in use for several decades.

with high-performance aircraft were launched between America and Europe.

The first aircraft with jet engines increased the possibilities of civil aviation. The British Comet 4B, Russian Tu-104, American Boeing 707 and French Caravelle introduced the age of the jetliner.

Today Jules Verne's literary journey around the world in 80 days can be completed in a tiny fraction of that time, and we are about to see the arrival of the scheduled service on the world's biggest passenger aircraft, the A380.supremacy.

Perspectives in international air travel

So what problems still face international air travel today, and what lines of development are already apparent?

With regard to military aircraft, the tendency is again moving away from universal multi-purpose aircraft and towards specialisations. The all-rounder that had to be able to alter its task during a mission if at all possible did so at the cost of its combat abilities, since it is technically impossible to solve all problems equally well.

The high level of manoeuvrability of the fighter aircraft prevents it from carrying as much weaponry as a fighter bomber should. One possible solution is to have as many different modifications as possible on a single platform.

And yet much of what is technically possible is never successfully turned into reality, although modified versions of some types may appear decades later. Supersonic flight, the standard in military aviation, has failed in civil aviation for economic and environmental reasons. Today Russian developers have the Tu-444, a supersonic business aircraft, on their drawing boards, and renowned market institutes foresee sales of 400 to 700. The only condition is that the costs must not be more than 20 per cent higher than those of other aircraft.

With the exception of the Me 163, rocket aircraft have been used only as experimental aircraft in aviation history. Extreme flight performances in flight heights and speeds were achieved with them. Nor will rocket power play a part in serial aircraft in the future.

There have also been experiments with atomic-powered aircraft. There were projects in the Soviet Union, USA and Great Britain early in the 1950s. It is believed that there have been trials with reactor engines in the Soviet Union and USA. The hopes that were linked to these projects were dashed. Nor are there plans to take up the idea of building atomic-powered aircraft again in the foreseeable future. This is not only for economic reasons, but also because of environmental, safety and political issues.

One alternative to kerosene could be hydrogen technology. There have been experiments in the USA and Soviet Union, and work on this project has undoubtedly continued in Russia.

So is the battle for market shares going to produce ever-bigger and ever-faster aircraft? It is not expected that there will be a bigger aircraft than the A380 for some time to come. Various empirical facts support statements about possible further development.

Aircraft that are currently under trial and about to be type approved will be in operational use for the next 30 to 40 years. Some examples are these: the Boeing 747 has so far been in service for 37 years, the F-4 Phantom for 48, and the F-8 Crusader and MiG-21 for an impressive 51 years. The B-52 has also been flying for a very long time, and there have been several series constructions of modernised versions of the C-130 transporter. Of course individual aircraft do not reach these impressive ages, but the type certainly does. Over the course of long periods of operation, there are constant modernisations and upgrades of features, and modifications to the jets and cell. And often older versions of a particular type are upgraded to the latest standards.

There are also favourable development perspectives for regional aircraft. In Africa, Asia and America there are still many areas that are not served by air. There regional traffic has a completely difference meaning from that in the middle of Europe, for instance with regard to the expansion of the countries such as Brazil. It is no wonder that impulses for aircraft construction and aviation development should come from these so-called threshold countries.

However the growth in air travel also increases the risks that are inherent to a greater traffic density. Although flying is widely known to be the safest way to travel, even one accident is one too many. International air transport founded the International Civil Aviation Organization (ICAO) in 1944, and it is becoming ever more important.

Thanks to its administrative structure, it is also able to control the safety of aircraft flows and the density in take-off and landing areas at major airports.

The North American X-15 was used to research high-speed aircraft (3 October 1967: 4545 mph) at great heights (22 August 1963: 107,960 m). An additional jet control made it easier to steer the aircraft at great heights.

In 1987 the unmotorised muscle-powered aircraft Daedalus 88 (built in 1987), which was developed and built by professors and students at the Massachusetts Institute of Technology (MIT), covered a distance of 124 miles from the air force base of Herakleion on Crete to the island of Santorini in 3 hours 54 minutes, setting new records for distance and flight duration for muscle-powered aircraft.

About choices and organisation of the book

The more than 500 aircraft are divided into seven chapters. Every classification has its advantages and disadvantages. Although clarity is an advantage, the disadvantage is that it may be at the cost of possible associations. It is not always easy to define something as belonging to one chapter or another, and classification is rarely straightforward. The individual aircraft families (of a manufacturer, builder or construction office) are shown in association provided the basic allocation to the chapters permits that. Within the chapters the aircraft are classified individually by manufacturer and constructor. Several types by the same manufacturer appear in order of their maiden flight, the time they were first trialled or the year of construction. This was made more difficult in some instances by companies being sold or merging, or being renamed for various reasons. In these cases if the type name is used as a brand name (such as Beechcraft, Gulfstream or Learjet) then the established brand name will be given priority over the new manufacturer's name.

Frequently used abbreviations:

kN	kilo Newton
kp	kilopond
kW	kilowatt
MG	machine gun
MK	automatic cannon
HP	horsepower
RAF	Royal Air Force
RLM	Reichsluftfahrtministerium (Reich Air Ministry)
STOL	Short Take-off and Landing
STOVL	Short Take-off and Vertical Landing
USAAC	US Army Air Corps
USAAF	US Army Air Force
USAF	US Air Force
VSTOL	Vertical Short Take-off and Landing
VTOL	Vertical Take-off and Landing
WHP	wave hp

Passenger and freight aircraft

Passenger and freight aircraft

This chapter is about aircraft that have been adapted for use in the civilian transportation of passengers, freight and loads, or for special tasks (such as aerial photography, patrol services or agricultural aviation), and operate from land. Not all of the aircraft are commercial aircraft as such. The chapter also includes transport aircraft if they belong to a specific 'family'. There are also business and multi-role aircraft from the extensive division of general aviation if they are deemed to represent major segments of civil aviation, based on the number of aircraft and flight movements. As is so often the case, it is not always possible to draw clear divisions. Many types are used for scheduled services by major airlines as well as privately in general aviation; some freight and transport aircraft are derived from commercial aircraft, just as many aircraft that were originally used for civilian aviation have been converted for military operations and vice versa. Wherever possible – and this was determined by the selection – development lines and aircraft 'families' have been left together, even though occasionally this may have gone against a precise form of systemisation.

152 (Dresden 152)

Four-jet shoulder-wing passenger aircraft (maiden flight of the first prototype 4.12.1958). The 152 (also called the BB-152 for the designers Baade/Bonin, or Dresden 152) was the first German jet-powered passenger aircraft; the DEFA even made a film of its creation: *Menschen mit Flügeln (People with Wings)*. The design was based on a military construction developed by former Junkers staff under the management of Brunolf Baade in the Soviet Union. Three prototypes were built in Dresden, starting in 1958. However, following the crash of the first prototype (4.3.1959), the project was repeatedly delayed. The second prototype (152/II V4) – with numerous changes to the nose, nacelles and undercarriage – was tested in the air (maiden flight 26.8.1960), and the third one (152/II V5) only on the ground. Series production commenced in 1961, but was stopped later the same year without any further operational aircraft being delivered. Although it had initially indicated its interest in buying this aircraft, the Soviet Union later withdrew; there were no orders from other countries or airlines either.

Type: 152/II V4
Country of origin: GDR
Use: passenger aircraft
Wingspan: 27.00 m
Length: 31.42 m
Powered by: 4 Pirna 014, each providing 31 kN (3150 kp) thrust
Max. take-off weight: 46,500 kg
Cruising speed: 500 mph
Range: max. 1550 miles
Ceiling: 10,700 m
Passengers: 58–72

AASI Jetcruzer 450/500 P

Single-engine business aircraft (maiden flight 11.1.1989). The most striking features are the 'canard' design, which has no conventional tail unit, and the pusher propeller at the rear. The FAA classified the 450 as the first spin-resistant aircraft. Although the 450 did not go into series production, it served as the prototype for the 500 P, which has a pressurised cabin (maiden flight 22.8.1997).

Type: AASI Jetcruzer 500 P
Country of origin: USA
Use: business aircraft
Wingspan: 12.86 m (fore flap: 5.77 m)
Length: 9.20 m
Powered by: 1 Pratt & Whitney Canada PT6A 66A turboprop, 1200 kW (1572 hp)
Max. take-off weight: 2495 kg
Maximum speed: 370 mph
Range: 1865 miles
Ceiling: 9140 m
Passengers: 5 + 1 pilot

Adam A500

Twin-engine business aircraft (maiden flight 11.7.2002); the push–pull configuration of two engines gives it flying characteristics that are similar to those of a single-engine aircraft. The carbon wings are connected via two wing supports to the lateral rudder and tail unit. Built largely of graphite-composite materials.

Type: Adam A500
Country of origin: USA
Use: business aircraft
Wingspan: 13.41 m
Length: 11.15 m
Powered by: 2 Teledyne Continental TSIO-550 E, each 255 kW (346 hp)
Max. take-off weight: 4420 kg
Cruising speed: 265 mph
Range: 1815 miles
Ceiling: 7620 m
Passengers: 4 + 2 pilots

Aero Ae270

Single-engine passenger and freight aircraft (maiden flight 25.7.2000) with a pressurised cabin and additional cargo hold. The Executive Transport version accommodates five passengers in the 'club' arrangement. The Aero Ae270 is also available in a combined freight/passenger version, as an ambulance aircraft and with floats.

Type: Aero Ae270 Ibis
Country of origin: Czechoslovakia
Use: multi-role aircraft
Wingspan: 13.8 m
Length: 12.24 m
Powered by: 1 Pratt & Whitney Canada PT6A-42A engine, 634 kW (860 hp)
Max. take-off weight: 3300 kg
Cruising speed: 205 mph
Range: 1365 miles
Ceiling: 9300 m
Passengers: 5–8 + 2 pilots

Aerospatiale/BAe Concorde

Four-jet shoulder-wing long-haul supersonic passenger aircraft, designed and constructed to travel at twice the speed of sound (maiden flight prototype 001 on 2.3.1969). The aircraft was a joint production between the French and British aviation industries, and started scheduled operations in 1976. The aircraft is made largely of aluminium with a heat-resistant nickel alloy, stainless steel and titanium. The 'nose' can be raised and lowered for take-off and landing. Concorde has no elevator on the rear, and the rudder and combined pitch and yaw rudders are on the trailing edges of the wings. The transatlantic flying time was 3 to 3½ hours, which – when flying west – meant that Concorde landed before she took off in Europe. However, Concorde failed to be a financial success. Construction was halted in 1979 after just 20 aircraft. When a Concorde crashed on take-off in Paris (25.7.2000), a number of safety defects on the landing gear and fuel tanks had to be resolved. Supersonic flying then became even less economical. The last Air France Concorde flew on 24 June 2003, while the era of the British Airways Concorde ended on 24 October 2003.

Type: Concorde
Country of origin: France, Great Britain
Use: supersonic passenger aircraft
Wingspan: 25.56 m
Length: 62.74 m
Powered by: 4 Rolls-Royce Olympus 593-Mk-610 turbojets with afterburner, each producing 189.4 kN (19,312 kp) thrust
Max. take-off weight: 185,000 kg
Cruising speed: max. 1360 mph
Range: 4140 miles
Ceiling: 19,000 m
Passengers: 100–125

Aerospatiale ATR 72

Twin-engine high-wing short-haul passenger aircraft, based on the ATR 42, although the construction was based on the extended version (4.5 m longer). The ATR 72-200 (1989) was followed by the ATR 72-210 (1992) with more powerful engines, and the longer-range ATR 72-500 (1997) with sound insulation and a modernised cabin interior. The ATR 72 does not have an APU (auxiliary power unit); instead it has a propeller brake (referred to as 'hotel mode') that stops the propeller on the no. 2 (right-hand) engine, allowing the turbine to continue running and provide power and air to the aircraft.

Type: Aerospatiale ATR 72-200
Country of origin: France, Italy
Use: passenger aircraft
Wingspan: 27.05 m
Length: 27.17 m
Powered by: 2 Pratt & Whitney Canada PW124, each 1610 kW (2190 hp)
Max. take-off weight: 22,500 kg
Cruising speed: 315 mph
Range: 870 miles
Ceiling: 8000 m
Passengers: 66–72

Airbus A300

Twin-jet wide-body mid- to long-haul passenger aircraft (maiden flight of the A300 B1 in 1972). With it, Airbus Industrie gave new impulse to the market for wide-body aircraft, which in 1970 was dominated by Boeing. Design work began in 1965 as an Anglo-French joint project, which the Federal Republic of Germany joined with the agreement of 26 September 1967. However, since 1984 only the modernised A300-600 and A300-600R (long range) have been built. There is also a freight version, the A300-600F.

Type: Airbus A300-600R
Country of origin: EU
Use: passenger aircraft
Wingspan: 44.48 m
Length: 54.08 m
Powered by: 2 turbofans, each 249 kN to 273.6 kN (25,390 kp to 27,900 kp)
Max. take-off weight: 165,000 kg (with PW4156 jet engines)
Cruising speed: 540 mph
Range: 4789 miles (with 267 passengers)
Ceiling: 12,200 m
Passengers: 247–375

Airbus A310

Twin-jet passenger aircraft, shortened version of the Airbus A300 (maiden flight 3.4.1982). The fully digitalised cockpit and winglets on the wings were new. The first version was the A310-200 for medium and long haul. The long-haul version A310-300 (additional tank in the tail unit) first came onto the market in 1985.

Type: Airbus A310-200
Country of origin: EU
Use: passenger aircraft
Wingspan: 43.91 m
Length: 46.65 m
Powered by: 2 Pratt & Whitney PW4000 or General Electric CF6-80C2, each producing 222.3 kN (22,675 kp) thrust
Max. take-off weight: 142,000 kg
Cruising speed: 535 mph
Range: 4600 miles
Ceiling: 12,500 m
Passengers: 218–262

Airbus A320

Twin-jet short- and medium-haul passenger aircraft (maiden flight 1987), the foundation of the entire A320 family. The A320 was the first aircraft after Concorde to be controlled by fly-by-wire rather than mechanically using conventional yokes. The improved A-320-200 carries more fuel and has more powerful engines.

Type: Airbus A320-200
Country of origin: EU
Use: passenger aircraft
Wingspan: 33.91 m
Length: 37.57 m
Powered by: 2 General Electric/SNECMA CFM56-5 or IAE V2500 turbofans, each producing 110 kN (11,216 kp) thrust
Max. take-off weight: 73,500–77,000 kg
Cruising speed: 525 mph
Range: 4600 miles
Ceiling: 12,500 m
Passengers: 153–179

Airbus A321

Twin-jet short- and medium-haul passenger aircraft (maiden flight March 1993). The A321 is basically a stretched version of the A320. The wings, landing gear and supporting parts on the cell had to be stronger than on the first design. The development of the A321-200 began in 1995; its maiden flight was on 12 December 1996.

Type: Airbus A321-200
Country of origin: EU
Use: passenger aircraft
Wingspan: 34.10 m
Length: 44.50 m
Powered by: 2 General Electric/SNECMA CFM56-5B1 or IAE V2500-A5 turbofans, each producing 133 kN (13,561 kp) thrust
Max. take-off weight: 89,000 kg
Cruising speed: max. 560 mph
Range: 3420 miles
Ceiling: 12,500 m
Passengers: 188–220

Airbus A319

Twin-jet short- to medium-haul passenger aircraft (maiden flight 25.8.1995). The A319 is shorter than the first design. Operators can choose from several options for the take-off weight, which accordingly determines the range.

Type: Airbus A319
Country of origin: EU
Use: passenger aircraft
Wingspan: 33.91 m
Length: 32.84 m
Powered by: 2 CFMI CFM56-5A or IAE V2527-A5 turbofans, each producing 99.7 kN (10,166 kp) thrust

Max. take-off weight: 56,000–75,000 kg
Cruising speed: 520 mph
Range: 2115–4350 miles
Ceiling: 11,280 m
Passengers: 124–156

Airbus A318

Twin-jet passenger aircraft (maiden flight 15.1.2002). This version is again shorter than the A319. The 'Baby Bus' is currently used mainly on short-haul routes. The operators have several choices of take-off weight. At the end of 2005, Airbus Industrie presented the modified A318 Elite of the Airbus Corporate Jetliner family.

Type: Airbus A318
Country of origin: EU
Use: passenger aircraft
Wingspan: 34.10 m
Length: 31.44 m
Powered by: 2 General Electric/SNECMA CFM56 or P & W PW6000 turbofans, each producing 98 kN (9996 kp) thrust
Max. take-off weight: 59,000–68,000 kg
Cruising speed: 535 mph
Range: max. 2300 miles
Ceiling: 12,500 m
Passengers: 107–117

Airbus Corporate Jetliner (ACJ)

Twin-jet long-haul business aircraft based on the A319. The ACJ is much used by major international companies, but also extremely popular with many governments as a VIP aircraft. In November 2005, Airbus announced the A318 Elite as a smaller ACJ and the A320 as a larger one.

Type: Airbus A319ACJ
Country of origin: EU
Use: business aircraft
Wingspan: 33.91 m
Length: 32.84 m
Powered by: 2 IAE V2527-A5, each providing 99.7 kN (10,166 kp) thrust
Max. take-off weight: 75,500 kg
Cruising speed: 520 mph
Range: 5175 miles
Ceiling: 11,280 m
Passengers: 124–156

Airbus A330

Twin-jet long-haul passenger aircraft (maiden flight of A330-200 on 1.11.1992, A330-300 on 13.8.1997). The A330 was developed together with the A340. The starting point was the body of the A300, which was extended. The A330-200 (long haul) and A330-300 have different body lengths (and passenger capacities).

Type: Airbus A330-300
Country of origin: EU
Use: passenger aircraft
Wingspan: 60.30 m
Length: 63.60 m
Powered by: 2 CF6-80E1 or PW4000 or RR Trent 700 turbofans, each producing 303–320 kN (30,900–32,630 kp) thrust
Max. take-off weight: 217,000 kg
Cruising speed: 560 mph
Range: 6525 miles
Ceiling: 12,500 m
Passengers: 295–335

Airbus A340

Four-jet long-haul passenger aircraft (maiden flight of A340-300 on 25.10.1991). One of the main differences between this and the A330 is that the wings have been reinforced around the engines. The A340-200 (long haul; maiden flight 1.4.1992) and A340-300 have different body lengths. The A340-500 (maiden flight 11.1.2002) and A340-600 (maiden flight 23.3.2001) again have a longer body and greater wingspan, and can carry up to 440 passengers.

Type: Airbus A340-200
Country of origin: EU
Use: passenger aircraft
Wingspan: 60.30 m
Length: 59.39 m
Powered by: 4 CFM56-5C4 turbofans, each producing 140 kN (14,275 kp) thrust
Max. take-off weight: 257,000 kg
Cruising speed: 545 mph
Range: 9195 miles
Ceiling: 12,500 m
Passengers: 239–375

Airbus A350

Twin-jet wide-body long-haul passenger aircraft (project). Originally planned simply as a further development of the A330-200, the aircraft was subsequently virtually reconstructed. The aerodynamics of the body are to be improved and made of new aluminium–lithium alloys. The wings – this is an Airbus 'first' – will be made of carbon-fibre composites.

Type: Airbus A350-800
Country of origin: EU
Use: passenger aircraft (project)
Wingspan: 61.10 m
Length: 58.80 m
Powered by: 2 General Electric GEnx 1A or Rolls-Royce Trent 1711 turbofans, each producing 280–334 kN (28,550–34,057 kp) thrust
Max. take-off weight: 245,000 kg
Cruising speed: 610 mph
Range: 10,130 miles
Passengers: 253

Airbus A300-600ST Beluga

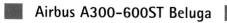

Twin-jet low-wing transport aircraft designed to carry oversized or bulky cargo. The Beluga can easily carry large Airbus parts around the various Airbus Industrie plants. The cargo hold totals more than 1400 m³. When the special versions of the Boeing B-377 (Super Guppy) were no longer big enough, the company started developing its own special transport aircraft based on the A300-600. The by-name 'Beluga' is a reference to its resemblance to a Beluga whale. Five Airbus A300-600ST have been built, and all fly mainly for Airbus Industrie.

Type: Airbus Super Transporter
Country of origin: EU
Use: transport aircraft
Wingspan: 44.84 m
Length: 54.16 m
Powered by: 2 Turbofans General Electric CF6-80C2A1 each producing 262.4 kN (26,756 kp) thrust
Max. take-off weight: 155,000 kg
Cruising speed: 465 mph
Range: 1055 miles
Ceiling: 10,760 m
Load: 47,000 kg

Airbus A380

Four-jet long-haul wide-body passenger aircraft (maiden flight 27.4.2005, entered service in 2008). The dimensions of the A380 far exceed those of the Boeing 747. Up to 850 passengers can be accommodated on the two full-length decks of the A380's body. The cockpit of the A380 is situated between the two decks and accessed via a staircase on the lower deck. A higher arrangement would make it difficult to see out. A camera assists the pilots when taxiing. The use of laminate and carbon-fibre materials and sandwich constructions for the structure have reduced the weight of the A380, so the operating costs should be 15 per cent lower than the usual standards of this class. Work is already underway on other versions (such as freight and long haul with a shorter body).

Type: Airbus A380-800
Country of origin: EU
Use: passenger aircraft
Wingspan: 79.80 m
Length: 73.00 m
Powered by: 4 Rolls-Royce Trent 900 or Engine Alliance GP7000, each producing 298 kN (30,386 kp) thrust
Max. take-off weight: 560,000 kg
Cruising speed: 560 mph
Range: 9320 miles
Ceiling: 12,500 m
Passengers: 555–850

Airspeed AS 57 Ambassador

British twin-engine medium-haul commercial aircraft (maiden flight 1950). On short-haul routes, it is noteworthy for its low operating costs. The aircraft were also extremely pleasant to maintain. Excellent short-start properties and an above-average performance on a single engine made it one of the safest and most popular aircraft of its time.

Type: Airspeed AS 57 Ambassador
Country of origin: Great Britain
Use: passenger aircraft
Wingspan: 35.05 m
Length: 25.05 m
Powered by: 2 Bristol Centaurus 661 18-cylinder radial engines, each 1929 kW (2625 hp)
Max. take-off weight: 23,800 kg
Cruising speed: 260 mph
Range: 1365 miles
Ceiling: 7600 m
Passengers: 47–60

Albatros L 73

Twin-engine passenger aircraft that was called a 'sleeper' because of its – by the standards of the day – very comfortable passenger cabin. The eight seats in the cabin could be turned into beds to sleep four. From 1927 the L 73 flew the Berlin–Moscow route overnight, as well as Berlin–Lübec-Copenhagen–Malmö and Berlin–Brünn–Vienna.

Type: Albatros L 73
Country of origin: Germany
Use: passenger aircraft
Wingspan: 19.70 m
Length: 14.60 m
Powered by: 2 BMW IV, each 230 kW (312 hp) and others
Max. take-off weight: 4600 kg
Cruising speed: 100 mph
Range: 375 miles
Ceiling: 3000 m
Passengers: 8 or 4 bunks + 2 crew

Antonov An-2

Single-engine passenger and freight aircraft with STOL and good slow-flying properties; often referred to as a biplane, but because of the differing sizes of the wings also known as a 1½ wing (maiden flight 31.8.1947). The wings are covered in fabric. The An-2 was used both for civilian and military purposes, and it is estimated that more than 18,000 units were built.

Type: Antonov An-2P
Country of origin: Soviet Union
Use: passenger and transport aircraft
Wingspan: top 18.18 m, bottom 14.24 m
Length: 12.74 m
Powered by: 1 Shvetzov 9-cylinder ASch-62IR radial engine, 736 kW (1000 hp)
Max. take-off weight: 5500 kg
Maximum speed: 160 mph
Range: 560 miles
Ceiling: 4400 m
Passengers: 8–12 + 2 crew

Antonov An-12

Soviet four-engine transport aircraft, originally developed from the An-10 passenger aircraft for military purposes (maiden flight 16.12.1956). There was no fixed loading ramp in the back, and the military version had two 23 mm cannons as rear weaponry. Over 200 of the total of 1250 units built were used for civilian purposes, and very many were exported.

Type: Antonov An-12BP
Country of origin: Soviet Union
Use: transport aircraft
Wingspan: 38.00 m
Length: 33.10 m
Powered by: 4 Ivchenko AI-20M turboprops, each 3126 kW (4250 hp)
Max. take-off weight: approx. 61,000 kg
Cruising speed: 415 mph
Range: 2235 miles
Ceiling: 10,200 m
Passengers: 132 (or payload 22 t) + 5 crew

Antonov An-22 Antæus

Four-engine transport aircraft, cantilevered shoulder wing (maiden flight 27.2.1965), at the time of its maiden flight the world's largest aircraft; designed as a transport aircraft for heavy loads and long distances. Between 1965 and February 1976, 68 units were delivered. The aircraft has a rear loading gate with a hydraulic ramp, and can operate on rough airstrips.

Type: Antonov An-22
Country of origin: Soviet Union
Use: transport aircraft
Wingspan: 64.40 m
Length: 57.80 m
Powered by: 4 Kusnezov NK-12MA turboprops, each 11,185 kW (15,200 hp)
Max. take-off weight: 250,000 kg
Cruising speed: 360 mph
Range: 3105–6805 miles
Ceiling: 11,000 m
Passengers: 29 + 5 crew (80 t payload)

Antonov An-124 Ruslan

Four-jet transport aircraft developed as a military transporter; at the time of its maiden flight on 26 December 1982 it was the biggest aircraft in the world. It can take off and land on rough terrain. It is able to 'kneel' for easier loading. A number of An-124 Ruslans have been flying for civilian companies since the 1990s.

Type: Antonov An-124
Country of origin: Soviet Union
Use: transport aircraft
Wingspan: 73.30 m
Length: 69.10 m
Powered by: 4 Lotarev D-18T turbofans, each producing 229.5 kN (23,350 kp) thrust
Max. take-off weight: 392,000 kg (civilian)
Cruising speed: 500–530 mph
Range: 2985 miles with a payload of 120 t
Ceiling: 11,600 m
Passengers: 88 + 6 crew (max. 150 t)

Antonov An-225 Mrija

Six-jet transport aircraft, cantilevered shoulder wing, further development of the An-124 Ruslan. It was designed to carry the Buran space shuttle. The body and wings were all extended by around 15 m. The wings were given a new middle section, additional engines were fitted on each side and a double tail unit was constructed, making it currently the largest aircraft in the world.

Type: Antonov An-225
Country of origin: Soviet Union/Ukraine
Use: transport aircraft
Wingspan: 88.40 m
Wingspan rear tail unit: 32.65 m
Length: 84.00 m

Powered by: 6 Lotarev D-18T, each producing 229.5 kN (23,409 kp) thrust
Max. take-off weight: 600,000 kg
Maximum speed: 530 mph
Range: max. 9570 miles
Ceiling: 11,000 m
Crew: 7 (max. payload 250 t)

Antonov An-24

Twin-engine short-haul passenger and transport aircraft (maiden flight April 1960). The aircraft was intended to replace the Ilyushins Il-12 and Il-14, and the Lissunov Li-2, and to be able to operate from small and rough airstrips. A total of more than 1300 units were built. In addition to the basic version, the An-24T was built as a freight aircraft, and the An-24P for firefighting.

Type: Antonov An-24
Country of origin: Soviet Union
Use: passenger aircraft
Wingspan: 29.20 m
Length: 23.50 m
Powered by: 2 Ivchenko AI-24, each 1875 kW (2550 hp)
Max. take-off weight: 21,000 kg
Cruising speed: 280 mph
Range: 465 miles
Ceiling: 8400 m
Passengers: 44–50 + 4 crew

Antonov An-26

Twin-engine transport aircraft, cantilevered high wing that was based on the An-24 (maiden flight 1967). The rear fuselage was raised so a loading ramp could be fitted. Some versions can carry people and freight together. There is a small additional turbojet in the right nacelle (APU and climb rate/high altitude cruise booster).

Type: Antonov An-26
Country of origin: Soviet Union
Use: transport aircraft
Wingspan: 29.20 m
Length: 28.30 m
Powered by: 2 Ivchenko AI-24WT, each 2103 kW + RU 19A-300 booster of 7.85 kN (801 kp)
Max. take-off weight: 24,000 kg
Cruising speed: 275 mph
Range: 685–1460 miles
Ceiling: 8400 m
Crew: 4–5
Load: 5500–6300 kg or 39 passengers/30 paratroopers

Antonov An-72

Twin-engine short- and medium-haul STOL transport aircraft (maiden flight 31.8.1977), cantilevered high wing, engines on the middle of the wings. The aircraft has a retractable nose wheel undercarriage and a short, sturdy main landing gear on the rear, and can also operate on unpaved airstrips.

The two turbofans are positioned high up, guiding the airflow over the wings, which helps to increase the lift. There is a loading ramp on the rear under the T-rudder. Later variants included a version for VIP flights (An-72S) and for sea monitoring (An-72P).

Type: Antonov An-72
Country of origin: Soviet Union/Ukraine
Use: transport aircraft
Wingspan: 31.89 m
Length: 28.7 m
Powered by: 2 ZMKB Progress D36, each providing 63.7 kN (6425 kp) thrust
Max. take-off weight: 34,500 kg
Cruising speed: 340–375 mph
Range: 1245 (up to 7.5 t payload) to 2985 miles
Ceiling: 11,800 m
Passengers: up to 68

Antonov An-140

Twin-engine short-haul passenger aircraft (maiden flight 17.9.1997) with APU and an air-conditioned pressurised cabin. It performs well at high-altitude airports (above 1700 m) and in hot climates (45 °C). The aircraft can take off and land on rough terrain. It is intended to replace the An-24 and its variants.

Type: Antonov An-140
Country of origin: Ukraine
Use: passenger aircraft
Wingspan: 25.50 m
Length: 22.60 m
Powered by: 2 Klimov TW3-117WMA-SBM1, each 1838 kW (2500 hp) or others
Max. take-off weight: 21,500 kg
Cruising speed: 355 mph
Range: 860–1895 miles
Ceiling: 7200 m
Passengers: 52

Antonov An-148

Twin-jet high-wing passenger aircraft with a T-rudder (maiden flight prototype 17.12.2004); with APU and air-conditioned pressurised cabin. The aircraft is to replace the aged Tu-134 and Jak-42 as a regional aircraft. Thanks to modern avionics, it can operate on poor airstrips and in all-weather conditions, and it is available in a number of different versions.

Type: Antonov An-148-100E
Country of origin: Ukraine
Use: passenger aircraft
Wingspan: 28.91 m
Length: 29.13 m

Powered by: 2 Progress D-436-148, each providing 65.6 kN (6600 kp) thrust
Max. take-off weight: 42,600 kg
Maximum speed: 540 mph
Range: 3170 miles
Ceiling: 12,500 m
Passengers: 75

Armstrong Whitworth AW 650/660 Argosy

Four-engine high-wing freight aircraft (maiden flight 8.1.1959). For financial reasons, existing modules were used in its construction; the wings were taken from the Avro Shackleton bomber, the nacelles from the Vickers Viscount 800. The freight deck with the pressurised cabin could be loaded both from the front and the rear, and the cockpit – which was visually striking – was in an elevated position above the freight deck. Of the military version AW 660 (maiden flight March 1961), 56 units flew for the Royal Air Force 1961–1975 (see illustration), primarily in Aden and the Persian Gulf.

Type: Armstrong Whitworth
AW 650-100 Argosy
Country of origin: Great Britain
Use: transport aircraft
Wingspan: 35.05 m
Length: 26.44 m
Powered by: 4 Rolls-Royce Dart RDa.7/2 526, each 1567 kW (2130 hp)
Max. take-off weight: 39,917 kg
Maximum speed: 295 mph
Range: 2700 miles
Ceiling: 6900 m
Crew: 2–3

Type: Armstrong Whitworth AW 660 Argosy
Country of origin: Great Britain
Use: transport aircraft
Wingspan: 35.05 m
Length: 27.12 m
Powered by: 4 Rolls-Royce Dart RDa.8 Mk 101, each 1820 kW (2475 hp)
Max. take-off weight: 46,720 kg
Maximum speed: 270 mph
Range: 3250 miles
Ceiling: 5500 m
Load: up to 69 military personnel (or 13 t freight) + 4–5 crew

Aviation Traders Limited ATL-98

British four-engine low-wing freight aircraft, developed and built on the basis of the Douglas DC-4 (maiden flight 21.6.1961). In the conversion of the DC-4, the cockpit was moved up (in a cone over the cargo area), the body extended and the lateral tail unit raised. A total of 21 DC-4s were constructed between 1961 and 1969.

Type: Aviation Traders Limited ATL-98
Country of origin: Great Britain
Use: transport aircraft
Wingspan: 35.81 m
Length: 31.27 m
Powered by: 4 PW R-2000-7M2 Twin Wasp, each 1081 kW (1470 hp)
Max. take-off weight: 33,475 kg
Maximum speed: 250 mph
Range: 2300 miles
Ceiling: 5700 m
Crew: 4
Load: 8035 kg

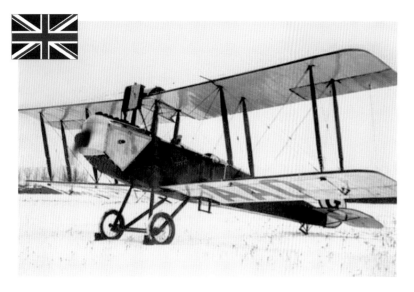

Avro 548

Single-engine passenger biplane, developed as the civilian version of the military type Avro 504 after WWI (maiden flight October 1919). Avro produced seven units by 1924; other manufacturers converted the 504 type into the 548 under licence (approx. 30 units). The various aircraft differ in features and engines.

Type: Avro 548
Country of origin: Great Britain
Use: passenger aircraft
Wingspan: 10.97 m
Length: 8.97 m
Powered by: 1 PD Renault in-line engine, 60 kW (81 hp)
Max. take-off weight: 880 kg
Maximum speed: 80 mph
Range: 175 miles
Ceiling: 3000 m
Passengers: 2 + 1 pilot

Avro 688/689 Tudor

Four-engine passenger and transport aircraft, and the first British transport aircraft to have a pressurised cabin (maiden flight June 1945). The wings of the Avro 694 Lincoln were used for the construction. With its payload of 9.5 t, the Avro Tudor was one of the heaviest aircraft in the Berlin Airlift 1948/9.

Type: Avro 688 Tudor IV
Country of origin: Great Britain
Use: passenger and transport aircraft
Wingspan: 36.58 m
Length: 25.99 m
Powered by: 4 Rolls-Royce Merlin 621, each 1267 kW (1723 hp)
Max. take-off weight: 36,288 kg
Cruising speed: 210 mph
Range: 4000 miles
Ceiling: 8350 m
Passengers: 32

Avro 748

Twin-engine short-haul commercial aircraft (maiden flight 24.6.1960), an all-metal low wing with a pressurised cabin and propelled by turboprops. Design work for a replacement for the DC-3 commenced in 1958. After the first series of 18 units had been delivered, Avro was taken over by Hawker-Siddeley. The type remained in production as the Hawker-Siddeley HS 748. From 1961, a series 2 with a higher take-off weight was built and 198 units were sold; this was followed by the smaller series 2A (71 units) and 2C (25 units). In the mid-1970s Hawker-Siddeley became a division of British Aerospace, and the former Avro 748 remained in development as the BAe 748.

Type: Avro 748
Country of origin: Great Britain
Use: passenger aircraft
Wingspan: 30.02 m
Length: 20.42 m
Powered by: 2 Rolls-Royce Dart RDa.7 Mk 536-2, each 1700 kW (2310 hp)
Max. take-off weight: 23,133 kg
Cruising speed: 280 mph
Range: 905 miles
Ceiling: 7620 m
Passengers: 48

Avro RJ100

Four-jet short-haul passenger aircraft (maiden flight 13.5.1992); known as the BAe 146-300 until 1992. The British Aerospace subsidiary Avro International Aerospace continued producing the type, which was redesigned in 1992, as the Avro RJ (regional jet). The new RJ100 had quieter engines than the BAe original, and modern digital avionics. Its body was extended by 2.39 m over the RJ85.

Type: Avro 146-RJ100
Country of origin: Great Britain
Use: passenger aircraft
Wingspan: 26.21 m
Length: 30.99 m
Powered by: 4 Textron Lycoming LF507 turbofans, each producing 31.1 kN (3160 kp) thrust
Max. take-off weight: 44,225–46,000 kg
Cruising speed: 475 mph
Range: max. 1715 miles
Passengers: 100–120

BAC 1-11

Twin-jet low-wing passenger aircraft with a T-rudder (maiden flight prototype 20.8.1963). The aircraft was the 'changing of the guard' (the first design was by Hunting Percival Aircraft, which later became part of BAC) for the Vickers Viscount turboprop. The 200 and 300 series with more powerful engines and designed for a greater payload, plus the 400 series (for the American market), were approved in 1965; all other dimensions remained the same. The 500 series (1968) had a longer body (+ 4.11 m) and greater wingspan (+ 1.20 m), and could hold up to 97 passengers – 119 if seated close together. The 475 series had the body of the 400 and the wings of the 500. Series production of the 1-11 in Great Britain ended in 1980; nine more units were manufactured under licence in Romania.

Type: BAC 1-11 Series 500
Country of origin: Great Britain
Use: passenger aircraft
Wingspan: 28.50 m
Length: 32.61 m
Powered by: 2 Rolls-Royce Spey 512DW turbofans, each providing 55.8 kN (5690 kp) static thrust
Max. take-off weight: 47,700 kg
Cruising speed: 490 mph
Range: 1705 miles with max. load
Ceiling: 9000 m
Passengers: 98–119

Beechcraft 18/Super 18

Twin-engine low-wing passenger and transport aircraft in all metal semimonocoque construction (maiden flight 1937). The 18 series was built and continuously updated for more than 30 years. The completely redesigned Super 18 flew for the very first time on 10 December 1953. From 1963 the Super 18 was supplied with a nose wheel units and radar as standard.

Type: Beechcraft Super 18
Country of origin: USA
Use: passenger aircraft
Wingspan: 15.10 m
Length: 10.70 m
Powered by: 2 Pratt & Whitney R-985 AN-14, each 330 kW (450 hp)
Max. take-off weight: 4490 kg
Cruising speed: 220 mph
Range: max. 1490 miles
Ceiling: 6500 m
Passengers: 5-7 + 2 crew

Beechcraft Bonanza

Single-engine business aircraft, all-metal semimonocoque construction (maiden flight 6.12.1945), launched on the market after WWII as the first four-seater all-metal de-luxe business aircraft. The V35 and F33 versions of the Bonanza seat 4–5 people; the A36/A36TC seats 6. Amongst other things, the F33A was used as a training aircraft by Deutsche Lufthansa.

Type: Beechcraft Bonanza A36
Country of origin: USA
Use: business aircraft
Wingspan: 10.21 m
Length: 8.38 m
Powered by: 1 Teledyne-Continental IO-550-B, 220 kW (300 hp)
Max. take-off weight: 1415 kg
Cruising speed: 190 mph
Range: 530 miles
Ceiling: 5630 m
Passengers: 5 + 1 pilot

Beechcraft 99

Twin-engine cantilevered low-wing passenger and transport aircraft (maiden flight prototype July 1966; series production since 1968) that was originally designed as a commuter aircraft. The 99 type was intended to replace the Beechcraft 18. The Executive version with a particularly comfortable interior has been available since 1969. Some of the 239 aircraft built were later converted to freight transporters.

Type: Beechcraft C99 Commuter
Country of origin: USA
Use: passenger aircraft
Wingspan: 13.98 m
Length: 13.58 m
Powered by: 2 Pratt & Whitney Canada PT6A-36, each 405 kW (550 hp)
Max. take-off weight: 5126 kg
Cruising speed: 285 mph
Range: max. 1050 miles
Ceiling: 6100 m
Passengers: 16 + 2 crew

Beechcraft 1900 Airliner

Twin-engine commuter and business turboprop aircraft, derived from the Beechcraft 99. There is room for up to 19 passengers. In addition to the 1900C basic version, there is the 1900D with a higher cabin ceiling (more headroom), the 1900D Executive, a comfortably fitted-out business aircraft, and the 1900C Cargo version.

Type: Beechcraft 1900D
Country of origin: USA
Use: passenger aircraft
Wingspan: 17.67 m
Length: 17.63 m
Powered by: 2 Pratt & Whitney Canada PT6A-67D turboprops, each 955 kW (1300 hp)
Max. take-off weight: 7688 kg
Cruising speed: 300 mph
Range: max. 1725 miles
Ceiling: 7620 m
Passengers: 19 + 2 crew

Beechcraft 200 Super King Air

Twin-engine turboprop business aircraft (maiden flight 27.10.1972), renamed King Air B200 after Beechcraft was taken over by Raytheon. It has a pressurised cabin and conference seating, and needs only a short runway (from 600 m). The aircraft has been in construction for over 30 years, constantly improved and – thanks to its reliability and economy – is a successful seller.

Type: B200 King Air
Country of origin: USA
Use: business aircraft
Wingspan: 16.61 m
Length: 13.36 m
Powered by: 2 Pratt & Whitney Canada PT6A-42, each 634 kW (862 hp)
Max. take-off weight: 5693 kg
Cruising speed: 325 mph
Range: max. 2000 miles
Ceiling: 10,000 m
Passengers: 7–9

Beriev Be-30

Twin-engine high-wing STOL passenger aircraft (maiden flight 3.3.1967 with radial engines, 13.7.1968 with turboprops). Approximately half of the wing consists of a honeycomb-like composite material. The large rectangular windows of the passenger cabin are a striking feature. A total of just three units were built.

Type: Beriev Be-30
Country of origin: Soviet Union
Use: passenger aircraft
Wingspan: 17.00 m
Length: 15.70 m
Powered by: 2 Glushenkov TVD-10, each 698 kW (950 hp) take-off power
Max. take-off weight: 5860 kg
Cruising speed: 282 mph
Range: max. 810 miles
Passengers: 15 + 1–2 crew

Blériot SPAD S.33

Single-engine single-bay passenger biplane (maiden flight 12.12.1920). The passengers sat in wicker chairs in the closed cabin. The open cockpit (there was one other seat apart from the pilot's) was roughly in the middle of the body behind the upper wing. There were 41 series aircraft constructed. The S.33 flew with several small airlines for a long time, and also served as the basic design for a number of successful developments of single-engine aircraft.

Type: Blériot SPAD S.33
Country of origin: France
Use: passenger aircraft
Wingspan: 11.66 m
Length: 9.08 m
Powered by: 1 Salmson CM.9 radial engine, 191 kW (260 hp)
Max. take-off weight: 2062 kg
Cruising speed: 100 mph
Range: max. 670 miles
Ceiling: 13,700 m
Passengers: 4–5 + 1 pilot

Bloch 120

Triple-engine shoulder-wing passenger and transport aircraft in all metal construction (maiden flight 1932). Flown by Air France from the end of 1934. It could also be used as a freight aircraft, and was intended for use in the French colonies.

Type: Bloch MB-120
Country of origin: France
Use: passenger aircraft
Wingspan: 20.54 m
Length: 15.30 m
Powered by: 3 Lorraine 9Na Algol, each 220 kW (300 hp)
Max. take-off weight: 6000 kg
Cruising speed: 125 mph
Range: 620 miles
Ceiling: 6300 m
Passengers: 10

Blohm & Voss Ha 139

Four-engine transport aircraft with folding wings (maiden flight 1936). The mid-wing (with the fuel tanks) was covered in metal, the outer wings in fabric. The aircraft was catapult launched and designed as a transatlantic mail carrier. According to the specifications, it was to transport 400–500 kg of freight up to 3100 miles at 155 mph. The versions Ha 139 V1 Nordwind and HA 139 V2 Nordmeer (delivered in the summer of 1937 to Luft Hansa) were built. The aircraft took off from the mail ships *Friesenland* and *Schwabenland*. The final unit (delivered at the end of 1938) with the registration Ha 139B Nordstern had a slightly modified wing geometry, which meant that the engines were positioned somewhat lower.

Type: Blohm & Voss Ha 139
Country of origin: Germany
Use: mail carrier
Wingspan: 27.00 m
Length: 19.50 m
Powered by: 4 Jumo 205C two-stroke diesel engines, each 447 kW (600 hp)
Max. take-off weight: 17,500 kg
Cruising speed: 160 mph
Range: max. 3295 miles
Ceiling: 6600 m
Crew: 4–5

Boeing 247

Twin-engine cantilevered all-metal low-wing passenger aircraft (maiden flight 8.2.1933). The aircraft was already fitted out with an autopilot, echo sounder, ADF system and blind flying instruments. The low-wing construction, de-icing system, pitch propeller and retractable landing gear were innovations in this class. A total of 76 were built. Because of an exclusive agreement with United Airlines, only a relatively small number of this type were sold.

Type: Boeing 247
Country of origin: USA
Use: passenger aircraft
Wingspan: 22.56 m
Length: 15.72 m
Powered by: 2 Pratt & Whitney R-1340 Wasp radial engines, each 404 kW (550 hp)
Max. take-off weight: 6192 kg
Cruising speed: 190 mph
Range: approx. 745 miles
Ceiling: 7700 m
Passengers: 10 + 2–3 crew

Boeing 307 Stratoliner

Four-engine transport aircraft, cantilevered low wing with a conventional tail unit (maiden flight 31.12.1938), and the first civilian aircraft to have a pressure-ventilated cabin. The experience gained in the construction of the B-17 bomber was incorporated in the construction of the B-307 during the period 1938 to 1940. The wings, engines and tail unit of the B-17 remained largely unchanged; only the body with the pressurised cabin was a new construction. Just 10 Stratoliners were built. The USA's entry into WWII prevented more extensive use of this modern aircraft.

Type: Boeing 307
Country of origin: USA
Use: passenger aircraft
Wingspan: 32.61 m
Length: 22.66 m

Max. take-off weight: 19,050 kg
Powered by: 4 Wright GR-1820 Cyclone radial engines, each 671 kW (912 hp)
Maximum speed: 245 mph

Range: 2385 miles
Ceiling: 7985 m
Passengers: 33

Boeing 377 Stratocruiser

Four-engine passenger aircraft. The construction combined the wings, tail unit and engines of the B-29 bomber with a newly constructed, spacious body with two decks. The B-377 – built between 1947 and 1950 – was the first to fly non-stop from New York to London. Some aircraft of this type were later converted into the Guppy.

Type: Boeing 377
Country of origin: USA
Use: passenger aircraft

Wingspan: 43.05 m
Length: 33.63 m
Powered by: 4 Pratt & Whitney R-4360B Wasp Major 28 radial engines, each 2610 kW (3500 hp)
Max. take-off weight: 66,134 kg
Cruising speed: 340 mph
Range: 4195 miles
Ceiling: 9750 m
Passengers: 55–112

Boeing 707

Four-jet long-haul commercial aircraft, cantilevered low wing with a conventional tail unit (maiden flight 20.12.1957). In October 1958, PanAm started a scheduled service from New York to Paris on the 707. Over the course of its production period to 1992, 1012 aircraft were built in a number of variations. The basic type was the 707-120. The series 707-320 and 420 had bigger wings and a longer range.

Type: Boeing 707-120
Country of origin: USA
Use: passenger aircraft
Wingspan: 39.87 m
Length: 44.04 m
Powered by: 4 Pratt & Whitney PW JT3C-6, each providing 62.3 kN (6322 kp) thrust
Max. take-off weight: 116,575 kg
Cruising speed: 555 mph
Range: 4225 miles
Ceiling: 12,800 m
Passengers: 181

Boeing 720

Four-jet passenger aircraft for longer medium-haul flights (maiden flight 23.11.1959). It was derived from the Boeing 707 (work designation 707-020), and although many systems remained unchanged there were several innovations. The adjustment of the wing geometry improved its slow-flying behaviour and shortened the take-off and landing distance. This meant that the Boeing 720 could also be used on small airfields.

Type: Boeing 720B
Country of origin: USA
Use: passenger aircraft
Wingspan: 39.88 m
Length: 41.68 m
Powered by: 4 Pratt & Whitney JT3D-1, each providing 75.6 kN (7711 kp) thrust
Max. take-off weight: 103,874 kg
Cruising speed: 540 mph
Range: 4200 miles
Ceiling: 12,200 m
Passengers: 140–156

Boeing 727

Triple-jet cantilevered low-wing short- and medium-haul commercial aircraft with a T-rudder (maiden flight 6.2.1963). The positioning of the engines on the rear produced a 'clean' wing with various flaps. The type was constantly further developed during the period of its production (to 1984). The freight version 727-200F was the final new launch, in 1981.

Type: Boeing 727-100
Country of origin: USA
Use: passenger aircraft
Wingspan: 32.92 m
Length: 40.59 m
Powered by: 3 Pratt & Whitney JT8D-1, each providing 62.3 kN (6322 kp) thrust
Max. take-off weight: 68,946 kg
Cruising speed: 575 mph
Range: 1895 miles
Ceiling: 11,400 m
Passengers: 131

Boeing 737

Twin-jet short- and medium-haul commercial aircraft (maiden flight 9.4.1967). Developed since 1964, to date 4000 aircraft of every version and generation of this type have been sold. The 'next generation' versions have been in operation since 1993. The 737-600 was presented in 1998 as the smallest version of this modernised series; it has a higher landing gear, different wing geometry and a glass cockpit. The Boeing 737-700C (Convertible) can be converted from a passenger to a freight aircraft in less than one hour.

Type: Boeing 737-600
Country of origin: USA
Use: passenger aircraft
Wingspan: 43.05 m
Length: 33.63 m
Powered by: 2 CFMI CFM56-7 turbofans, each producing 101 kN (10,300 kp) thrust
Max. take-off weight: 66,000 kg
Cruising speed: 530 mph
Range: 3510 miles
Ceiling: 11,000 m
Passengers: 110

Boeing 757

Twin-jet low-wing medium-haul commercial aircraft (maiden flight 19.2.1982). The 757-200 was developed together with the Boeing 767, which optimised the financial operation of both types on the same fleet. The year 1998 brought the 757-300 with a body that is 7.10 m longer (maiden flight 2.8.1998). The last 757 was delivered in April 2005 (200 version); then production ceased due to lack of demand.

Type: Boeing 757-200
Country of origin: USA
Use: passenger aircraft
Wingspan: 38.05 m
Length: 47.32 m
Powered by: 2 Rolls-Royce RB211-535E4B, each producing 193.5 kN (19,680 kp) thrust
Max. take-off weight: 115,680 kg
Cruising speed: 545 mph
Range: 3605–4535 miles
Ceiling: 11,600 m
Passengers: 170–228

Boeing 747

Four-jet wide-bodied long-haul passenger aircraft with a conventional tail unit (maiden flight 9.2.1969). The aviation industry owes the development of this jet to the fact that Boeing came after the Lockheed C-5 Galaxy in a competition for a large military transport aircraft. Its 'hump' made the 747 famous and instantly recognisable all over the world, and earned it the nickname of 'Jumbo Jet'. This 'hump', situated above the lower passenger deck, contains the cockpit. Over the course of its development, the quiet room adjoining the cockpit became a second passenger deck with first and business-class seats. From the time of its maiden flight to the introduction of the Airbus A380, the Boeing 747 was the world's biggest passenger aircraft. The first 747-100 series was not a commercial success. The 747-200 was much more so, and – with better engines, larger fuel tanks and a longer range – was in production until 1992. In the 747-400 series (since 1988, and with sales of 650 units the best-selling version), the cockpit was largely redesigned. The wingspan was also increased and winglets added to the tips of the wings.

Type: Boeing 747-400ER
Country of origin: USA
Use: passenger aircraft
Wingspan: 64.40 m
Length: 70.70 m
Powered by: 4 GE CF6-80, each producing 274 kN (27,940 kp) thrust
Max. take-off weight: 412,800 kg
Cruising speed: 570 mph
Range: 8825 miles (with max. load)
Cruising height: 12,800 m
Passengers: 366–524

Boeing 767

Twin-jet low-wing medium- and long-haul commercial aircraft (maiden flight 26.9.1981). Three versions were constructed: the 767-200 was the basic version. The 767-300 and the 767-400 ER (extended range) were of different lengths, with different wingspans and engines. Military adaptations of this type – reconnaissance, refuelling and lead aircraft – have been in production since 2003.

Type: Boeing 767-400 ER
Country of origin: USA
Use: passenger aircraft
Wingspan: 51.90 m
Length: 61.40 m
Powered by: 2 General Electric CF6-80C2B8F turbofans, each producing 282.5 kN (28,807 kp) thrust
Max. take-off weight: 204,120 kg
Cruising speed: 530 mph
Range: max. 6495 miles
Ceiling: 13,145 m
Passengers: 250–305

Boeing 777

Twin-jet long-haul commercial aircraft (maiden flight 14.6.1994). The 777-200 is the basic version, the 777-200 ER the basic version with an extended range, and the 777-100 a shorter version of the basic version. The 777-200 LR (long range) is marketed as the Worldliner (range 10,840 km). The 777-300 is the extended basic version (up to 550 seats).

Type: Boeing 777-200
Country of origin: USA
Use: passenger aircraft
Wingspan: 60.90 m
Length: 63.70 m
Powered by: 2 Pratt & Whitney 4090 turbofans, each producing 349 kN (35,588 kp) thrust
Max. take-off weight: 247,210 kg
Cruising speed: 555 mph
Range: 5995 miles
Cruising height: 13,110 m
Passengers: 305

Boeing 717

Twin-jet short-haul commercial aircraft (maiden flight 2.9.1998). The plans went back to McDonnell Douglas in 1995. After the company was taken over by Boeing in 1997, the MD 95 project was continued as the Boeing 717; to date, around 120 units have been delivered. Production stopped in 2006 because of lack of demand.

Type: Boeing 717
Country of origin: USA
Use: passenger aircraft
Wingspan: 28.45 m
Length: 37.81 m
Powered by: 2 Rolls-Royce BR715-A1-30, each producing 82.3 kN (8360 kp) thrust
Max. take-off weight: 49,845 kg
Cruising speed: 505 mph
Range: 1580 miles
Ceiling: 11,200 m
Passengers: 106

Boeing BBJ

Twin-jet business aircraft for long-haul routes and more discerning passengers. Based on the Boeing 737, the aircraft was produced in co-operation between Boeing and General Electric (maiden flight 4.11.1996). The Boeing Business Jet has the body of the 737-700, and uses the larger wings, mid-wing section and landing gear of the 737-800. With the addition of up to nine further tanks, this is a long-haul aircraft with a maximum range of more than 6835 miles. After the BBJ and BBJ 2 (based entirely on the 737-800), a third design was announced: the BBJ 3 (based on the 737-900). It was to have up to 11 per cent more cabin space than the BBJ 2. Different features are planned for all three versions.

Type: Boeing BBJ
Country of origin: USA
Use: Firmenflugzeug
Wingspan: 35.80 m
Length: 33.63 m
Powered by: 2 CFM56-7B27 turbofans, each producing 122 kN (12,440 kp) static thrust

Max. take-off weight: 77 564 kg
Cruising speed: 530 mph
Range: 7000 miles
Cruising height: 12,500 m
Passengers: 8, 25 or up to 50

Boeing 787

Project for a twin-jet wide-body aircraft (programme was officially launched on 26.4.2004). The Boeing 787 (formerly the Boeing 7E7) was soon given the soubriquet of Dreamliner, which proved to be a successful marketing choice. There are currently plans for three versions: the medium-haul 787-3 and long-haul versions 787-8 and 787-9 with a greater wingspan. A freight version is also being worked on. Half of the aircraft (for which many orders had been received before its maiden flight) is to be constructed of modern composite materials.

Type: Boeing 787
Country of origin: USA
Use: passenger aircraft (in development)
Wingspan: 60.00 m
Length: 56.00 m
Max. take-off weight: 218,000 kg
Range: 9760 miles
Passengers: 223

Bombardier BD-100 Challenger 300

Twin-jet business aircraft for medium-haul intercontinental routes (maiden flight 14.8.2001). The aircraft's performance ranges from the small Learjet 60 to the large Challenger 604. The cross-section of the cell is very large for this class (2.18 m wide and 1.85 m high). The cabin also has a small galley.

Type: Bombardier BD-100 Challenger 300
Country of origin: Canada
Use: business aircraft
Wingspan: 19.46 m
Length: 20.97 m
Powered by: 2 Honeywell AS907 turbofans, each producing 28.91 kN (2950 kp) thrust
Max. take-off weight: 17,010 kg
Cruising speed: max. 560 mph
Range: max. 3575 miles
Ceiling: 13,700 m
Passengers: 8 (max. 16)

Bombardier Global 5000

Twin-jet low-wing business aircraft with a T-rudder. The aircraft is based on the Global Express, although it is around 80 cm shorter and designed for short- and medium-range destinations. The aircraft has modern avionics. The cabin interior is available with a choice of seating variants.

Type: Bombardier Global 5000
Country of origin: Canada
Use: business aircraft
Wingspan: 28.65 m
Length: 29.49 m
Powered by: 2 BMW/Rolls-Royce BR710-A2-20, each producing 65.6 kN (6690 kp) static thrust

Max. take-off weight: 39,780 kg
Cruising speed: 560 mph
Range: 5525 miles
Ceiling: 15,545 m
Passengers: 8–19

Bombardier Global Express XRS

Twin-jet low-wing business aircraft with a T-rudder (in service since 2006). The aircraft is a further development of the Global concept which began with the Global 5000, developed for very long routes. The jet is intended for companies and private clients.

Type: Bombardier Global Express XRS
Country of origin: Canada
Use: business aircraft
Wingspan: 28.60 m
Length: 30.30 m
Powered by: 2 Rolls-Royce BR710A2-20 turbofans, each producing 65.6 kN (6690 kp) thrust
Max. take-off weight: 44,450 kg
Cruising speed: 560 mph
Range: 7075 miles
Ceiling: 15,545 m
Passengers: 8–19

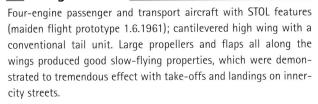

Breguet 941

Four-engine passenger and transport aircraft with STOL features (maiden flight prototype 1.6.1961); cantilevered high wing with a conventional tail unit. Large propellers and flaps all along the wings produced good slow-flying properties, which were demonstrated to tremendous effect with take-offs and landings on inner-city streets.

Type: Breguet 941
Country of origin: France
Use: passenger and transport aircraft
Wingspan: 43.00 m
Length: 29.90 m
Powered by: 4 Turmo III D-3 turboprops, each 1105 kW (1500 hp)
Max. take-off weight: 26,500 kg
Cruising speed: 300 mph
Range: max. 1925 miles
Ceiling: 8500 m
Passengers: 55-60

Bristol Britannia

British four-engine commercial aircraft (maiden flight 16.8.1952). The original plans were for a four-engine aircraft with 48 seats, but its size was soon increased. Ten units of the 102 series were sold to BOAC. The 310 series with a longer range – it could fly non-stop over the North Atlantic in both directions – was produced in 1956. Military transport versions (series 252 and 253) flew for the RAF.

Type: Bristol Type 175 Britannia (Serie 310)
Country of origin: Great Britain
Use: passenger aircraft
Wingspan: 43.36 m
Length: 37.87 m
Powered by: 4 Bristol Proteus 765 turboprops, each 2775 kW (3770 PS)
Max. take-off weight: 88,915 kg
Cruising speed: 405 mph
Range: 4270 miles
Ceiling: 9700 m
Passengers: 84–139

British Aerospace ATP

Twin-engine low-wing passenger and transport aircraft, created as an extended version (body is 5.50 m longer) of the Avro/HS-748 (maiden flight 6.8.1986). The ATP (Advanced Technology turboprop) has modern avionics and an EFIS glass cockpit. The slow-turning six-blade propellers create less noise.

Type: British Aerospace ATP
Country of origin: Great Britain
Use: passenger aircraft
Wingspan: 30.62 m
Length: 26.00 m
Powered by: 2 Pratt & Whitney Canada PW124A, each 1852 kW (2518 hp)
Max. take-off weight: 22,450 kg
Cruising speed: 305 mph
Range: 1430–2235 miles
Ceiling: 8100 m
Passengers: 64–72 + 1 pilot

British Aerospace BAe 125

Lightweight twin-jet multi-role aircraft, originally designed by De Havilland (maiden flight 1962), taken over by Hawker-Siddeley and then, after it was acquired by British Aerospace, remained in production with the new company from 1977. The BAe HS 125 is used in many modifications, both civilian and military: as a business and commuter aircraft, for medical services and as a training aircraft.

Type: British Aerospace BAe 125
Country of origin: Great Britain
Use: multi-role aircraft
Wingspan: 12.00 m
Length: 8.60 m
Powered by: 2 BS Viper 521, each 13.9 kN (1417 kp)
Max. take-off weight: 9300 kg
Cruising speed: 470 mph
Range: 1725 miles
Ceiling: 11,000 m
Passengers: 8 + 1 pilot

Britten-Norman BN-2 Islander

British twin-engine multi-role aircraft, cantilevered shoulder wing in an aluminium construction with STOL features. The aircraft was developed at the beginning of the 1960s, primarily to provide links for poorly developed areas with unpaved airfields. It proved itself both in passenger service and in freight traffic in areas that other aircraft were unable to access. The Islander was soon recognised as the ideal 'bush aircraft' that – as an ambulance aircraft, for instance – can transport two stretcher patients at the same time. In the roughly 40 years of its production history, the aircraft was improved several times (from 1979 to 1998 by Schweizer Pilatus AG as the Pilatus Britten-Norman). With over 1500 units produced, it is one of the most successful European aircraft developments of all time.

Type: Britten-Norman BN-2 Islander
Country of origin: Great Britain
Use: multi-role aircraft
Wingspan: 14.94 m
Length: 10.86 m
Powered by: 2 Lycoming O-540-E4C, each 195 kW (265 hp)
Max. take-off weight: 2993 kg
Cruising speed: max. 170 mph
Range: 870 miles
Ceiling: 4024 m
Passengers: max. 9

Britten-Norman BN-2A Mk III Trislander

British triple-engine short-haul passenger aircraft (maiden flight 11.9.1970). It was derived from the Britten-Norman BN-2 Islander. Obviously inspired by triple-engine passenger jets such as the DC-10 and the Lockheed L1011, a third propeller engine was mounted high on the rear; however, this made it so heavy – despite its having a longer body than the Islander – that additional support was required. Because there was no centre aisle, passengers entered through three doors on either side.

Type: BN-2A Mk III Trislander
Country of origin: Great Britain
Use: passenger aircraft
Wingspan: 16.15 m
Length: 15.01 m
Powered by: 3 Lycoming O-540-E4C5, each 195 kW (265 hp)
Max. take-off weight: 4500 kg
Cruising speed: 165 mph
Range: 995 miles
Ceiling: 4000 m
Passengers: 18

Canadair CRJ 100

Twin-jet regional commercial aircraft (maiden flight 10.5.1991). The aircraft in the RJ series were based on the successful Challenger business aircraft (longer body, bigger wings). In the aircraft family, the CRJ 100 was designed for long regional and little-used routes.

Type: CRJ 100
Country of origin: Canada
Use: regional commercial aircraft
Wingspan: 21.21 m
Length: 26.77 m
Powered by: 2 General Electric CF34-3A1, each with 40.7 kN (4150 kp) thrust
Max. take-off weight: 24,000 kg
Cruising speed: 530 mph
Range: 975 miles
Ceiling: 12,500 m
Passengers: 50 + 2 crew

Canadair (Bombardier) CRJ 900

Twin-jet low-wing regional commercial aircraft (maiden flight 21.2.2001); it is a stretched derivation of the CRJ 700 with a higher take-off weight. The CRJ 900E (extended range) and CRJ 900LR long-haul version are also available.

Type: CRJ 900
Country of origin: Canada
Use: regional commercial aircraft
Wingspan: 23.24 m
Length: 36.40 m
Powered by: 2 General Electric CF34-8C5, each 63.4 kN (6424 kp) thrust
Max. take-off weight: 36,514 kg
Cruising speed: 515 mph
Range: 1725 miles
Ceiling: 12,500 m
Passengers: 86

Cessna 208B Grand Caravan

Single-engine shoulder-wing multi-role aircraft with strut-braced wings (maiden flight 1986). The Cessna Grand Caravan is the longer – by 1.22 m – version of the Caravan (maiden flight 1982). Its uses include passenger and freight transportation, medical flights, surveying and mapping, and transporting parachutists; it can also be used as a seaplane by adding floats.

Type: Cessna 208B Grand Caravan
Country of origin: USA
Use: business aircraft
Wingspan: 15.90 m
Length: 12.70 m
Powered by: 1 Pratt & Whitney Canada PT6A-114A, 503 kW (685 hp)
Max. take-off weight: 3985 kg
Cruising speed: 210 mph
Range: 1045 miles
Ceiling: 7620 m
Passengers: 14

Cessna 404 Titan

Twin-engine low-wing passenger and freight aircraft with a V-rudder (maiden flight 26.2.1975). The basic version has seats for nine passengers, the Titan Ambassador for ten; the Titan Courier has been modified for transporting freight. Titans are also used for courier and patrol services.

Type: Cessna 404
Country of origin: USA
Use: business aircraft
Wingspan: 14.12 m (later model 14.23 m)
Length: 12.04 m
Powered by: 2 Continental GTSIO-520-M, each 280 kW (380 hp)
Max. take-off weight: 3810 kg
Cruising speed: 250 mph
Range: 1685–2120 miles
Ceiling: 7925 m
Passengers: 8 + 2 crew

Cessna 500 Citation

Twin-jet low-wing business aircraft (maiden flight 15.9.1969). The Cessna 500 was one of the first jet-engine business aircraft, and opened up a new era in corporate and business travel. It was the founder member of the Citation family, which is today the most comprehensive family of business jets.

Type: Cessna 500 Citation
Country of origin: USA
Use: business jet
Wingspan: 13.32 m
Length: 13.26 m
Powered by: 2 Pratt & Whitney JT15D-1 turbofans, each producing 9.79 kN (1016 kp) thrust
Max. take-off weight: 4920 kg
Cruising speed: 400 mph
Range: max. 1530 miles
Ceiling: 11,700 m
Passengers: 5–7 + 2 crew

Convair CV 440 Metropolitan

Twin-engine low-wing passenger aircraft with a conventional rudder (maiden flight 6.10.1955). The Convair CV 440 Metropolitan is a further development of the Convair CV 340. The longer body housed weather radar equipment. Thanks to the new exhaust system (thrust nozzle), the noise level in the cabin dropped.

Type: Convair CV 440 Metropolitan
Country of origin: USA
Use: passenger aircraft
Wingspan: 32.12 m
Length: 24.84 m
Powered by: 2 Pratt & Whitney R-2800 CB16 or CB17 18-cylinder double radial engines, each 1865 kW (2535 hp)
Max. take-off weight: 22,540 kg
Cruising speed: 290 mph
Range: 1740 miles
Ceiling: 7700 m
Passengers: 50

Convair CV 880

Four-jet low-wing passenger aircraft with a conventional rudder (maiden flight 27.1.1959). In comparison with its competitors Boeing and Douglas, the Convair CV 880 could carry fewer passengers because of its more slender body, but it was faster. Ultimately, though, this was not sufficient for it to survive against the financially more successful Boeing and Douglas aircraft. From 1960 the 880 M 131 flew with a larger fuel tank.

Type: Convair CV 880
Country of origin: USA
Use: passenger aircraft
Wingspan: 36.58 m
Length: 39.42 m
Powered by: 4 General Electric CJ-805-3, each producing 49.8 kN (5080 kp) thrust
Max. take-off weight: 87,900 kg
Cruising speed: 555 mph
Range: 4660 miles
Ceiling: 10,600 m
Passengers: 80–130

Dassault Falcon 900

Triple-jet long-haul business aircraft (maiden flight 21.9.1984). The Falcon 900 is available in several versions: in 2000, the 900C replaced the 900B, which had been in production for almost ten years. The main areas of use are business and adventure trips, 'shuttle' flights to/from cruise ships, and freight transportation. The aircraft is often used by charter companies.

Type: Dassault Falcon 900C
Country of origin: France
Use: business and freight aircraft
Wingspan: 19.30 m
Length: 20.20 m
Powered by: 3 Allied Signal TFE 731 5AR, each producing 19.6 kN (2000 kp) thrust
Max. take-off weight: 20,640 kg
Cruising speed: 515 mph
Range: 4350 miles
Ceiling: 15,500 m
Passengers: 19 + 2 crew

De Havilland DH.84 Dragon

Twin-engine transport and passenger biplane (maiden flight 24.11.1932), designed for passenger travel between southern England and Paris. It provided the first commercial air travel around the Highlands and distant islands of Scotland. In England 115 units were built, and in Australia 87. Some units were converted to police aircraft and used in the colonies.

Type: De Havilland DH.84 Dragon
Country of origin: Great Britain
Use: transport and business aircraft
Wingspan: 14.43 m
Length: 10.52 m
Powered by: 2 De Havilland Gipsy Major, each 97 kW (132 hp)
Max. take-off weight: 2041 kg
Cruising speed: 115 mph
Range: 545 miles
Ceiling: 4420 m
Passengers: 6 + 1 pilot

De Havilland DH.89 Dragon Rapide

Twin-engine passenger biplane (maiden flight 17.4.1934). Following the success of the DH.84 Dragon, De Havilland designed the smaller version of the DH.86. In Canada, some units were fitted with floats and aeroplane skis. In WWII, aircraft of this type were used for training, coastal patrols and reconnaissance. Production ended in 1946. Some units remained in operation until the 1960s.

Type: De Havilland DH.89 Dragon Rapide
Country of origin: Great Britain
Use: passenger aircraft
Wingspan: 14.63 m
Length: 10.51 m
Powered by: 2 De Havilland Gipsy Six, each 149 kW (202 hp)
Max. take-off weight: 2495 kg
Maximum speed: 155 mph
Range: 530 miles
Ceiling: 5800 m
Passengers: 8 + 2 crew

De Havilland DH.106 Comet

Four-jet low-wing passenger aircraft, the world's first jet-engine passenger aircraft (maiden flight 27.7.1949). In 1952, BOAC started a regular scheduled service with the Comet 1. Three serious accidents in 1954 – caused by material fatigue in the pressurised cabin, particularly around the square windows, and subsequent sudden loss in pressure – put an end to sales of this aircraft type. Although the at-risk versions of the Comet had already been withdrawn

and the Comet 4 (maiden flight 27.4.1958) was an extremely reliable substitute (with round windows, incidentally – as is the case with almost all jets today), De Havilland was unable to cope with the competition from the Boeing 707 and the DC 8. The maritime reconnaissance Nimrod was based on the Comet.

Type: De Havilland DH.106 Comet 4
Country of origin: Great Britain
Use: transport and passenger aircraft
Wingspan: 34.98 m
Length: 33.98 m
Powered by: 4 Rolls-Royce Avon 524, each 46.7 kN (4760 kp) thrust
Max. take-off weight: 73,480 kg
Cruising speed: 500 mph
Range: 3225 miles
Ceiling: 12,200 m
Passengers: 56–109

DHC-2 Beaver

Single-engine transport and liaison aircraft, strut-braced shoulder wing (maiden flight 16.8.1947). This sturdy aircraft – designed for operation on unpaved surfaces – could also be fitted with floats (see illustration), and so met the requirements of Canadian 'bush pilots'.

Type: De Havilland Canada DHC-2 Beaver
Country of origin: Canada
Use: transport and liaison aircraft
Wingspan: 14.63 m
Length: 9.22 m
Powered by: 1 Pratt & Whitney 895 Wasp 9-cylinder radial engine, 330 kW (450 hp)
Max. take-off weight: 2350 kg
Cruising speed: 135 mph
Range: 745 miles
Ceiling: 5500 m
Passengers: 4 + 2 crew

DHC-4 Caribou

Twin-engine transport and passenger aircraft with STOL characteristics (maiden flight 30.7.1958). The aircraft combines the STOL properties of the Beaver and Otter with a load capacity that approximates to that of a DC-3. The aircraft – including the military version – was also an export success. Production ended in 1973 after 307 units.

Type: De Havilland Canada DHC-4A Caribou
Country of origin: Canada
Use: multi-role aircraft
Wingspan: 29.15 m
Length: 22.13 m
Powered by: 2 Pratt & Whitney R-2000-7M2 Twin Wasp, each 1080 kW (1470 hp)
Max. take-off weight: 12,930 kg
Cruising speed: 180 mph
Range: 240–1300 miles
Ceiling: 7560 m
Passengers: 30 (or 3630 kg freight)

DHC-7

Four-engine high-wing regional STOL aircraft with a T-rudder (maiden flight 27.3.1975). Thanks to its high rate of climb, the aircraft was ideal for problematic airfields, and its low noise level (due to the slow-turning propellers) made it ideal for airports in close proximity to towns and cities.

Type: De Havilland Canada DHC Dash 7
Country of origin: Canada
Use: regional commercial aircraft
Wingspan: 28.40 m
Length: 24.60 m
Powered by: 4 Pratt & Whitney Canada PT6A-55 propeller turbines, each providing 904 kW (1230 PS) take-off power
Max. take-off weight: 21,319 kg
Cruising speed: 250 mph
Range: 940–1375 miles
Ceiling: 6400 m
Passengers: 50–54

DHC Dash 8Q-200

Twin-engine regional commercial aircraft. This version was given new engines, a higher speed and longer range. The Dash 8 is now made by Bombardier Aerospace, which acquired De Havilland Canada in 1992. From the second quarter of 1996, the 8-200 was also available as a 'Q' (for quiet) type with active noise and vibration insulation.

Type: De Havilland Canada DHC-8Q-200
Country of origin: Canada
Use: regional commercial aircraft
Wingspan: 25.90 m
Length: 22.30 m
Powered by: 2 Pratt & Whitney Canada PW123, each 1581 kW (2150 hp)
Max. take-off weight: 19,500 kg
Cruising speed: 340 mph
Range: 1365 miles
Cruising height: 7600 m
Passengers: 37–39

Dewoitine D-338

French triple-engine passenger aircraft (maiden flight 1935). Like the D-333, the aircraft was derived from the D-332. The body was around 3 m longer than that of the D-333, and the wingspan was also increased slightly. For Air France 31 units flew, including from Paris to Cannes, Damascus, Hanoi, Dakar and Hong Kong. After WWII, the nine remaining D-338s continued to fly the Paris–Nice route for some time.

Type: Dewoitine D-338
Country of origin: France
Use: passenger aircraft
Wingspan: 29.35 m
Length: 22.13 m
Powered by: 3 Hispano-Suiza 9V-10, each 423 kW (575 hp)
Max. take-off weight: 11,100 kg
Cruising speed: 160 mph
Range: 1210 miles
Ceiling: 5000 m
Passengers: 22

Dornier Do B Merkur

Single-engine passenger aircraft, shoulder wing with a conventional tail unit and fixed undercarriage (maiden flight 1925). Passengers travelled in a closed cabin, while the pilot sat in an open cockpit above it. Its short take-off and landing distance made it ideal for small airfields.

Type: Dornier Do B Merkur
Country of origin: Germany
Use: passenger aircraft
Wingspan: 19.60 m
Length: 12.80 m
Powered by: 1 BMW VI, 500 kW (680 hp)
Max. take-off weight: 3700 kg

Cruising speed: 110 mph
Range: 620 miles
Ceiling: 5200 m
Passengers: 6–8

Dornier Do 228

Twin-engine short-haul multi-role aircraft with STOL characteristics. The new wing is a point of interest (new technology wing). First came the 228-100 for 15 passengers, then the 228-200 for 19 passengers. The Do 228 is used for passengers and freight, and also for research and patrolling tasks (forest fires, environmental care and so on). Improved versions (101, 201, 202 and 212) were produced until 1989. Some units were also fitted with special equipment. The aircraft is popular because of its ease of maintenance and because it is not dependent on infrastructures. Production ended after 242 units. Around 30 units were built under licence in India.

Type: Dornier Do 228-200
Country of origin: Germany
Use: multi-role aircraft
Wingspan: 16.97 m
Length: 16.56 m
Powered by: 2 Garrett TPE331-10, each 570 kW (775 hp)
Max. take-off weight: 6400 kg
Cruising speed: 265 mph
Range: 1490 miles
Cruising height: 3000 m
Passengers: 19

Dornier Do 328

Twin-engine passenger aircraft for short-haul and regional air travel. The new style of wing gave this aircraft very good flying characteristics. In addition to the turbo-prop version 328-100, which has been available since 1993, the Do 328-300 (Do 328 Jet) with two jet turbines has been in production since 1999. In 2003, the American company Avcraft Aviation acquired the building rights to the Do 238 from Fairchild Dornier (bankrupt in 2002). The plans for a further development, the series 428, were cancelled.

Type: Dornier Do 328-100
Country of origin: Germany
Use: passenger aircraft
Wingspan: 20.98 m

Length: 21.11 m
Powered by: 2 Pratt & Whitney Canada PW119B turboprops, each 1380 kW (1877 hp)
Max. take-off weight: 13,900 kg

Cruising speed: max. 385 mph
Range: 840 miles
Ceiling: 9450 m
Passengers: 33

Douglas DC-1

Prototypes of a twin-engine commercial aircraft (maiden flight 1.7.1933); DC stands for Douglas Commercial, and was the name of the entire series. A single DC-1 was built, and trialled by TWA in scheduled service. However, it was the start of the famous series of successful developments. The design was stretched for series construction: this was the DC-2.

Type: Douglas DC-1
Country of origin: USA
Use: passenger aircraft
Wingspan: 25.91 m
Length: 18.29 m
Powered by: 2 Pratt & Whitney Hornet SDG-1690D, each 515 kW (700 hp)
Max. take-off weight: 7938 kg
Cruising speed: 190 mph
Range: 1000 miles
Ceiling: 7010 m
Passengers: 12

Douglas DC-3

Twin-engine low-wing commercial aircraft (maiden flight 17.12.1935). It dominated civilian air travel in the USA during the period before WWII – it was safe, easy to maintain and economical. The military version (called the Dakota by the RAF, and the C-47 by the USAF) was much used after WWII as a transport aircraft. There were 10,655 original units of the DC-3 built, and 4937 under licence.

Type: Douglas DC-3
Country of origin: USA
Use: passenger and transport aircraft
Wingspan: 28.90 m
Length: 19.70 m
Max. take-off weight: 11,431 kg

Powered by: 2 Pratt & Whitney Twin Wasp S1C3-G, each 895 kW (1217 hp)
Maximum speed: 185 mph
Range: 1350 miles
Ceiling: 6620 m
Passengers: 32 + 2 crew

Douglas DC-5

Twin-engine high-wing passenger aircraft designed for short-haul (maiden flight 12.2.1939). However, the outbreak of WWII caused the orders to stop coming in. Only 16 of these aircraft were built. But even its main competitor, William Boeing, acquired one in 1940 as his private aircraft.

Type: Douglas DC-5
Country of origin: USA
Use: passenger and transport aircraft
Wingspan: 23.77 m
Length: 19.07 m
Powered by: 2 Pratt & Whitney R-1690 or Wright Cyclone GR-1820-F62, each 634 kW (862 hp)
Max. take-off weight: 9072 kg
Maximum speed: 220 mph
Range: max. 1600 miles
Ceiling: 5790 m
Passengers: 16–22

Douglas DC-6

Four-engine passenger and transport aircraft with a pressurised cabin (maiden flight prototype 26.6.1945). The following were manufactured between 1946 and 1959: DC-6A transport version (maiden flight 29.9.1949), DC-6B passenger version (maiden flight 2.2.1951) and a combined freight/passenger version, the DC-6C. On the ST (Swing Tail) transport version, the entire rear section including the tail unit folded down for loading.

Type: Douglas DC-6B
Country of origin: USA
Use: passenger and transport aircraft
Wingspan: 35.81 m
Length: 32.18 m
Max. take-off weight: 48,534 kg
Powered by: 4 R-2800CB16, each 1765 kW (2400 hp)
Cruising speed: max. 315 mph
Range: max. 4715 miles
Ceiling: 7620 m
Passengers: 82–107

Douglas DC-7

Four-engine low-wing passenger aircraft, developed from the DC-6 (maiden flight 18.5.1953). The basic version of the DC-7 was 2.44 m longer than the DC-6 and had more powerful engines. Other versions were the DC-7B Intercontinental version with larger fuel tanks; the DC-7C with a longer body, greater wing span and inside engines situated further away from the cabin (also known as the 'Seven Seas'), and the DC-7F freight version. A total of 366 DC-7s were constructed.

Type: Douglas DC-7C
Country of origin: USA
Use: passenger and freight aircraft
Wingspan: 38.36 m
Length: 34.21 m
Max. take-off weight: 64,864 kg
Powered by: 4 Wright R-3350-988 TC-18-EA4, each 2500 kW (3400 hp)
Cruising speed: 360 mph
Range: 5220 miles
Ceiling: 9200 m
Passengers: 104

Douglas (McDonnell Douglas) DC-8

Four-jet low-wing passenger aircraft (maiden flight 30.5.1958). Less than a year after the Boeing 707 was commissioned, a total of 556 units in various versions were produced between 1959 and 1972. The DC-8 was further developed in the mid-1960s. The so-called Super Sixty could fly up to 259 passengers extremely long distances. Remarkable fact: on 21.8.1961 a DC-8-43 became the first civilian jet to break the sound barrier while in a controlled dive (Mach 1.012).

Type: Douglas DC-8-50
Country of origin: USA
Use: passenger aircraft
Wingspan: 43.41 m

Length: 45.87 m
Max. take-off weight: 147,415 kg
Powered by: 4 Pratt & Whitney JT3D3, each 80.1 kN (8170 kp) thrust

Cruising speed: max. 580 mph
Range: 5715–7000 miles
Passengers: 132, 144 or 179

Douglas (McDonnell Douglas) DC-9

Twin-jet low-wing short-haul commercial aircraft with a T-rudder (maiden flight 25.2.1965). The engines were both positioned on the rear, as with the French Caravelle. This facilitated a 'cleaner' wing. During the period of production (to 1982), many different civilian and military versions were built. In 1980 the successor, the MD-80 (developed as the DC-9-80) had her maiden flight. She has replaced the DC-9 since 1982. The MD-90 series later followed the MD-80 versions.

Type: Douglas DC-9-50
Country of origin: USA
Use: passenger aircraft
Wingspan: 28.47 m
Length: 40.72 m
Powered by: 2 JT8D-15, each providing 69 kN (7040 kp) or JT8D-17, each providing 71.2 kN (7260 kp) thrust
Max. take-off weight: 54,885 kg
Cruising speed: max. 560 mph
Range: max. 2070 miles
Cruising height: 10,000 m
Passengers: max. 139

Douglas (McDonnell Douglas) DC-10

Triple-jet long-haul commercial aircraft (maiden flight 29.8.1970). McDonnell Douglas entered the market for wide-bodied aircraft with the DC-10. In addition to the main version, the DC-10-10, the manufacturer also offered numerous other passenger, freight and military versions; the DC-10-30 long-haul version was particularly successful. The DC-10-40 long-haul version was given new jet engines. In December 1988, production of the DC-10 (466 units had been built) was stopped in favour of the MD-11. The characteristic engine arrangement was copied by a number of other aircraft manufacturers.

Type: Douglas DC-10-30
Country of origin: USA
Use: passenger and freight aircraft
Wingspan: 50.39 m
Length: 55.06 m
Powered by: 3 General Electric CF6-50C2, each 226.8 kN (23,127 kp) take-off power
Max. take-off weight: 251,815 kg
Maximum speed: 600 mph
Range: 4600 miles (full load) to 6525 miles
Ceiling: 9965 m
Passengers: 256–380

EADS Socata TB 20 Trinidad

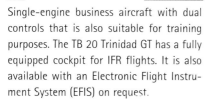

Single-engine business aircraft with dual controls that is also suitable for training purposes. The TB 20 Trinidad GT has a fully equipped cockpit for IFR flights. It is also available with an Electronic Flight Instrument System (EFIS) on request.

Type: EADS Socata TB 20
Country of origin: France
Use: business aircraft
Wingspan: 9.97 m
Length: 7.75 m
Powered by: 1 Textron Lycoming IO-540 C4D5D, 184 kW (250 hp)
Max. take-off weight: 1400 kg
Cruising speed: 185 mph
Range: 1275 miles
Ceiling: 6100 m
Passengers: 3–4 + 1 pilot

Embraer EMB 110 Bandeirante

Twin-engine passenger aircraft for regional air travel (maiden flight 9.8.1972). By 1990 a total of approx. 500 units had been built in a number of versions. Many of these aircraft are still in use today, particularly in Brazil, the Pacific area and Canada. A military version, the EMB 111 M, was built as a marine patrol aircraft.

Type: Embraer EMB 110P
Country of origin: Brazil
Use: passenger aircraft
Wingspan: 15.32 m
Length: 15.10 m
Powered by: 2 Pratt & Whitney PT6A-34, each 560 kW (760 hp)
Max. take-off weight: 5700 kg
Cruising speed: max. 260 mph
Range: 1220 miles
Passengers: 18 + 2 crew

Embraer EMB 120

Twin-engine low-wing passenger aircraft with a T-rudder for regional air travel (maiden flight 27.7.1983). Developed as a commuter aircraft, it quickly established itself on the European and US markets.

Type: Embraer EMB 120
Country of origin: Brazil
Use: passenger aircraft
Wingspan: 19.80 m
Length: 20.00 m
Powered by: 2 Pratt & Whitney Canada 115, each 872 kW (1185 shaft hp)
Max. take-off weight: 11,500 kg
Cruising speed: max. 340 mph
Range: 1085 miles
Ceiling: 9085 m
Passengers: 28–30 + 2 crew

Embraer ERJ 140

Twin-jet low-wing regional commuter aircraft with a T-rudder (maiden flight 27.6.2000). It is largely similar in construction to its 'relations', the small ERJ 135 and the large ERJ 145. Its body is 2.2 m longer than that of the ERJ 135.

Type: Embraer ERJ 140 ER
Country of origin: Brazil
Use: regional commercial aircraft
Wingspan: 20.04 m
Length: 28.45 m
Powered by: 2 Rolls-Royce/Allison AE3007A1/3, each 33.2 kN (3385 kp) take-off power
Max. take-off weight: 20,100 kg
Maximum speed: 530 mph
Range: 1900 miles
Ceiling: 11,200 m
Passengers: 44

Embraer EMB 175

Twin-jet commercial aircraft (maiden flight 14.6.2003); 1.78 m longer than the EMB 170. Segments were inserted in front of and behind the wings. In all other respects, the elongated version is 95% the same as the EMB 170. A choice of seating is offered with the EMB 175.

Type: Embraer EMB 175
Country of origin: Brazil
Use: medium-range commercial aircraft
Wingspan: 26.00 m
Length: 31.68 m
Powered by: 2 General Electric CF34-8E, each with 62.3 kN (6350 kp) take-off power
Max. take-off weight: 35,990 kg
Cruising speed: 540 mph
Range: 2070 miles
Ceiling: 10,700 m
Passengers: 78–86

Embraer EMB 195

Twin-jet commercial aircraft, elongated version of the EMB 190: two segments were inserted in front of and behind the wings (maiden flight December 2004). As well as the standard version, it is also available in a long-haul version (LR). The LR version has a greater fuel capacity, and its range is approx. 340 miles further.

Type: Embraer EMB 195 LR
Country of origin: Brazil
Use: medium-range commercial aircraft
Wingspan: 28.72 m
Length: 38.65 m
Powered by: 2 General Electric CF34-10E, each with 82.3 kN (8390 kp) take-off power
Max. take-off weight: 48,790 kg
Cruising speed: 540 mph
Range: 2070 miles
Ceiling: 10,700 m
Passengers: 108–118

Embraer CBA 123 Vector

Twin-engine passenger and transport aircraft for regional and commercial travel (maiden flight 1991). The low-wing aircraft has a T-rudder, and is powered by two pressure propellers on the rear of the aircraft.

Type: Embraer CBA 123
Country of origin: Brazil
Use: passenger aircraft
Wingspan: 17.93 m
Length: 18.09 m
Powered by: 2 TPF 351 20 propeller turbines, each 713 kW (970 shaft hp)
Max. take-off weight: 9500 kg
Cruising speed: 375 mph
Range: 870 miles
Ceiling: 12,200 m
Passengers: 19 + 2 crew

Focke-Wulf A 17 Möwe

Single-engine shoulder-wing passenger aircraft (maiden flight 1927). The A 17 proved to be more economical than almost every other commercial aircraft in operation at the time. The Möwe ('Seagull') was in service until 1937 (including on the Berlin–Zurich and Berlin–Paris routes). Over the course of its construction period, the aircraft was given more powerful engines.

Type: Focke-Wulf A 17
Country of origin: Germany
Use: passenger aircraft
Wingspan: 20.00 m
Length: 13.00 m
Powered by: 1 Gnome-Rhône Jupiter 9 Ab, 310 kW (420 hp)
Max. take-off weight: 3610 kg
Cruising speed: 100 mph
Range: 435 miles
Ceiling: 4300 m
Passengers: 8–9 + 2 crew

Focke-Wulf Fw 200 Condor

Four-engine, low-wing, cantilevered passenger aircraft. The first trials in 1937 were promising, and Luft Hansa immediately ordered the first series. Nine Fw 200As and the first export orders followed: two each for Denmark (illustration) and Brazil. This was followed by the Fw 200B, the first major series version with more powerful BMW engines. In August 1938 the long-haul version (Fw 200S-1), a converted V-1, flew from Berlin to New York in slightly less than 25 hours.

Type: Fw 200A (Serie)
Country of origin: Germany
Use: passenger aircraft
Wingspan: 32.84 m
Length: 23.85 m
Powered by: 4 BMW 132G-1, each 530 kW (720 hp)
Max. take-off weight: 14,600 kg
Cruising speed: 210 mph
Range: 900 miles
Ceiling: 7200 m
Passengers: 26 + 4 crew

Fokker F.III

Single-engine high-wing passenger aircraft (maiden flight 1921), based on a construction by chief designer Reinhold Platz. The F.III was Fokker's first independent passenger aircraft. This aircraft type was used on numerous routes within Europe (such as Amsterdam–London from April 1921). On 30 April 1922 a Fokker F.III took off from Königsberg for Moscow, opening up a regular flight connection between Germany and the Soviet Union.

Type: Fokker F.III
Country of origin: Netherlands
Use: passenger aircraft
Wingspan: 17.60 m
Length: 11.07 m
Powered by: 1 Armstrong Siddeley Puma, 176 kW (240 hp)
Max. take-off weight: 1900 kg
Cruising speed: 85 mph
Range: 620 miles
Ceiling: 3200 m
Passengers: 5 + 1 crew

Fokker F.XXXVI

Four-engine high-wing passenger and transport aircraft (maiden flight 22.6.1934). The most striking aspect of this aircraft is the wheels on the landing gear: their diameter of 1.80 m was extremely large for the time. The generously dimensioned wing was made of wood. The four cabins for 32 passengers could be converted into 16 bunks.

Type: Fokker F.XXXVI
Country of origin: Netherlands
Use: passenger aircraft
Wingspan: 32.92 m
Length: 23.60 m
Powered by: 4 Wright Cyclone F2, each 569 kW (760 hp)
Max. take-off weight: 16,500 kg
Cruising speed: 175 mph
Range: 840 miles
Ceiling: 4400 m
Passengers: 32 + 4 crew

Fokker/Fairchild F.27 Friendship

Twin-engine high-wing commercial aircraft (maiden flight proto-type 24.11.1955), originally developed as the replacement for the much-used DC-3. It was a multi-functional aircraft with a pressurised cabin in a number of civilian and military versions. The body was extended to increase the passenger capacity from 44 to 52. In 1956 Fokker signed a contract with Fairchild to produce the aircraft in the USA. The first aircraft built there (illustration) flew in 1958. With more than 800 units built and sold, the Fokker F.27 was one of the most successful turboprop aircraft of all time.

Type: Fokker F.27-200
Country of origin: Netherlands, USA
Use: passenger and transport aircraft
Wingspan: 29.00 m
Length: 23.50 m
Powered by: 2 Rolls-Royce Dart Mk.528 propeller turbines, each 1730 kW (2350 hp)
Max. take-off weight: 19,050 kg
Cruising speed: max. 270 mph
Range: 915 miles
Ceiling: 9935 m
Passengers: 44 + 2 crew

Fokker F.28 Fellowship

Twin-jet low-wing short-haul commercial aircraft with a T-rudder (maiden flight 9.5.1967). Production was in co-operation with MMB and Short with the final assembly being completed in Amsterdam; it ended in 1987 after 241 units. It was built in the following versions: the 1000; the 2000 for 79 passengers, which was 2.50 m longer; the 5000 and 6000 with more powerful engines and pre-wings, and the 3000 and 4000 with longer wings.

Type: Fokker F.28-3000
Country of origin: Netherlands
Use: passenger aircraft
Wingspan: 25.07 m
Length: 27.40 m
Powered by: 2 Rolls-Royce RB1832 Spey Mk.55515P, each producing 44 kN (4486 kp) thrust
Max. take-off weight: 33,110 kg
Cruising speed: max. 530 mph
Range: 1520 miles
Ceiling: 10,675 m
Passengers: 64

Fokker 50

Twin-engine passenger aircraft (maiden flight 1985). Although similar to the F-27 on the outside, the Fokker 50 is primarily a new aircraft, designed and built for regional and short-haul routes (the versions 50-100 and 50-300; also configurations for combined passenger and freight traffic). Production of the Fokker 50 ended in 1997 after 205 units.

Type: Fokker 50-100
Country of origin: Netherlands
Use: passenger aircraft
Wingspan: 29.00 m
Length: 25.25 m
Powered by: 2 Pratt & Whitney Canada PW125B, each 1864 kW (2535 hp)
Max. take-off weight: 19,950 kg
Cruising speed: max. 330 mph
Range: 1275 miles
Ceiling: 4400 m
Passengers: 50–58 + 2 crew

Fokker 100

Twin-jet low-wing passenger aircraft with a T-rudder (maiden flight 30.11.1986); developed from the Fokker F-28. It received much acclaim for its extremely low (for the time) noise load – 'whisper jet'. From 1994 there was a version with a freight hatch on the front left side of the body that quickly converted from passengers to freight traffic.

Type: Fokker 100
Country of origin: Netherlands
Use: passenger aircraft
Wingspan: 28.08 m
Length: 35.31 m
Powered by: 2 Rolls-Royce Tay Mk.650-15, each producing 68 kN (6934 kp) thrust
Max. take-off weight: 44,500 kg
Cruising speed: 470 mph
Range: 2670 miles
Ceiling: 11,900 m
Passengers: 95–107

(Grumman G-159) Gulfstream I

Twin-engine turboprop business aircraft (maiden flight 14.8.1958). This aircraft holds 10–14 passengers in comfort, and is designed for long haul. The commercial version is for 19–24 passengers. There have also been two military versions, one for the US Navy and one for the Coast Guard.

Type: Grumman G-159 Gulfstream 1
Country of origin: USA
Use: business aircraft
Wingspan: 23.90 m
Length: 19.40 m
Powered by: 2 Rolls-Royce RDa-7/2, each 1485 kW (2020 hp)
Max. take-off weight: 15,935 kg
Cruising speed: 350 mph
Range: 2540 miles
Ceiling: 10,760 m
Passengers: 10–14 (or 19–24) + 2 crew

Gulfstream G 550

Twin-jet long-haul business aircraft; like the G 500 it was developed from the Gulfstream V-SV. The G 550 has new Honeywell avionics with LCD displays, Cursor Control Devices, Enhanced Vision System (IR) and an additional cabin window; it also has a greater take-off weight and longer range. Some are also produced for military use (such as reconnaissance).

Type: Gulfstream G 550
Country of origin: USA
Use: business aircraft
Wingspan: 28.50 m
Length: 29.40 m
Powered by: 2 Rolls Royce BR 710, each providing 68.4 kN (6975 kp) thrust
Max. take-off weight: 41,277 kg
Cruising speed: 560 mph
Range: 7770 miles
Ceiling: 15,545 m
Passengers: 14–18 + 2 crew

Guppy

Four-engine transport aircraft, based on the Boeing 377. The individual aircraft were converted by Conroy Aircraft to various modifications and engine configurations. At the end of the Apollo space programme, the Super Guppy Turbine (it had propeller turbines instead of piston engines), which NASA had used to transport rocket components (such as stages of the Saturn V rocket), was sold to Aerospatiale in France. There it was used to transport aircraft components between Airbus Industrie's various production sites until the company had developed its own wide-bodied aircraft (cf. Airbus A300ST Beluga).

Type: Boeing 377 SGT-201 Super Guppy Turbine
Country of origin: USA
Use: transport aircraft
Wingspan: 47.61 m
Length: 46.84 m
Powered by: 4 Allison 501 D22C, each 3610 kW (4910 hp)
Max. take-off weight: 77,100 kg
Cruising speed: 285 mph
Range: 505 miles
Ceiling: 7600 m
Load: 24,500 kg

Hamburger Flugzeugbau HFB 320 Hansa Jet

Twin-jet mid-wing business aircraft with a T-rudder; by Hamburger Flugzeugbau GmbH (maiden flight 21.4.1964); the first German passenger jet to go into series construction (in Hamburg-Finken-werder since 1967) and be delivered. Most notable feature: the forward-swept wing (15°). Although the aircraft remained in production after the takeover by Messerschmitt-Boelkow-Blohm (MBB), only 45 units were sold in all.

Type: HFB 320
Country of origin: Germany
Use: business aircraft
Wingspan: 14.49 m
Length: 16.61 m
Powered by: 2 General Electric CJ 601-9, each producing 12.7 kN (1295 kp) thrust
Max. take-off weight: 9200 kg
Cruising speed: 530 mph
Range: 1430 miles
Ceiling: 11,600 m
Passengers: 12 + 2 crew

Handley Page Hermes

British four-engine mid-range passenger aircraft (maiden flight 2.9.1947). The Hermes was developed from the Hastings transport aircraft. The prototype Hermes I crashed on its maiden flight in 1945. It did not go into series production until the IV version, and was used by BOAC. However, as better-performing aircraft were already available in the USA, the Hermes was soon shifted onto 'second-rate' airlines.

Type: Handley Page H.P.81 Hermes IV
Country of origin: Great Britain
Use: passenger aircraft
Wingspan: 34.44 m
Length: 29.52 m
Powered by: 4 Bristol Hercules 763, each 1566 kW (2130 hp)
Max. take-off weight: 39,000 kg
Cruising speed: 270 mph in 6100 m
Range: 2000 miles
Ceiling: 7670 m
Passengers: 82

Hawker Siddeley Trident

Three-jet passenger aircraft (maiden flight of the 2E on 27.7.1967). Its course of development led from the Trident 1 (103 passengers, 1962) and Trident 1E to the Trident 2E. With a total of 50 units built, it is the most commercially successful Trident. The extended successor Trident 3B (1970) had an additional engine at the rear as a boost on take-off.

Type: Hawker Siddeley HS 121 Trident 2E
Country of origin: Great Britain
Use: passenger aircraft
Wingspan: 29.87 m; **Length:** 34.98 m
Powered by: 3 Rolls-Royce RB163-25 Spey 512, each producing 53.15 kN (5420 kp) thrust
Max. take-off weight: 65,000 kg
Cruising speed: max. 600 mph
Range: 2580 miles
Ceiling: 8990 m
Passengers: 128 + 3 crew

Heinkel He 70 Blitz

Fast, single-engine commercial aircraft (maiden flight 1.12.1932), competitor's answer to the Lockheed Orion 9 C. The He 70 was faster than the fighters in use at the time, and was the first commercial aircraft in the world to have a retractable undercarriage. The aircraft set eight international records in 1933. Four passengers sat opposite each other on two double seats, with a fifth behind the pilot.

Type: Heinkel He 70
Country of origin: Germany
Use: passenger aircraft
Wingspan: 14.80 m
Length: 12.00 m
Powered by: 1 BMW VI 7.3, 552 kW (750 hp)
Max. take-off weight: 3460 kg
Cruising speed: 200 mph
Range: 555-1300 miles
Ceiling: 5500 m
Passengers: 5 + 1 pilot

Ilyushin Il-12

Twin-engine passenger and transport aircraft (maiden flight 7.1.1946). The aircraft was intended as the replacement for the Li-2, and there are structural similarities between the two. Some 3000 aircraft were produced in total, and flew under the most diverse weather and operational conditions. They were used for scheduled flights by Aeroflot, in Poland and in Czechoslovakia.

Type: Ilyushin Il-12
Country of origin: Soviet Union
Use: passenger aircraft
Wingspan: 31.70 m
Length: 21.30 m
Powered by: 2 ASch-82FN, each 1360 kW (1850 hp)
Max. take-off weight: 17,000 kg
Cruising speed: 200 mph
Range: 1180 miles
Ceiling: 6700 m
Passengers: 24 (to max. 32) + 4–5 crew

Ilyushin Il-18

Four-engine mid- to long-haul passenger aircraft (maiden flight 4.6.1957). The aircraft was powered by propeller turbines, and had a pressurised cabin. The basic version (from 1959) was designed for 75 passengers. The Il-18B had space for 84 passengers. The D and E versions had an extended cabin, and the D also had additional tanks for long flights. The aircraft was widely regarded as being strong and reliable, and was extremely popular.

Type: Ilyushin Il-18D
Country of origin: Soviet Union
Use: passenger aircraft
Wingspan: 35.90 m
Length: 37.40 m
Powered by: 4 Ivchenko AI-20M, each 3125 kW (4250 hp)
Max. take-off weight: 64,000 kg
Cruising speed: 390 mph
Range: 2655 miles
Ceiling: 9000 m
Passengers: 110–122 + 5 crew

Ilyushin Il-76

Four-jet shoulder-wing transport aircraft (maiden flight 25.3.1971). The military version is able to transport heavy equipment, and can also land on unpaved runways. Apart from the Soviet Union and its successor states, the Il-76 flew – or flies – in various modifications (including a fire-fighting version). The latest modernised version is the Il-76-TD with Perm PS-90A-76 jet engines (maiden flight 5.8.2005).

Type: Ilyushin Il-76
Country of origin: Soviet Union
Use: transport aircraft
Wingspan: 50.30 m
Length: 46.30 m
Powered by: 4 Soloviev D-30KP, each 120 kN (12,236 kp) thrust
Max. take-off weight: 190,000 kg
Cruising speed: 530 mph
Range: 2985 miles
Ceiling: 13,000 m
Load: 47 t
Crew: 7

Ilyushin Il-96

Four-jet wide-bodied long-haul passenger aircraft (maiden flight 30.8.1988). On the exterior, the main differences between the Il-96 and Il-86 are the much greater wingspan, higher lateral rudder and eye-catching winglets. The cross-section of the body is the same as that of the Il-86. Several other versions were built in addition to the basic one (including a freight transporter). There are plans for a double-decker version for up to 550 passengers.

Type: Ilyushin Il-96-300
Country of origin: Russia
Use: passenger aircraft
Wingspan: 60.10 m; Length: 55.30 m
Powered by: 4 Aviadvigatel PS-90A, each producing 156.9 kN (16,000 kp) thrust
Max. take-off weight: 216,000 kg
Cruising speed: 610 mph
Range: 5530 miles with max. load
Cruising height: 12,000 m
Passengers: 235–270; max. 300

Jakovlev Jak-42

Soviet triple-jet low-wing passenger aircraft with a T-rudder (maiden flight 7.3.1975). The Jak-42 was based on the Jak-40, and intended to replace types such as the Tu-124, Tu-134 and Il-18 on short- and long-haul routes. It went into operation in 1980. The larger Jak-42D (for 120 passengers) appeared in 1989. The latest version with avionics by Allied Signal, the Jak-142, has been in service since 1993.

Type: Jakovlev Jak-42D (Jak-142)
Country of origin: Soviet Union
Use: passenger aircraft
Wingspan: 34.88 m
Length: 36.38 m
Powered by: 3 Lotarev D-36 turbofans, each producing 63.7 kN (6500 kp) thrust
Max. take-off weight: 56,500 kg
Cruising speed: max. 505 mph
Range: max. 2485 miles
Ceiling: 9600 m
Passengers: 104–120

Junkers F 13

Single-engine low-wing passenger aircraft, the first all-metal civilian aircraft (maiden flight 28.6.1919), and the first aircraft in the world to be designed specifically for passenger travel. Riveted Duralumin struts were used for the structure. The closed cabin had upholstered or wicker armchairs, heating and interior lighting. The aircraft could also be fitted with floats or skis. Although the engine performance of 118 kW was modest at first, it increased over the course of construction (total of more than 60 variants of the F 13a to F 13k) to 420 kW. About one-third of the 330 F 13s built flew with German markings.

Type: Junkers F 13a
Country of origin: Germany
Use: passenger aircraft
Wingspan: 17.80 m
Length: 10.50 m
Powered by: 1 Junkers L2, 170 kW (230 hp) from 1924
Max. take-off weight: 1850 kg
Maximum speed: 105 mph
Ceiling: 4000 m
Range: 750 miles
Passengers: 4 + 2 crew

Junkers G 23/G 24

Triple-engine cantilevered low-wing all-metal passenger aircraft (1923). The Junkers G 23 (illustration) is a close relative of the G 24. Although designed for civil aviation, because of the Allied powers' limitations on German aircraft construction, the less powerful Mercedes D IIIa engines had to be fitted. Most of the aircraft went to Sweden, where they were upgraded to the technical level of the G 24 and then reimported to Germany with Swedish approval. From May 1926 the G 24 could be assembled in Dassau, and the Swedish conversion system was halted.

Type: Junkers G 23
Country of origin: Germany
Use: passenger aircraft
Wingspan: 28.50 m
Length: 15.28 m
Powered by: 1 Junkers L2, 2 Mercedes D IIIa with an additional 378 kW (515 hp)
Max. take-off weight: 5500 kg
Maximum speed: 105 mph
Ceiling: 4000 m
Passengers: 9 + 2 crew

Type: Junkers G 24a
Country of origin: Germany
Use: passenger aircraft
Wingspan: 28.50 m
Length: 15.23 m
Powered by: 3 Junkers L2 mit je 170 kW (230 PS)
Max. take-off weight: 5500 kg
Maximum speed: 110 mph
Range: 810 miles
Ceiling: 4000 m
Passengers: 9 + 2 crew

Junkers W 33/W 34

The W 33 was originally developed as a freight and mail carrier, and as a cantilevered low wing in a further development of the F 13 (maiden flight 17.6.1926). However, the aircraft could also be used for passengers. The differences between the W 33 and W 34 were the engines and wingspan. A triple-seater bomber and reconnaissance version was built in Sweden.

Type: Junkers W 34hi
Country of origin: Germany
Use: transport and passenger aircraft
Wingspan: 17.75 m
Length: 10.27 m
Powered by: 1 BMW 132 A, 485 kW (660 hp)
Max. take-off weight: 3200 kg
Maximum speed: 165 mph
Range: 560 miles
Ceiling: 6300 m
Passengers: 6 + 2 crew

Junkers G 38

Four-engine mid-wing commercial aircraft with a box tail unit (maiden flight 6.11.1929). There was room in the so-called 'thick wing' (2 m at the base of the wing) – a Junkers patent – for engines, fuel and passengers. The engines were later replaced by more powerful ones. The first of just two G 38s built crashed on landing at Dessau. The second G 38 was used as a transport aircraft in WWII, and destroyed while on the ground in Athens in a British air attack in May 1941.

Type: Junkers G 38
Country of origin: Germany
Use: passenger aircraft
Wingspan: 44.00 m
Length: 23.20 m
Powered by: 2 L55 12-cylinder V engines, each 441 kW (600 hp), and 2 L8 6-cylinder in-line engines, each 294 kW (400 hp)
Max. take-off weight: 21,500–23,000 kg
Cruising speed: 130 mph
Range: 2175 miles
Passengers: 30–34 + 7 crew

Junkers Ju 52/3m

Triple-engine low-wing passenger aircraft, all-metal construction (maiden flight 7.3.1932). The cell was largely the same as that of the Ju 25/1m; it was adapted for passenger traffic. The cabin could hold 17 people (including emergency seats). It had hot-air heating and ventilation. There was also storage space for baggage and freight, a washroom and WC. The cockpit had dual controls and modern radio equipment. Over the course of time, the aircraft was given different engines to suit purchasers' requirements. Later, large numbers of military transport versions were manufactured and commissioned in addition to the civilian aircraft.

Type: Junkers Ju 52/3m
Country of origin: Germany
Use: passenger aircraft
Wingspan: 29.25 m
Length: 18.50 m
Powered by: 3 BMW 132A, each 485 kW (660 hp)
Max. take-off weight: 9200 kg
Maximum speed: 180 mph
Range: 810 miles
Ceiling: 6300 m
Passengers: 15 (17) + 2 crew

Junkers Ju 60

Single-engine cantilevered low-wing passenger aircraft with a smooth metal body (maiden flight 8.11.1932). The Ju 60 – the last design in which Hugo Junkers was directly involved – failed to meet expectations for a fast commercial aircraft, and so only three prototypes were built. One aircraft initially flew freight routes, and was then used for passengers from 1934 to 1936. The third prototype was used as the model for the Ju 160.

Type: Junkers Ju 60
Country of origin: Germany
Use: fast commercial aircraft
Wingspan: 14.30 m
Length: 11.84 m
Powered by: 1 Pratt & Whitney Hornet radial engine, 404 kW (550 hp)
Max. take-off weight: 3090 kg
Maximum speed: 175 mph
Range: 620 miles
Ceiling: 5200 m
Passengers: 6 + 2 crew

Junkers Ju 160

Single-engine cantilevered low-wing passenger aircraft with a smooth metal body (maiden flight 30.1.1934); developed from the Ju 60. Great attention was paid to achieving a smooth fit of the details on the outer surfaces, and it was given a pitch propeller. Only small numbers of this aircraft were produced in four series.

Type: Junkers Ju 160
Country of origin: Germany
Use: fast commercial aircraft
Wingspan: 14.30 m
Length: 12.30 m
Powered by: 1 BMW 132A, 490 kW (666 hp)
Max. take-off weight: 3540 kg
Maximum speed: 210 mph
Range: 685 miles
Ceiling: 5200 m
Passengers: 6 + 2 crew

Junkers Ju 90

Four-engine passenger aircraft with a twin lateral rudder (maiden flight 28.8.1937), the result of the plans for a strategic bomber (Ju 89, development halted). It was intended to compete with the Douglas DC-3 as a passenger aircraft. It was also called 'Der Grosse Dessauer' after its place of origin. Two prototypes crashed during trials. However, six units were delivered to Luft Hansa before war broke out.

Type: Junkers Ju 90
Country of origin: Germany
Use: passenger aircraft
Wingspan: 35.30 m
Length: 26.42 m
Powered by: 4 BMW 132h radial engines, each 550 kW (750 hp)
Max. take-off weight: 23,000 kg
Maximum speed: 215 mph
Range: 1300 miles
Ceiling: 5750 m
Passengers: 40 + 4 crew

Kalinin K 5

Single-engine strut-braced shoulder-wing passenger aircraft with elliptic wings (maiden flight April 1929). The aircraft had a comfortable passenger cabin. A total of 260 units were built.

Type: Kalinin K 5
Country of origin: Soviet Union
Use: passenger aircraft
Wingspan: 20.50 m
Length: 15.80 m
Powered by: 1 M22 engine, 355 kW (482 hp)
Max. take-off weight: 4000 kg
Cruising speed: 105 mph
Range: 635 miles
Ceiling: 5560 m
Passengers: 6 + 2 crew

Learjet 23

Single-engine low-wing business aircraft (maiden flight 7.10.1963). William P. Lear created an entirely new type of aircraft, based on a Swiss construction. A whole range of other, similar aircraft used in general aviation was also based on it. There is room in the cabin for up to six passengers (typically four). By 1966, 104 series aircraft of this type had been built.

Type: Learjet 23
Country of origin: USA
Use: business aircraft
Wingspan: 10.84 m
Length: 13.18 m
Powered by: 2 General Electric CJ-610-4, each producing 12.7 kN (1295 kp) thrust
Max. take-off weight: 5675 kg
Cruising speed: 510 mph
Range: 1655 miles
Ceiling: 13,750 m
Passengers: 4–6 + 2 crew

Learjet 31

Twin-jet low-wing business aircraft (maiden flight 11.5.1987). Body and engines were derived from the type 35, and the wings from the 55. The Learjet 31A – with improved avionics and faster cruising speeds – was announced in 1990. The 31ER operates with a greater range. A revised version of the Learjet 31A became available in 2000.

Type: Learjet 31A
Country of origin: USA
Use: business aircraft
Wingspan: 13.35 m
Length: 14.84 m
Powered by: 2 Honeywell TFE731-23B, each providing 15.56 kN (1588 kp) thrust
Max. take-off weight: 7484 kg
Cruising speed: 490 mph
Range: 1800 miles
Ceiling: 15,545 m
Passengers: 8 + 2 crew

Learjet (Bombardier) 45

Twin-jet low-wing business aircraft with a T-rudder, built by the Canadian manufacturer Bombardier in co-operation with many other companies (maiden flight 7.10.1995). Unlike the derivations based on the original Learjet 23, the 45 is a completely new construction. A long-haul version, the 45 XR (with a greater take-off weight and range) is also produced.

Type: Learjet 45
Country of origin: USA
Use: business aircraft
Wingspan: 14.56 m
Length: 17.68 m
Powered by: 2 Allied Signal TFE731-20, each providing 15.7 kN (1586 kp) thrust
Max. take-off weight: 9163 kg
Cruising speed: 510 mph
Range: max. 2530 miles
Ceiling: 14,545 m
Passengers: 8–9

Learjet (Bombardier) 60

Twin-jet medium-haul business aircraft (maiden flight 15.6.1992), based on the 55 version of 1979 but with a longer body. Its features include satellite telephone/fax/Internet, a monitor with Airshow 400, cabin video system, DVD/CD player, separate WC and washing facilities. The standard cabin configuration can easily be converted to a cabin with bunks for overnight flights.

Type: Learjet 60
Country of origin: USA
Use: business aircraft
Wingspan: 13.35 m
Length: 17.89 m
Powered by: 2 Pratt & Whitney PW305A, each providing 20.46 kN (2086 kp) thrust
Max. take-off weight: 10,319 kg
Cruising speed: 525 mph
Range: max. 2875 miles
Ceiling: 15,545 m
Passengers: 8–10 + 2 crew

Let L-200 Morava

Twin-engine multi-role low-wing aircraft with twin lateral rudder (maiden flight prototype 8.4.1957) which was used as a business, commuter and ambulance (with 2 stretchers) aircraft; it was – and is still – also used for many other functions in general aviation. More than 1000 Moravas were produced.

Type: Let L-200 A Morava
Country of origin: Czechoslovakia
Use: multi-role aircraft
Wingspan: 12.00 m
Length: 8.60 m
Powered by: 2 Walter Minor M 337, each 154 kW (210 hp)
Max. take-off weight: 1950 kg
Cruising speed: 185 mph
Range: 1055 miles
Ceiling: 6400 m
Passengers: 4 + 1 pilot

Let L-410 Turbolet

Twin-engine commercial short-haul aircraft for passengers and freight (maiden flight prototype 16.4.1969). It can take off and land on grass. The L-410 was supplied in many versions (the most successful of which is the L-410UVP with an elongated body and greater wingspan) and special fittings (such as an ambulance or survey aircraft). To date, more than 1100 units of every version of the L-410 have been built.

Type: Let L-410 UVP
Country of origin: Czechoslovakia
Use: multi-role aircraft
Wingspan: 19.48 m
Length: 14.47 m
Powered by: 2 Walter M601B, each 544 kW (740 hp)
Max. take-off weight: 5800 kg
Cruising speed: 235 mph
Range: 1055 miles
Ceiling: 1040 m
Passengers: 17–19 + 1 pilot

Let L-610

Twin-engine shoulder-wing passenger aircraft with a T-rudder; used for short haul and as a commuter aircraft (maiden flight 28.12.1988). The further development of the Let L-410 was designed for extreme climate conditions. After the end of the Soviet Union, it was adapted to the requirements of the western market (maiden flight of the L-610G on 18.12.1992).

Type: Let L-610
Country of origin: Czechoslovakia
Use: multi-role aircraft
Wingspan: 28.50 m
Length: 29.40 m
Powered by: 2 Motolet M-602, each 1340 kW (1820 hp)
Max. take-off weight: 14,000 kg
Cruising speed: 250 mph
Range: 1490 miles
Ceiling: 10,250 m
Passengers: 40 + 2 crew

Lockheed Vega

Single-engine high-wing passenger air-craft, wood-frame construction (maiden flight 4.7.1927). Pilot and passengers sat in a closed cabin. Amelia Earhart became the first person to circumnavigate the globe solo in a Vega 5B NC7952. By the time production ceased, a total of 128 Vegas had been built.

Type: Lockheed Vega 5C
Country of origin: USA
Use: business aircraft
Wingspan: 12.50 m
Length: 8.38 m
Powered by: 1 Pratt & Whitney Wasp SC-1 radial engine, 330 kW (450 hp)
Max. take-off weight: 2155 kg
Maximum speed: 185 mph
Range: 550 miles
Ceiling: 5485 m
Passengers: 6 + 1 pilot

Lockheed 10/12 Electra

Twin-engine low-wing passenger aircraft with a double lateral rudder (maiden flight 23.2.1934). The aircraft could hold ten passengers and their baggage. A smaller version, the model 12, was used as a commuter and business aircraft, and its shorter cabin could accommodate six passengers.

Type: Lockheed 10 Electra
Country of origin: USA
Use: passenger aircraft
Wingspan: 16.76 m
Length: 11.76 m
Powered by: 2 Pratt & Whitney R985-SB, each 335 kW (456 hp)
Max. take-off weight: 4773 kg
Maximum speed: 220 mph
Range: 945 miles
Ceiling: 6100 m
Passengers: 10 + 2 crew

Lockheed Constellation

Four-engine long-haul commercial aircraft with a triple lateral rudder and pressurised cabin (maiden flight prototype 9.1.1943). Initially used by the military (C-69), it was later sold to numerous civilian operators (L.049). On 19 April 1946 the first Constellation for civilian flights, the L.649, took off. The L.749 with a longer range followed in 1947.

Type: Lockheed Constellation L.749A
Country of origin: USA
Use: passenger aircraft
Wingspan: 37.90 m
Length: 29.00 m
Powered by: 4 18-cylinder Curtiss-Wright R-3350-BD1 double-star engines, each 1838 kW (2500 hp)
Max. take-off weight: 48,535 kg
Cruising speed: 325 mph
Range: 3980 miles
Ceiling: 8300 m
Passengers: 44–80 + 6–8 crew

Lockheed Super Constellation

Four-engine commercial aircraft (maiden flight 13.10.1950) with the elongated body of the Constellation (additional segments inserted before and behind the wings) and with rectangular cabin windows. The performance of the jets was improved by adding exhaust turbines. The freight version, the L.1049D, was produced in 1954. The L.1049G (from the end of 1954) was the most successful.

Type: Lockheed Super Constellation L.1049G
Country of origin: USA
Use: passenger aircraft
Wingspan: 37.50 m
Length: 34.60 m
Powered by: 4 18-cylinder Curtiss-Wright R3350-972TC-18DA double-star engines, each 2389 kW (3250 hp)
Max. take-off weight: 62,370 kg
Cruising speed: 300 mph
Range: 4025 miles
Ceiling: 7050 m
Passengers: 76–99 + 7–10 crew

Lockheed L.188 Electra

Four-engine passenger aircraft (maiden flight prototype 6.12.1957). The first series aircraft were delivered to the airlines in October 1958. After a number of accidents in 1959, certain changes had to be made. A total of 170 series aircraft were produced, including the versions L.180A and L.180C.

Type: Lockheed L.188A Electra
Country of origin: USA
Use: passenger aircraft
Wingspan: 30.18 m
Length: 31.81 m
Powered by: 4 Allison turboprop 501 D-13, each 2800 kW (3800 hp), or 501 D-15, each 3022 kW (4110 hp)
Max. take-off weight: 52,665 kg
Cruising speed: 405 mph
Range: 2765 miles
Ceiling: 8650 m
Passengers: 67–85 + 3 crew

Lockheed L.1011 Tristar

Triple-jet low-wing passenger aircraft with a conventional rudder (maiden flight 16.11.1970). This medium-sized wide-bodied aircraft was intended to help the manufacturer regain lost market shares. It was also available in a long-haul version and one with a shorter (by 4.11 m) body. Lock-heed ended the series after 250 units, and then withdrew from civilian aviation.

Type: Lockheed L.1011-1 Tristar
Country of origin: USA
Use: passenger aircraft
Wingspan: 47.35 m
Length: 54.35 m
Powered by: 3 Rolls-Royce RB211-22-02, each producing 180.6 kN (18,416 kp) thrust
Max. take-off weight: 195,000 kg
Cruising speed: max. 590 mph
Range: 3290 miles
Ceiling: 12,800 m
Passengers: max. 400

Martin 2-0-2

Twin-engine low-wing passenger aircraft (maiden flight 22.11.1946). After an accident in 1948, a number of structural errors had to be rectified. The improved version flew in 1950, but only 12 were delivered. Some 103 units of a version extended by 1 m and with more powerful engines then left the production belt as the M 4-0-4 (photo: M 4-0-4).

Type: Martin 2-0-2
Country of origin: USA
Use: passenger aircraft
Wingspan: 28.24 m
Length: 21.80 m
Powered by: 2 Pratt & Whitney R2800 CA, each 1765 kW (2400 hp)
Max. take-off weight: 18,100 kg
Cruising speed: 275 mph
Range: 1555 miles
Ceiling: 6890 m
Passengers: 36 + 2 crew

McDonnell Douglas MD-83

Twin-jet medium-haul commercial aircraft (maiden flight 17.12.1984). From 1979 to 1999, over 1190 units of the 80 series were built in five versions, including one for freight. The MB-83 has a higher take-off weight and longer range, but in all other respects (apart from the jet engines) it is the same as the MD-82.

Type: McDonnell Douglas MD-83
Country of origin: USA
Use: passenger aircraft
Wingspan: 32.87 m
Length: 45.09 m
Powered by: 2 Pratt & Whitney JT8D-219, each 93.4 kN (9525 kp) thrust
Max. take-off weight: 72,560 kg
Cruising speed: 500 mph
Range: 2880 miles
Cruising height: 10,670 m
Passengers: 137–172

McDonnell Douglas MD-11

Triple-jet low-wing long-haul passenger aircraft with a conventional tail unit (maiden flight 10.1.1990). The MD-11 was designed as the successor to the DC-10. It has a longer body, improved aerodynamics (including the winglets), and a glass cockpit. Boeing stopped production in 2001 (after the takeover by McDonnell Douglas), when some 200 units had been produced. Many MD-11s have now been converted to freighters.

Type: McDonnell Douglas MD-11
Country of origin: USA
Use: passenger aircraft
Wingspan: 16.76 m
Length: 61.21 m
Powered by: 3 Pratt & Whitney PW 4450, each producing 267 kN (27,216 kp) thrust
Max. take-off weight: 273,290 kg
Cruising speed: 580 mph
Range: max. 9480 miles
Ceiling: 13,100 m
Passengers: 323–405 + 2 pilots

Messerschmitt M 20

Single-engine commercial aircraft for passengers or freight; cantilevered high wing in Duralumin all-metal construction (maiden flight prototype 26.2.1928). A total of 15 M 20s were built, and it was in service with Luft Hansa until the 1940s. The freight version had small, round 'bull's-eyes' instead of rectangular cabin windows.

Type: Messerschmitt M 20 a
Country of origin: Germany
Use: passenger aircraft
Wingspan: 25.50 m
Length: 14.90 m
Powered by: 1 BMW VI, 500 kW (680 hp)
Max. take-off weight: 4500 kg
Cruising speed: 100 mph
Range: 590 miles
Ceiling: 4700 m
Passengers: 8–10 + 2 crew

NAMC YS-11

Twin-engine low-wing short-haul commercial aircraft with a T-rudder (maiden flight 1962) that was designed and built on the initiative of the Japanese government. The production and marketing company was founded specifically for this aircraft. A total of 182 units of this Japanese turbo-prop aircraft were manufactured, and a large number of them were exported.

Type: NAMC YS-11
Country of origin: Japan
Use: passenger aircraft
Wingspan: 32.00 m
Length: 26.30 m
Powered by: 2 Rolls-Royce Dart, each 2200 kW (3000 hp)
Max. take-off weight: 24,500 kg
Cruising speed: 330 mph
Range: 2020 miles
Cruising height: 9450 m
Passengers: 64

Piaggio P.166

Twin-engine business aircraft, mid-wing with supporting wings on the bow; elongated wings and elevator positioned towards the rear (maiden flight 23.12.1986). The aircraft is made mainly of light metal and laminates. Its turboprop propulsion helps it to reach jet speeds.

Type: Piaggio P.166 DL3
Country of origin: Italy
Use: business aircraft, patrol aircraft
Wingspan: 14.69 m
Length: 11.90 m
Powered by: 2 Avco Lycoming LTP 101 600, each 432 hp (587 kW)
Max. take-off weight: 4300 kg
Maximum speed: 260 mph
Range: approx. 1410 miles
Ceiling: 7925 m
Passengers: 8–10 + 1–2 crew

Piaggio P.180 Avanti

Twin-engine business aircraft, mid-wing with supporting wings on the bow; elongated wings and elevator that is positioned towards the rear (maiden flight 23.12.1986). The aircraft is made mainly of light metal and laminates. Its turboprop propulsion helps it to reach jet speeds.

Type: Piaggio P.180 Avanti
Country of origin: Italy
Use: business aircraft
Wingspan: 14.03 m
Length: 14.41 m
Powered by: 2 Pratt & Whitney Canada PT6A-66, each 634 kW (862 shaft hp)
Max. take-off weight: 5239 kg
Maximum speed: 455 mph
Range: approx. 1615–1865 miles
Ceiling: 12,500 m
Passengers: 7–8 + 1–2 crew

Pilatus PC-12

Single-engine multi-role aircraft (maiden flight 31.5.1991). The aircraft combines a single high-performance turboprop engine with a spacious cell. This concept makes it ideal for a wide range of uses in general aviation: from commercial and ambulance versions through to use by the police and the US immigration authorities. Its versatility has made it a great commercial success.

Type: Pilatus PC-12
Country of origin: Switzerland
Use: multi-role aircraft
Wingspan: 16.23 m
Length: 14.40 m
Powered by: 1 Pratt & Whitney Canada PT6A-67B, 1327 kW (1800 hp)
Max. take-off weight: 4000 kg
Maximum speed: 310 mph
Range: 1840 miles
Ceiling: 7620 m
Passengers: 6–9 + 2 crew

Piper PA 23 Apache

A twin-engine business aircraft (maiden flight 1954), the Apache was the manufacturer's first twin-engine four-seater aircraft. The first series versions were delivered in 1954. The aircraft, much modified, remained in production until 1982.

Type: Piper PA 23-235 Apache
Country of origin: USA
Use: business aircraft
Wingspan: 11.32 m
Length: 8.41 m
Powered by: 2 Lycoming O-540-B1A5, each 175 kW (238 hp)
Max. take-off weight: 2177 kg
Cruising speed: 190 mph
Range: 1180 miles
Ceiling: 5240 m
Passengers: 3 + 1 pilot

Piper PA 28 Cherokee

Twin-engine cantilevered low-wing business aircraft (maiden flight prototype 10.2.1961). The Cherokee in all its various modifications remains Piper's most frequently built aircraft, and is widely regarded as one of the most important and most popular aircraft in general aviation.

Type: Piper PA 28-140
Country of origin: USA
Use: business aircraft
Wingspan: 9.14 m
Length: 7.16 m
Powered by: 1 Lycoming O-320-E3D, 132 kW (150 hp)
Max. take-off weight: 975 kg
Cruising speed: 140 mph
Range: 775 miles
Ceiling: 4160 m
Passengers: 3 + 1 pilot

Piper PA 31 Navajo

Twin-engine cantilevered low-wing business aircraft (maiden flight prototype 30.9.1964); from its appearance it is Piper's largest aircraft. The PA 31P was given a pressurised cabin in 1970. The PA 31-350 Navajo Chieftain (1973) was extended (10 passengers) and given more powerful engines. Many derivations and licence constructions were based on the basic PA 31, including the Embraer 820.

Type: Piper PA 31-350 Chieftain
Country of origin: USA
Use: business aircraft
Wingspan: 12.40 m
Length: 10.55 m
Powered by: 2 Lycoming TIO-540-J2BD, each 260 kW (353 hp)
Max. take-off weight: 3175 kg
Cruising speed: 270 mph
Range: 1390 miles
Ceiling: 9260 m
Passengers: 9–10 + 2 crew

Piper PA 42 Cheyenne

Twin-engine low-wing turboprop business aircraft (maiden flight of customer aircraft 15.5.1979); the turboprop version of the Piper PA 31. The cell contains a comfortable pressurised cabin. The Cheyenne IIIA is also used as a training aircraft by various airlines and air forces, including Lufthansa and Germany's Bundesluftwaffe.

Type: Piper PA 42 Cheyenne III
Country of origin: USA
Use: business aircraft
Wingspan: 14.53 m
Length: 13.23 m
Powered by: 2 Pratt & Whitney Canada PT6A-41, each 535 kW (727 hp)
Max. take-off weight: 5125 kg
Cruising speed: 255 mph
Range: 1925 miles
Ceiling: 10,060 m
Passengers: 6–9 + 2 crew

Polikarpow Po-2

Single-engine multi-role aircraft, strut-braced wood construction (maiden flight 7.1.1928). It was fitted out for use as a training and sports aircraft, as a crop-duster and as a passenger aircraft with a closed cabin. In 1941 the Soviet Union also used it as a reconnaissance aircraft and fighter; over 40,000 units were produced. Probably the most frequently produced aircraft in the world.

Type: Polikarpow Po-2
Country of origin: Soviet Union
Use: multi-role aircraft
Wingspan: 11.40 m
Length: 8.20 m
Powered by: 1 5-cylinder M-11, 75 kW (102 hp)
Max. take-off weight: 1355 kg
Maximum speed: 155 mph
Range: 410 miles
Ceiling: 7300 m
Passengers: 1–2 + 1 pilot

PZL M-15 Belphegor

Jet-powered agricultural biplane (maiden flight 9.1.1974). The M-15 Belphegor is the only jet turbine-powered biplane in aviation history. The high position of the turbine was intended to reduce the 'vacuum cleaner effect' on unpaved surfaces. Although originally 3000 units were to be built, it remained a small series of 120.

Type: PZL M 15 Belphegor
Country of origin: Poland
Use: agricultural biplane
Wingspan: 22.33 m (top)
Length: 12.72 m
Powered by: 1 AI-25 jet engine, producing 15 kN (1530 kp) thrust
Max. take-off weight: 5650 kg
Working speed: approx. 110 mph
Range: 250 miles
Load: 2 1450 l containers (2500 kg chemicals)
Crew: 1–2

PZL M-28 Skytruck

Twin-engine short-haul transport aircraft, a development of the licence-built Antonov An-28 (1994). The PZL M-28 Skytruck has STOL properties and can operate from unpaved surfaces. It is available as a passenger version, a freight version, an ambulance aircraft and a military transporter.

Type: PZL M-28 Skytruck
Country of origin: Poland
Use: multi-role aircraft
Wingspan: 22.06 m
Length: 13.10 m
Powered by: 2 Pratt & Whitney PT6A-65B, each 687.5 kW (935 hp)
Max. take-off weight: 7500 kg
Maximum speed: 220 mph
Range: 930 miles
Ceiling: 6200 m
Passengers: 19 (or payload 3085 kg)

Saab 340

Twin-engine cantilever low-wing turboprop aircraft; used for short haul and as a commuter aircraft (maiden flight of series version 5.3.1984). The aircraft was initially developed in co-operation with Fairchild, but the American partner withdrew from the project in 1985.

Type: Saab 340
Country of origin: Sweden
Use: passenger aircraft
Wingspan: 21.44 m
Length: 19.73 m
Powered by: 2 General Electric CT-7-9A/9B, each 1275 kW (1733 hp)
Max. take-off weight: 13,200 kg
Maximum speed: 300 mph
Range: 1865 miles
Ceiling: 8200 m
Crew: 33–37

Savoia Marchetti SM.95

Italian four-engine low-wing commercial aircraft with a tail wheel undercarriage arrangement (maiden flight May 1943). This aircraft, which was still in construction during WWII, was used afterwards to rebuild Italy's airline industry. It was used on transcontinental routes, e.g. to Venezuela.

Type: Savoia Marchetti SM.95
Country of origin: Italy
Use: passenger aircraft
Wingspan: 34.28 m
Length: 24.77 m
Powered by: 4 Alfa Romeo 128 RC.18, each 641 kW (860 hp)
Max. take-off weight: 21,600 kg
Cruising speed: 200 mph
Range: 1240 miles
Ceiling: 6800 m
Passengers: 18 + 5 crew

Short 360

Twin-engine passenger aircraft (maiden flight 1.6.1981) for short routes; improved version of the Short 330. The body was extended by 91 cm, the wingspan increased. The aircraft was designed for commuter travel. The 360 Advanced with more powerful engines (later known as the Short 360-200) appeared in November 1985, followed in February 1987 by the Short 360-300.

Type: Short 360-300
Country of origin: Great Britain
Use: passenger aircraft
Wingspan: 22.08 m
Length: 21.58 m
Powered by: 2 Pratt & Whitney PT6A-67R, each 1062 kW (1444 hp)
Max. take-off weight: 12,290 kg
Cruising speed: 250 mph
Range: 465 miles
Ceiling: 3050 m
Passengers: 36 + 2 crew

Sukhoi SSJ 100 (formerly Sukhoi RRJ)

Project for a twin-jet low-wing passenger aircraft with a conventional tail unit. The Russian Regional Jet was intended to replace the obsolete Tu-134, Jak-40, Jak-42 and other designs. This project is a collaboration between Sukhoi and Boeing. Initial plans are for three versions with various cell lengths and take-off weights.

Aeroflot ordered the first 30 units of the longest version, the SSJ 95, in December 2005.

Type: Sukhoi SSJ,100
Country of origin: Russia
Use: passenger aircraft
Wingspan: 29.87 m
Length: 23.87 m

Powered by: 2 Pratt & Whitney 800 or PowerJet SM146, each producing 62.4 kN or 70.8 kN (6363 kp or 7219 kp) thrust
Max. take-off weight: 42,500 kg
Cruising speed: 530 mph
Range: 2000 miles
Ceiling: 12,500 m
Passengers: 105 + 2 crew

Sukhoi Su-80

Twin-engine multi-role aircraft (maiden flight prototype 4.9.2001). The nacelles for the engines are carried in two wing supports, and the double tail unit is connected to a lifting body. The aircraft is the ideal replacement for the ageing An-24/26/28 type and other even older designs, and can be fitted out for a wide range of uses.

Type: Sukhoi Su-80GP
Country of origin: Russia
Use: passenger and transport aircraft
Wingspan: 23.18 m
Length: 18.26 m
Powered by: 2 CT7-9B propeller turbines, each 1287 kW (1750 shaft hp)
Max. take-off weight: 14,200 kg
Cruising speed: 290 mph
Range: 810 miles
Ceiling: 7600 m
Passengers: 30 + 2 crew

Sud Aviation Caravelle

Twin-jet short- and medium-haul commercial aircraft; low wing with a cruciform rudder and the first jet-propelled aircraft of this classification (maiden flights of prototypes on 25.5.1955 and 6.5.1956). The tail arrangement of the engines was highly innovative at the time. Not only did this give the Caravelle its proverbial elegance, but it also enabled the designers to create what was known as a 'cleaner' wing with a moderate degree of swing with no turbulence from the jet turbines. The basic version for 52 passengers later led to a number of other versions with increased passenger capacity. The Caravelle Super 12 (body 2.31 m longer; maiden flight 1970) held 129–138 passengers.

Type: Sud Aviation Caravelle VI
Country of origin: France
Use: passenger aircraft
Wingspan: 34.30 m
Length: 32.01 m
Powered by: 2 Rolls-Royce Avon 531R turbojets, each 54.7 kN (5535 kp) thrust
Max. take-off weight: 50,000 kg
Cruising speed: 490 mph
Range: 1645 miles
Ceiling: 12,000 m
Passengers: 64–99 + 5–7 crew

Sud Est Languedoc

Four-engine passenger aircraft (maiden flight 17.9.1945). First designed by Bloch before the war, it was built in Toulouse after the war. From 1946 it flew from Paris to Algiers and Casablanca as well as to various European capitals. Some aircraft were also used by the Polish airline LOT. Until 1970 a number of units were also used in trials for engines and control units.

Type: Sud Est SE.161 Languedoc
Country of origin: France
Use: passenger aircraft
Wingspan: 29.38 m
Length: 24.24 m
Powered by: 4 Pratt & Whitney Twin Wasp, each 880 kW (1200 hp)
Max. take-off weight: 23,700 kg
Cruising speed: 250 mph
Range: 2000 miles
Ceiling: 7200 m
Passengers: 33 + 5 crew

Tupolev ANT-9

Triple-engine shoulder-wing passenger aircraft (maiden flight April 1929). Many of the 70 units built flew international routes to European capitals and inner-Soviet long-haul routes. It was also used for transport and medical tasks during WWII. An extended version (for 36 passengers) with five engines, the ANT-14, was built once and used mainly for propaganda purposes and aerial tours. There was no requirement in the Soviet Union at the time for aircraft with greater passenger capacities.

Type: Tupolev ANT-9
Country of origin: Soviet Union
Use: passenger aircraft
Wingspan: 23.80 m

Length: 16.65 m
Powered by: 3 Wright Whirlwind, each 224 kW (305 hp)
Max. take-off weight: 5690 kg

Maximum speed: 130 mph
Range: 434 miles
Ceiling: 4500 m
Passengers: 9 + 2 crew

Tupolev ANT-20 Maxim Gorki

Eight-engine cantilevered mid-wing multi-role aircraft (maiden flight 17.6.1934) that was used for propaganda purposes and as a commercial aircraft. It contained printing machinery, a photographic laboratory, cinema, library, telephone switchboard and cabins, and could accommodate 72 passengers; at the time it was the biggest land aircraft in the world. Each of the two wings contained three engines that could be worked on in-flight through corridors inside the wings, and two more acted as tandem engines on a frame above the body. Large landing flaps reduced the landing speed to 60 mph, and thanks to its strong wheel brakes the aircraft needed just 400 m to land. In 1935 the ANT-20 landed at an air show after colliding with an accompanying fighter. Everyone on board, including many Soviet dignitaries and their families, was killed. Its successor, the ANT-20bis (illustration), was given stronger engines (no tandem engines on the body), and so required only six of them. The aircraft was used on Soviet long-haul routes until 1942.

Type: Tupolev ANT-20/ANT-20bis
Country of origin: Soviet Union
Use: multi-role aircraft
Wingspan: 63.00 m/64.00 m
Length: 33.00 m/34.10 m
Powered by: 8 AM-34FRN/6 AM-34FRNW, each 671 kW (900 PS)/895 kW (1200 hp)
Max. take-off weight: 42,000 kg/ 44,000 kg
Maximum speed: 150 mph/170 mph
Range: 1365 miles/560 miles
Ceiling: 4500 m/5500 m
Passengers: 72 + 8 crew/64 + 9 crew

Tupolev Tu-104

Twin-engine cantilevered low-wing passenger aircraft (maiden flight 17.6.1955). The aircraft was developed from the Tu-16 bomber. The engines were integrated in the wings. The aircraft was produced in several versions with various body lengths and engines. It was one of the first jet-powered commercial aircraft to be used for scheduled services.

Type: Tupolev Tu-104
Country of origin: Soviet Union
Use: passenger aircraft
Wingspan: 34.54 m; Length: 38.85 m
Powered by: 2 Mikulin AM-3(M), each producing 66.2 kN (6750 kp) thrust
Max. take-off weight: 76,000 kg
Maximum speed: 560 mph
Range: 1645 miles with max. load
Cruising height: 10,000 m
Passengers: 70 + 5 crew

Tupolev Tu-114

Four-engine low-wing long-haul passenger aircraft, structurally based on the Tu-20/Tu-95 bomber. The Tu-114 was and still is the biggest and fastest propeller-driven commercial aircraft (maiden flight 3.11.1957). The turbines powered four contra-rotating propellers. Due to the large diameter of the propellers (5.60 m), the landing gear had to be very high up. The 31 units manufactured were replaced in 1975 by the Ilyushin Il-62.

Type: Tupolev Tu-114
Country of origin: Soviet Union
Use: passenger aircraft
Wingspan: 51.10 m
Length: 54.10 m
Max. take-off weight: 171,000 kg
Powered by: 4 Kuznetsov NK-12, each 10,889 kW (14,800 hp)
Maximum speed: 545 mph
Range: 5590 miles
Ceiling: 12,000 m
Passengers: 170–220

Tupolev Tu-134

Twin-jet low-wing short- and medium-haul commercial aircraft with a T-rudder (maiden flight autumn 1963). The Tu-134 was derived from the Tu-124, but had an altered engine arrangement (at the rear) and thus a redesigned landing gear. The aircraft was produced in a number of civilian and military versions.

Type: Tupolev Tu-134A
Country of origin: Soviet Union
Use: passenger aircraft
Wingspan: 29.00 m
Length: 37.05 m
Powered by: 2 Soloviev D30-II, each producing 66.7 kN (6730 kp) thrust
Max. take-off weight: 47,000 kg
Cruising speed: 560 mph
Range: 1875 miles
Ceiling: 12,100 m
Passengers: 76–84 + 3 crew

Tupolev Tu-144

Four-jet supersonic passenger aircraft (maiden flight 31.12.1968). On 26 May 1970 it became the first commercial aircraft to exceed Mach 2. The last unit was completed in 1981; it later served as a test aircraft for the Buran space shuttle. In December 1975 the Tu-144 commenced freight operation, and in November 1977 passenger travel between Moscow and Alma-Ata. By 1978 the 16 aircraft produced had transported a total of 3284 passengers, so it was not really a commercial success.

Type: Tupolev Tu-144S
Country of origin: Soviet Union
Use: passenger aircraft
Wingspan: 28.80 m
Length: 65.70 m
Powered by: 4 Kusnezov NK-144, each producing 196 kN (20,000 kp) thrust
Max. take-off weight: 207,000 kg
Maximum speed: 1555 mph
Range: 1560 miles
Ceiling: 18,000 m
Passengers: 108–135 + 3–4 crew

Tupolev Tu-204

Twin-jet medium-haul passenger and transport aircraft (maiden flight 2.1.1989) that was and is built in various versions, and is the successor to the Tu-154. The Tu-204-300 long-haul version first flew on 18 August 2003. The cockpit has modern avionics, and meets western standards. The Tu-204C freight version can carry up to 27 tonnes of freight.

Type: Tupolev Tu-204-100
Country of origin: Russia
Use: passenger aircraft
Wingspan: 42.00 m
Length: 46.00 m
Powered by: 2 Perm PS-90A, each producing 154 kN (15,700 kp) thrust
Max. take-off weight: 103,000 kg
Cruising speed: 505 mph
Range: 4040 miles
Ceiling: 12,600 m
Passengers: 210 + 2 crew

Tupolev Tu-334

Twin-jet short- and medium-haul commercial aircraft (maiden flight prototype 25.8.1995). The body – much shortened and with a lower landing gear – was used for the Tu-204, as were the cockpit and other systems. The aircraft received type approval at the end of 2003, and is to replace the obsolete Tu-134.

Type: Tupolev Tu-334-120
Country of origin: Russia
Use: passenger aircraft
Wingspan: 29.80 m
Length: 31.10 m
Powered by: 2 Rolls-Royce RB710-48, each producing 68.2 kN (6954 kp) thrust
Max. take-off weight: 46,100 kg
Cruising speed: 510 mph
Range: 1555 miles
Ceiling: 11,100 m
Passengers: 102 + 2 crew

VFW Fokker 614

Twin-jet short-haul commercial aircraft, cantilevered low wing (maiden flight 14.7.1971). The engines are mounted on pylons on the wings in order to prevent the 'vacuum cleaner' effect of the turbines. Despite successful tests and a number of orders, the aircraft was a financial failure. The German government cut its funding in favour of the Airbus. Two units were converted to test aircraft.

Type: VFW Fokker 614
Country of origin: Germany
Use: passenger aircraft
Wingspan: 21.50 m
Length: 20.60 m
Powered by: 2 Rolls-Royce M45 H, each producing 33.8 kN (3446 kp) thrust
Max. take-off weight: 18,600 kg
Cruising speed: 435 mph
Range: 745 miles
Ceiling: 7600 m
Passengers: 40–44

Vickers Viking

Twin-engine passenger aircraft – Britain's first new construction after WWII (maiden flight 22.6.1945). Of the various series built, the IB was the most successful with 113 units sold. The Viking was built until 1948.

Type: Vickers Viking 1B
Country of origin: Great Britain
Use: passenger aircraft
Wingspan: 27.20 m
Length: 19.86 m
Powered by: 2 Bristol Hercules 634, each 1260 kW (1713 hp)
Max. take-off weight: 15,350 kg
Cruising speed: 210 mph
Range: 520 miles
Ceiling: 7240 m
Passengers: 24

Vickers Viscount

Four-engine passenger and transport aircraft (maiden flight prototype 16.7.1948), low wing with a conventional rudder; at the time of its maiden flight it was the first ever turboprop-driven passenger aircraft. Of the 700 (maiden flight 28.8.1950), 700D, 770D and 771D prototypes, 287 Viscounts were built; the 800 and 810 series have had more powerful engines since 1958.

Type: Vickers Viscount 700/800
Country of origin: Great Britain
Use: passenger aircraft
Wingspan: 28.56 m/28.56 m
Length: 24.94 m/26.11 m
Powered by: 4 Rolls-Royce Dart R.Da.3 505, each 1154 kW (1570 hp)/R.Da.6 Mk.510, each 1327 kW (1805 hp)
Max. take-off weight: 29,257 kg/32,840 kg
Cruising speed: 330 mph/365 mph
Range: 1330 miles/1725 miles
Ceiling: 7770 m/7620 m
Passengers: 40–63/65–75

Vickers Vanguard

Four-engine short- to medium-haul passenger aircraft (maiden flight 20.1.1959). It was planned to be the successor to the Vickers Viscount, was faster and could hold more. However, the arrival of the large passenger jets prevented it from being a financial success. Production ended in 1962, with 43 units in three versions. Nine units were later converted to freighters (Merchantman) by Aviation Traders.

Type: Vickers Vanguard V.952
Country of origin: Great Britain
Use: passenger aircraft
Wingspan: 36.15 m
Length: 37.45 m
Powered by: 4 Rolls-Royce Tyne 512, each 4076 kW (5545 hp)
Max. take-off weight: 66,440 kg
Cruising speed: 425 mph
Range: 2735 miles
Ceiling: 9145 m
Passengers: 139 + 3 crew

Vickers VC10

Four-jet long-haul passenger aircraft (maiden flight 1962). Originally designed for 135 passengers, the body was soon lengthened and the capacity increased (Super VC10). Some 64 units were built in both versions, and flew scheduled services until 1981. The military adaptations of the civilian aircraft as a transporter, and particularly a refuelling aircraft, were far more successful.

Type: Vickers VC10/Super VC10
Country of origin: Great Britain
Use: passenger aircraft
Wingspan: 44.55 m/44.55 m
Length: 48.52 m/52.32 m
Powered by: 4 Rolls-Royce Conway 540, each producing 94.1 kN (9595 kp)/Conway 550, each producing 100.1 kN (10,207 kp) thrust
Max. take-off weight: 141,500 kg/152,000 kg
Maximum speed: 550 mph/580 mph
Range: 6065 miles/7125 miles
Ceiling: 11,580 m/11,580 m
Passengers: 135/176–220

Zeppelin E-4/20 Staaken

Four-engine shoulder-wing commercial aircraft; the world's first ever four-engine all-metal aircraft (maiden flight 9.11.1920). It was intended to fly the Berlin–Friedrichshafen route. However, the E-4/20 had to be destroyed as the Allies designated it a weapon of war.

Type: Zeppelin E-4/20 Staaken
Country of origin: Germany
Use: passenger aircraft
Wingspan: 31.00 m
Length: 16.60 m
Powered by: 4 MB-IVa, each 190 kW (258 hp)
Max. take-off weight: 8500 kg
Cruising speed: 130 mph
Passengers: 12–18

Sports and training aircraft

Sports and training aircraft

Ever since its early days, motorised flying has been seen as a sporting challenge. Here it is not a matter of payload and passenger capacities, ever heavier and ever bigger, but the opposite – mobility, lightness (even ultra-lightness) and, if you like, goodwill. Sport includes training, and flying has to be learnt, whether general aviation or passenger and military flying. The features of training aircraft are constantly changing, and tomorrow's military and commercial pilots start their training in the same aircraft as amateur and leisure pilots.

3Xtrim

Single-engine lightweight aircraft, strut-braced hign-wing aeroplane with a fixed triple-point chassis. There are three versions of this aircraft: the 450 Ultra, the 495 Ultra + (both meet the criteria in some countries for ultra-lightweight aircraft), and the 550 Trainer. The seats in all three versions are side by side. The aircraft are sold either as kits or fully constructed machines.

Type: 3Xtrim 550 Trener
Country of origin: Poland
Use: training and sports aircraft
Wingspan: 10.03 m
Length: 6.87 m

Powered by: Bombardier-Rotax 912S with 73.6 kW (100 hp) take-off power
Max. take-off weight: 550 kg
Cruising speed: max. 120 mph

Range: 465 miles
Passengers: 1 + 1 pilot

Aerostyle Breezer

Single-engine ultra-light aircraft in aluminium/plastic construction. This low-wing aircraft is available with various engines (Rotax, Jabiro, BMW, VW or Hirth). The Breezer is one of the most frequently sold metal kits, but can be supplied as a finished aircraft. It is also available in a banner- and glider-towing version. In addition to the ultra-light version, there is a slightly heavier experimental version.

Type: Aerostyle Breezer Rotax 912 S
Country of origin: Germany
Use: ultra light aircraft
Wingspan: 8.71 m
Length: 6.40 m
Powered by: 1 Rotax 4-cylinder 4-stroke engine, 73 kW (100 hp)
Max. take-off weight: 472.50 kg
Cruising speed: 200 mph
Passengers: 1 + 1 pilot

Airspeed AS 8 Viceroy

Twin-engine lightweight low-wing sports aircraft (maiden flight in August 1934). The only Viceroy was a special construction for the MacRobertson air race, and was based on the Airspeed AS 6 Envoy. However the Viceroy had stronger engines, there were no windows in the body, and additional tanks in the body meant that more fuel could be carried.

Type: Airspeed AS 8 Viceroy
Country of origin: Great Britain
Use: sports aircraft
Wingspan: 15.90 m
Length: 10.50 m

Powered by: 2 turbocharged Armstrong Siddeley Cheetah VI radial engines, each 206 kW (280 hp)
Max. take-off weight: 2860 kg
Maximum speed: 210 mph
Range: 1400 miles
Ceiling: 3850 m
Crew: 2

Airspeed AS 10 Oxford

Twin-engine sports and training aircraft, wood construction, based on the AS 6 Envoy (maiden flight of prototype 19.6.1937). Crews of multi-engine aircraft trained on the Oxford. It was also used as an auxiliary bomber, air ambulance and liaison aircraft. By 1948, of the more than 8500 units constructed, over 100 were modified for civilian operators as the AS 65 Consul.

Type: Airspeed AS 10 Oxford
Country of origin: Great Britain
Use: training aircraft
Wingspan: 16.26 m
Length: 10.52 m

Powered by: 2 Pratt & Whitney R-985-AN6 Wasp Junior of 330 kW (450 hp)
Max. take-off weight: 3630 kg
Maximum speed: 200 mph
Range: 500 miles
Ceiling: 5830 m
Passengers: 2 + 2 crew

Blackburn B-2

Single-engine biplane sports and training aircraft, all-metal shell construction (maiden flight 10.12.1931). The aircraft was used for basic training. The two seats in the open cockpit for the instructor and student are side by side.

Type: Blackburn B-2
Country of origin: Great Britain
Use: training aircraft
Wingspan: 9.19 m
Length: 7.39 m
Powered by: 1 De Havilland Gipsy Major in-line engine, 97 kW (132 hp)
Max. take-off weight: 839 kg
Maximum speed: 110 mph
Range: max. 320 miles
Crew: 2

Blériot XI

Single-engine sports aircraft, wood construction (maiden flight 23.1.1909). On 25 July 1909 Blériot became the first person ever to fly the English Channel – and did so in an aircraft of this type. There was then a tremendous increase in demand for Blériot's aircraft; in 1913 alone some 800 were built (more than 60 per cent of France's entire aircraft production). Blériot developed a larger twin-seater version with a more powerful engine from the XI: the XI-2.

Type: Blériot XI/Blériot XI-2
Country of origin: France
Use: sports aircraft
Wingspan: 7.81 m/10.25 m
Length: 7.05 m/10.25 m
Powered by: 1 Anzani engine, 18.4 kW (25 hp)/Gnôme-7B rotary engine, 52 kW (70 hp)
Max. take-off weight: 320 kg/625 kg
Maximum speed: 45 mph/65 mph
Crew: 1–2

Bücker Bü 131 Jungmann

Single-engine, fully aerobatic biplane sports and training aircraft (maiden flight 27.4.1934). The aircraft was used for basic training. The body consisted mainly of a fabric-covered steel framework; the wings were fabric-covered wood. The serial version was used by training schools, by Germany's newly formed Luftwaffe (air force), and in 19 other countries. In Germany alone 3000 units were produced, and in total (including licensed constructions) around 5000.

Type: Bücker Bü 131 Jungmann
Country of origin: Germany
Use: training aircraft
Wingspan: 7.40 m
Length: 6.62 m
Powered by: 1 Hirth HM 60 R, 60 kW (80 hp)
Max. take-off weight: 630 kg
Maximum speed: 105 mph
Range: 425 miles
Ceiling: 3500 m
Crew: 1–2

Cessna 172 Skyhawk

Single-engine, high-wing four-seater sports and travel aircraft (1955); the US Air Force used it as the T-41 for pilot training. The more sophisticated luxury version was known as the Skyhawk. The version developed from the Cessna 170B was built until 1983 (over 35,000 units), including under licence in France (2144 units by Reims Aviation). It has been back in production since 1997 with modern aviation electronics. In 1987 the Cessna Skyhawk made headlines all over the world when Mathias Rust of Germany landed one on Red Square in Moscow.

Type: Cessna 172
Country of origin: USA
Use: sports and training aircraft
Wingspan: 10.92 m
Length: 8.28 m
Powered by: 1 Continental O 300 C, 107 kW (145 hp)
Max. take-off weight: 1043 kg
Cruising speed: 130 mph
Range: 595–685 miles
Ceiling: 4000 m
Passengers: 3 + 1 pilot

De Havilland Canada DHC-1 Chipmunk

Single-engine, fully aerobatic low-wing sports and training aircraft (maiden flight in 1946) that was intended to replace the Tiger Moth training biplane. Of these 218 were built in Canada, 1014 in Great Britain and 60 in Portugal. One-third of the aircraft were used by the RAF for basic training. Deutsche Lufthansa also used five Chipmunks as basic trainers.

Type: DHC-1
Country of origin: Canada
Use: training aircraft
Wingspan: 10.47 m
Length: 7.75 m
Powered by: 1 De Havilland Gipsy Major 8, 108 kW (146 hp)
Max. take-off weight: 914 kg
Maximum speed: 140 mph
Range: 260 miles
Ceiling: 4820 m
Crew: 1–2

De Havilland DH.82 Tiger Moth

Single-engine biplane sports and training aircraft (in use by the RAF Royal Flying School since 1931). The successor to the DH 60 Moth and developed from it, it became the RAF's standard training aircraft. Series production ended in 1945, and many of the former military aircraft were sold to private users as sports aircraft.

Type: De Havilland DH.82
Country of origin: Great Britain
Use: training aircraft
Wingspan: 8.94 m
Length: 4.34 m
Powered by: 1 De Havilland Gipsy Major l, 100 kW (130 hp)
Max. take-off weight: 828 kg
Maximum speed: 110 mph
Range: 300 miles
Ceiling: 4145 m
Crew: 1–2

Gotha Go-150

Twin-engine low-wing cantilever sports aircraft, wood construction. The body was an almost rectangular wooden construction with plywood planking; the wings and tail unit were also made of wood. This very lightweight two-seater won many prizes and set many records in flying competi-tions (including the single-seater altitude record of 8048 m in 1939).

Type: Gotha Go-150
Country of origin: Germany
Use: sports aircraft
Wingspan: 11.80 m
Length: 7.15 m

Powered by: 2 Zündapp Z 9-092, each 37 kW (50 hp) take-off power
Max. take-off weight: 936 kg
Cruising speed: 115 mph
Range: 560 miles
Ceiling: 4200 m
Crew: 2

Great Lakes 2T-1A-2

Single-engine sports aircraft, open two-seater biplane. The aircraft is suitable for aerobatics (maiden flight of prototype in 1928). Some 200 were built before 1933, but then production was halted because of the global economic crisis. Construction of the famous Great Lakes biplane recommenced in 1973.

Type: Great Lakes 2T-1A-2
Country of origin: USA
Use: sports aircraft
Wingspan: 8.13 m
Length: 6.45 m
Powered by: 1 Lycoming AEIO 360 BIGS, 134 kW (182 hp)
Max. take-off weight: 816 kg
Maximum speed: 130 mph
Range: 300 miles
Crew: 2

Gyroflug SC01 Speed Canard

Single-engine two-seater sports canard-configured mid-wing aircraft (so-called duck aircraft with strikingly short wings). The aircraft is made of fibreglass-reinforced laminate. The body was based on a glider cell. The aircraft is powered by a thrust propeller on the tail. The winglets on the tips of the wings support the side rudders.

Type: Gyroflug SC01 B 160
Country of origin: Germany
Use: sports aircraft
Wingspan: 7.70 m
Length: 5.20 m
Powered by: 1 Lycoming O-235-P2A, 88 kW (120 hp)
Max. take-off weight: 715 kg
Cruising speed: 170 mph
Range: 800–1300 miles
Ceiling: 4000 m
Crew: 2

Ilyushin Il 103

Single-engine low-wing sports aircraft, all-metal construction (maiden flight 17.5.1994); in series production since 1997. The aircraft has a fixed-nose wheel unit. It can also be used as a light freight aircraft.

Type: Ilyushin Il 103
Country of origin: Russia
Use: sports and training aircraft
Wingspan: 10.56 m
Length: 7.95 m
Powered by: 1 Teledyne Continental IO-360ES 6-cylinder boxer engine, 160 kW (218 hp)
Max. take-off weight: 1285 kg
Cruising speed: 125 mph
Range: 500 miles
Ceiling: 3000 m
Passengers: 3 + 1 pilot

Jakovlev Jak-18

Single-engine twin-seater training and sports aircraft (series production from 1947). By the time production of the 'classic' Jak 18 halted at the end of 1967, 6760 units had been built; together with the four-seater Jak 18T (since 1967), over 8000 were built in total. Since 1993 small quantities of the Jak 18T have again been produced, and its uses include training purposes.

Type: Jakovlev Jak-18A
Country of origin: Soviet Union
Use: training and sports aircraft
Wingspan: 10.60 m
Length: 8.18 m
Powered by: 1 Ivchenko AI-14R, 194 kW (263 hp)
Max. take-off weight: 1316 kg
Maximum speed: 160 mph
Range: 650 miles
Ceiling: 4000 m
Crew: 2

Jakovlev UT-2

Single-engine low-wing sports and training aircraft (developed in 1935) that was used for training purposes by the Soviet air forces during WWII. It is also a standard aircraft for many Soviet flying clubs. The cabin has a fabric-covered steel tube construction, the wings are fabric-covered wood. Floats can be added if required.

Type: Jakovlev UT-2
Country of origin: Soviet Union
Use: sports and training aircraft
Wingspan: 10.20 m
Length: 7.00 m
Powered by: 1 M-11 5-cylinder radial engine, 75 kW (100 hp)
Max. take-off weight: 856 kg

Maximum speed: 130 mph
Range: 310 miles
Ceiling: 3500 m
Crew: 1–2

Junkers A 48

Single-engine low-wing two-seater sports and training aircraft, all-metal construction with smooth metal body (maiden flight 15.9.1929). A total of seven were constructed and approved in Germany. The parts for seven more were delivered to the branch in Limmhamn (Sweden), where they were converted to Junkers K 47 fighter bombers. Various engines were used.

Type: Junkers A 48
Country of origin: Germany
Use: training aircraft
Wingspan: 12.40 m
Length: 8.55 m
Powered by: 1 Bristol Jupiter VII, 441 kW (600 PS)
Max. take-off weight: 1650 kg
Maximum speed: 170 mph
Range: 310 miles
Ceiling: 7500 m
Passengers: 1 + 1 pilot

Junkers A 50

Single-engine, low-wing two-seater sports aircraft, duralumin corrugated-sheet planking (maiden flight 13.2.1929). The second seat was covered when in single-seat use. In several versions 69 units were produced, 50 of which were sold. The A 50 with floats set eight FAI world records in 1930.

Type: Junkers A 50
Country of origin: Germany
Use: sports aircraft
Wingspan: 10.00 m
Length: 7.12 m
Powered by: 1 Armstrong Siddeley Genet, 59 kW (80 hp)
Max. take-off weight: 600 kg
Cruising speed: 105 mph
Ceiling: 4600 m
Crew: 1–2

Junkers T 26

Single-engine high-wing training aircraft, the follow-on to the T 23 (maiden flight 1925). A second, smaller underwing was fitted to create a biplane for basic training. However this version proved to be too expensive for flying schools, so it never became a commercial success.

Type: Junkers T 26
Country of origin: Germany
Use: training aircraft
Wingspan: 13.15 m
Length: 7.54 m
Powered by: 1 Junkers L1a, 59 kW (80 hp)
Max. take-off weight: 730 kg/805 kg
Cruising speed: 80 mph (monoplane)/70 mph (biplane)
Passengers: 1 + 1 pilot

Klemm Kl 35

Single-engine sports and training aircraft (maiden flight 1935). This cantilevered low-wing aircraft was fully aerobatic, and was used by several air forces as a trainer as well as by private individuals and flying clubs. From version D it had a tripod chassis.

Type: Klemm Kl 35 D
Country of origin: Germany
Use: training and sports aircraft
Wingspan: 10.40 m

Length: 7.35 m
Powered by: 1 4-cylinder in-line engine Hirth HM 504 A, 77 kW (105 hp)
Max. take-off weight: 705 kg
Maximum speed: 190 mph
Range: 500 miles
Ceiling: 4600 m
Crew: 2

Letov S-18

Single-engine biplane sports and training aircraft (maiden flight 1925). The original version had a wooden body. The S-118 was given a more powerful engine. The cell was completely reconstructed in steel tube for the D-218 (1926). The aircraft was used by private owners and flying clubs.

Type: Letov S-18
Country of origin: Czechoslovakia
Use: sports aircraft
Wingspan: 10.00 m
Length: 6.68 m
Powered by: 1 Walter NZ 60 radial engine, 44 kW (60 hp)
Max. take-off weight: 555 kg
Cruising speed: 65 mph
Range: 200 miles
Ceiling: 3500 m
Crew: 2

Messerschmitt M 17

Single-engine sports aircraft, wood construction, and first aeroplane to be created by Willy Messerschmitt (1925). Between six and eight were produced. In 1926 the M 17 became the first lightweight aircraft to cross the central Alps.

Type: Messerschmitt M 17
Country of origin: Germany
Use: sports aircraft
Wingspan: 11.60 m
Length: 5.85 m
Powered by: 1 Bristol Cherub III, 26.5 kW (36 hp)
Max. take-off weight: 370 kg
Cruising speed: 95 mph
Range: 310 miles
Ceiling: 4000 m
Passengers: 1 + 1 pilot

Messerschmitt Bf 108

Single-engine low-wing sports and training aircraft (1934). Several altitude and course records were set by this aircraft. Initially many private pilots used it as a travel aircraft before the Luftwaffe awarded a major order for it. During WII the Bf 108 was used as a liaison and retraining aircraft for the Bf 109.

Type: Messerschmitt Bf 108
Country of origin: Germany
Use: sports and training aircraft
Wingspan: 10.62 m
Length: 8.30 m
Powered by: 1 8-cylinder Argus As 10 C, 177 kW (240 hp) take-off power
Max. take-off weight: 1380 kg
Maximum speed: 185 mph
Range: approx. 590 miles
Ceiling: 5000 m
Passengers: 3 + 1 pilot

Piaggio P.148/149

Single-engine sports aircraft, cantilever, all-metal low-wing (maiden flight 12.2.1951), trainer used for basic flying training and aerobatics training. The improved version P.149 (maiden flight 19.6.1953) was the standard training aircraft used by Germany's Luftwaffe and various other armed forces. In Germany it was built under licence by Focke Wulf.

Type: Piaggio P.148/P.149
Country of origin: Italy
Use: sports and training aircraft
Wingspan: 11.12 m/11.12 m
Length: 8.44 m/8.80 m
Powered by: 1 Lycoming O-435-A, 142 kW/1 Lycoming GO 480, 202 kW
Max. take-off weight: 1280 kg/1680 kg
Maximum speed: 145 mph/190 mph
Range: approx. 575 miles/675 miles
Ceiling: 5000 m/6050 m
Passengers: 3–4 + 1 pilot

Pilatus PC-7

Single-engine multi-purpose training aircraft, originally with piston drive (further development of the P-3), the PC-7 with propeller turbine first took off in August 1966; the first series version flew in 1978. The turboprop trainer is valued for its qualities in training, instrument, aerobatics and night flying to this day.

Type: Pilatus PC-7 Mk.II
Country of origin: Switzerland
Use: training aircraft
Wingspan: 10.19 m
Length: 10.14 m
Powered by: 1 Pratt & Whitney PT 6A-25A, 410 kW (556 hp)
Max. take-off weight: 2250 kg
Maximum speed: 345 mph
Range: 930 km
Ceiling: 7600 m
Passengers: 1 + 1 pilot

Pilatus PC-21

Single-engine turboprop low-wing sports and training aircraft (maiden flight of the prototypes 2002 and 2004). The aerodynamic characteristics of the PC-21 are far superior to those of other turboprop aircraft. This is why this new trainer is suitable both for basic and advanced training, and also for some aspects of jet training.

Type: Pilatus PC-21
Country of origin: Switzerland
Use: training aircraft
Wingspan: 8.77 m
Length: 11.00 m
Powered by: 1 Pratt & Whitney Canada PT6A-68B, 1195 kW (1625 hp)
Max. take-off weight: 4250 kg
Maximum speed: 425 mph
Range: 805 miles
Ceiling: 11,580 m
Crew: 2

Piper J3c Cub

Single-engine high-wing sports aircraft that originated in the 1930s; from 1937 approx. 20,000 units were produced. The initial engine with a modest 30 kW was later increased to over 60 kW.

Type: Piper J3c-65
Country of origin: USA
Use: sports aircraft
Wingspan: 10.74 m
Powered by: 1 Continental, 48.5 kW (66 hp)
Max. take-off weight: 550 kg
Cruising speed: 70 mph
Range: 185 miles
Ceiling: 7000 m
Crew: 1

Platzer Kiebitz

Single-engine ultra-light aircraft, single-span biplane, composite construction. The aircraft has two seats, one behind the other. It is available in the classifications 330 kg and 400 kg; various engines have been approved for it. The aircraft is a self-assembly kit with no pre-assembled components. Instead the manufacturer offers a licence with a planning record.

Type: Platzer Kiebitz
Country of origin: Germany
Use: ultra- light aircraft
Wingspan: 7.60 m
Length: 6.90 m
Powered by: 1 Nissan MA-12-P or other
Max. take-off weight: 330 kg/400 kg
Maximum speed: 125 mph
Crew: 2

Ruschmeyer R90

Single-engine low-wing sports aircraft. This is the first time that vinyl ester resin and glass and carbon fibres have been used as a composite material. Ruschmeyer is Solaris Aviation in the USA, and this aircraft is called the Solaris Sigma 230.

Type: Ruschmeyer R90 230RG
Country of origin: Germany
Use: sports aircraft
Wingspan: 9.50 m
Powered by: 1 Textron Lycoming
IO540C4D5, 170 kW (230 hp)
Max. take-off weight: 1350 kg
Maximum speed: 200 mph
Range: 1000 miles
Ceiling: 4875 m
Passengers: 3 + 1 pilot

SAI KZ-2

Single-engine low-wing sports aircraft (maiden flight 11.12.1937); plywood and fabric-covered steel tube construction. The Coupé version (see illustration) had a closed cockpit and the two seats were side by side; the Sport version had an open cockpit and one seat was behind the other.

Type: SAI KZ-2 Kupé
Country of origin: Denmark
Use: sports aircraft
Wingspan: 10.50 m
Powered by: 1 4-cylinder in-line Gipsy Minor/Cirrus Minor I, 66 kW (90 hp)

Max. take-off weight: 750 kg
Maximum speed: 110 mph
Range: 560 miles
Ceiling: 5000 m
Crew: 2

Spirit of St. Louis

Single-engine shoulder-wing aircraft, fabric-covered steel tube and wood construction; flown by Charles Lindbergh when he crossed the Atlantic on 20–21 May 1927. Because the main tank was positioned in front of the instrument panel, Lindbergh – who did not want to have it behind him in case of an accident – had to use a periscope to see out of the front. The Spirit of St Louis held a total of 1705 litres of fuel – over half its total weight.

Type: Spirit of St. Louis
Country of origin: USA
Use: racing aircraft
Wingspan: 14.00 m
Length: 8.00 m
Powered by: 1 Wright Whirlwind J-5C, 223 hp, 194 kW (260 hp)
Max. take-off weight: 2330 kg
Maximum speed: 240 mph
Range: 3610 miles
Crew: 1

Suchoi Su-26

Single-engine low-wing sports aircraft (maiden flight 30.6.1984); first development by the Suchoi construction studio – which specialises in military jets – for the civilian aircraft market. This fully aerobatic aircraft was based on the Jak 50, and has also been exported to the West.

Type: Suchoi Su-26
Country of origin: Soviet Union
Use: sports aircraft
Wingspan: 7.80 m
Length: 6.83 m
Powered by: 1 VKOBM MP-14 P, 268 kW (364 hp)
Max. take-off weight: 962 kg
Maximum speed: 195 mph
Range: 515 miles
Ceiling: 4000 m
Crew: 1

Zlin Z-XII

Single-engine low-wing sports aircraft (1935); wood construction. It was available with an open cockpit or with a canopy. Over 200 units were built, and a large number exported.

Type: Zlin Z-XII
Country of origin: Czechoslovakia
Use: sports aircraft
Wingspan: 10.00 m
Length: 7.80 m
Powered by: 1 Persy II, 33 kW (45 hp)
Max. take-off weight: 520 kg
Cruising speed: 85 mph
Range: 185 miles
Ceiling: 3800 m
Crew: 2

Flying boats, seaplanes, hydroplanes and amphibians

Flying boats, seaplanes, hydroplanes and amphibians

For a long time amphibious aircraft and flying boats had the edge over their land-based counterparts, at least as far as size and transport capacities were concerned. These gigantic flying transporters – which were really more like flying boats – had their heyday from the 1920s to the 1940s. Operation from the water is ideal in parts of the world without a developed infrastructure where there are large areas of water, even though it is no longer used by the major airlines.

Aichi E16A Zuiun

Single-engine seaplane with two large floats (maiden flight 1942); fitted with dive brakes because it was used as a dive bomber, although its primary function was as a reconnaissance seaplane. A prototype replacement of the Aichi E13A had been built by 1942; series production commenced in January 1944, and 256 units were built by the end of the war.

Type: Aichi E16A1
Country of origin: Japan
Use: Reconnaissance seaplane
Wingspan: 12.81 m
Length: 10.83 m
Powered by: 1 14-cylinder Mitsubishi radial engine MK8A Kinsei 51, 970 kW (1319 hp)
Max. take-off weight: 3900 kg
Maximum speed: 275 mph
Range: 1500 miles
Ceiling: 10,000 m
Crew: 2
Weaponry: 2 MK 20 mm, 1 MG7.7 mm type 92, 250 kg bombs

Arado Ar 196

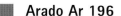

Single-engine low-wing seaplane with two floats and a body in welded-steel frame (sheet planking on the front, fabric on the rear). Used by the German navy from 1937 as a catapult-launched standard ship aircraft and successor to the He 50. A total of 541 were built.

Type: Arado Ar 196 A-1
Country of origin: Germany
Use: Ship aircraft
Wingspan: 12.47 m
Length: 11.00 m
Powered by: 9-cylinder BMW 132K radial engine, 706 kW (960 hp)
Max. take-off weight: 3730 kg
Maximum speed: 195 mph
Range: 665 miles
Ceiling: 7020 m
Crew: 2
Weaponry: 2 MK 20 mm, 1 MG17 7.92 mm, up to 100 kg bombs

Avro 510

Single-engine two-seater seaplane, of wooden construction, twin-spar covered biplane, in reality a one-and-a-half-decker (the upper wings were more than one-third longer than the lower ones). Steel spars connected the main, rear and supporting floats to the body. The British Admiralty ordered five of them, but they soon proved to be completely unsuitable.

Type: Avro 510
Country of origin: Great Britain
Use: Seaplane
Wingspan: top 18.30 m, bottom 11.60 m
Length: 11.58 m
Powered by: 1 Sunbeam Nubian engine, 111.8 kW (152 hp)
Max. take-off weight: 1270 kg
Maximum speed: 70 mph
Range: 310 miles
Ceiling: 950 m
Crew: 1 + 1 pilot

Beriev MBR-2

Single-engine shoulder-wing flying boat with a two-level boat body. The engine was positioned on a metal frame over the wing. From 1932 the naval reconnaissance craft had been put to use in Soviet coastal waters. The flying boat was easy to operate and maintain, and it was in production until 1942. A commercial derivative was spawned, the MP-1.

Type: Beriev MBR-2
Country of origin: Soviet Union
Use: flying boat
Wingspan: 18.90 m
Length: 13.50 m
Powered by: 1 12-cylinder M-17 in-line engine, 530–633 kW (720–860 hp)
Max. take-off weight: 4000 kg
Maximum speed: 175 mph
Range: 900 miles
Ceiling: 6600 m
Crew: 3–4
Weaponry: 2–4 MG, 600 kg bombs

Beriev Be-6

Twin-engine high-deck flying boat, all-metal construction (maiden flight 1947) that was used as a marine reconnaissance flying boat and bomber. As well as patrolling, the Be-6 could also be used as defence against submarines and to lay mines in coastal waters. A number of them were supplied to China, where they were in operation as the Qing 6.

Type: Beriev Be-6
Country of origin: Soviet Union
Use: flying boat
Wingspan: 33.00 m; **Length:** 23.50 m
Powered by: 2 Shvetzov ASch-73TK radial engines, each 1693 kW (2300 hp)
Max. take-off weight: 23,450 kg
Maximum speed: 260 mph
Range: 3000 miles
Ceiling: 6100 m
Weaponry: 4 or 5 23 mm NS-23 cannons; mines, depth charges, torpedoes on under-wing bomb racks

Beriev R-1

Soviet twin-jet flying boat with dual-level boat body and cruciform rudder (maiden flight 30.5.1952). The R-1 was the world's first single-jet flying boat. Its tasks were reconnaissance and fighting enemy targets. Four 23 mm cannons and a bomb load of 1000 kg were planned for this purpose. However, because of various recurring errors, the R-1 never became established; the experience gained from it was incorporated in the Beriev Be-10.

Type: Beriev R-1
Country of origin: Soviet Union
Use: flying boat
Wingspan: 21.40 m
Length: 19.43 m
Powered by: 2 Klimov VK-1, each with 26.87 kN (2740 kp) thrust
Max. take-off weight: 17,000 kg
Maximum speed: 500 mph
Range: 1240 miles
Ceiling: 11,500 m
Crew: 3
Weaponry: 4 23 mm cannons, bomb load up to 1000 kg

Beriev Be-12 Tschaika

Twin-engine turbo amphibian (maiden flight c. 1960). Originally developed for military use, most of the 150 craft are used for reconnaissance at sea and on coasts, and for hunting submarines. The Chayka (Seagull) was also used in emergencies at sea and for geological research. It replaced the Be-6 in the Soviet navy.

Type: Beriev Be-12
Country of origin: Soviet Union
Use: amphibious aircraft
Wingspan: 29.71 m
Length: 30.17 m
Powered by: 2 Iwtschenko Ai-20D mit je 3126 kW (4250 PS)
Max. take-off weight: 29,500 kg
Cruising speed: 200 mph
Range: 2500 miles
Ceiling: 11,300 m
Crew: 10
Weaponry: up to 5000 kg weapon load

Beriev Be-200

Twin-jet shoulder-wing amphibian with a T-rudder (maiden flight 24.9.1998). Apart from its variability – used both for passengers and freight, in environmental services and for sea patrolling – the Be-200 appeals in particular because of its suitability for rescue missions. Export version for Western markets has Rolls-Royce or Allison engines.

Type: Beriev Be-200
Country of origin: Russia
Use: amphibious aircraft
Wingspan: 32.78 m
Length: 32.05 m
Powered by: 2 Progress D-436TP turbofans, each with 73.6 kN (7444 kp) thrust
Max. take-off weight: 37,200 kg (from land), 43,000 kg (off water)

Cruising speed: 345–380 mph
Range: max. 1715 miles
Ceiling: 1700 m (with 7.5 t load) to 3850 m
Passengers: 64 (8 t freight/12 m³ water for fire-fighting)

Blackburn R.B.3A Perth

Three-engine biplane flying boat; designed as the successor to the Blackburn R.B.1 Iris as a long-distance reconnaissance flying boat. Due to recurring technical problems (particularly involving the rudder), it was used only from 1934 until 1938.

Type: Blackburn R.B.3A
Country of origin: Great Britain
Use: reconnaissance flying boat
Wingspan: 29.60 m
Length: 21.30 m
Powered by: 3 Rolls-Royce Buzzard IIMS, each 615 kW (836 hp)
Max. take-off weight: 14,740 kg
Maximum speed: 130 mph
Range: 1730 miles
Ceiling: 3500 m
Crew: 6
Weaponry: 1 MK 37 mm, 900 kg bomb load

Boeing 314 Clipper

Four-engine shoulder-wing flying boat for long distances (maiden flight 7.6.1938). Some of the fuel is stored in the stabilising floats on the sides. The Clipper was one of the biggest aircraft of its day – 12 units flew the Atlantic and Pacific routes for Pan American World Airways, and they had extremely luxurious interiors that included a dining salon and bathrooms. The cabin could accommodate 40 bunks for overnight trips in place of the 74 passenger seats. The Clippers were used by the military for logistics transportation purposes. In 1943 President Roosevelt of the US flew to the Casablanca Conference in a Boeing 314 (NC-18605 Dixie Clipper).

Type: Boeing 314
Country of origin: USA
Use: flying boat
Wingspan: 46.33 m
Length: 32.31 m
Powered by: 4 Wright GR-2600 Twin Cyclone, each 1192 kW (1600 hp)
Max. take-off weight: 37,422 kg
Cruising speed: 185 mph
Range: 3480 miles
Ceiling: 13,700 m
Passengers: 74

Breguet 521 Bizerte

Three-engine military biplane (maiden flight of prototype on 11.9.1933). Developed from the Short Calcutta, for which Breguet acquired the licence. Following the armistice in 1940, the German air force took on a number of units as marine rescue aircraft. The civilian counterpart to the Bizerte was the Breguet 530 Saigon.

Type: Breguet 521
Country of origin: France
Use: reconnaissance flying boat
Wingspan: 35.13 m (top), 18.90 m (bottom)
Length: 20.33 m
Powered by: 3 Gnome-Rhône 14N-11, each 671 kW (900 hp)
Max. take-off weight: 16,000 kg
Maximum speed: 145 mph
Range: 1300 miles
Ceiling: 6600 m
Crew: 8
Weaponry: 5 MG 7.5 mm, 200 kg bombs under the wings, torpedoes

Canadair CL 215

Twin-engine multi-purpose amphibian with a single-step boat body and supporting floats under the wings (maiden flight 23.10.1967). The aircraft was designed primarily for fighting forest fires (capacity 5455 l water/extinguishing agent). By the time production ceased in 1990, most of the 125 units had been fitted out for fire-fighting, ten had been modified for rescue operations and coastal surveillance, and two for passenger conveyance.

Type: Canadair CL 215
Country of origin: Canada
Use: multi-purpose amphibious aircraft
Wingspan: 28.60 m
Length: 19.82 m
Powered by: 2 Pratt & Whitney R-2800-CA6 radial engines, each 1566 kW (2130 hp)
Max. take-off weight: 19,731 kg (from land), 17,100 kg (from water)
Cruising speed: 180 mph
Range: max. 1300 miles
Crew: 2

Canadair CL 415

Twin-engine turboprop amphibious aircraft (maiden flight 6.12.1993). The aircraft is optimised for fighting forest fires; it takes just 12 seconds to fill the tanks with water. The CL 415 is also used for patrolling, and one version is used for passenger and freight transportation. This is currently the world's only large amphibious aircraft.

Type: Canadair CL 415
Country of origin: Canada
Use: amphibious aircraft
Wingspan: 28.61 m
Length: 19.82 m
Powered by: Pratt & Whitney Canada PW123AF propeller turbines, each 1750 kW (2380 hp)
Max. take-off weight: 19,800 kg (from land), 17,100 kg (from water)
Cruising speed: 180 mph
Range: max. 1510 miles
Ceiling: 9750 m
Passengers: up to 30 (or 4790 kg freight, or 6120 l water for fire-fighting) + 2 crew

Flying boats, seaplanes, hydroplanes and amphibians

Caproni Ca-60

Eight-engine triplane flying boat (maiden flight 4.3.1921). The three pairs of triplane wings on the body had a total wing area of 836 m² – twice as much as a B-52. With eight engines, four each in pusher and tractor sets, the aircraft took off just once, briefly, before crashing from a height of 20 m into Lake Maggiore.

Type: Caproni Ca-60
Country of origin: Italy
Use: flying boat
Wingspan: 30.50 m
Length: 23.45 m
Powered by: 8 Liberty L-12, each 293 kW (400 hp)
Max. take-off weight: 25,000 kg
Maximum speed: 70 mph
Range: 410 miles
Passengers: 60–100 + 8 crew

Consolidated PBY Catalina

Twin-engine high-wing amphibious aircraft with two floats (maiden flight 1935). The patrol flying boat was used in WWII for tasks such as accompanying convoys, and could remain airborne for up to 24 hours. Over 3300 units were built, making it the most frequently built amphibious aircraft.

Type: Consolidated PBY 5 A
Country of origin: USA
Use: amphibious aircraft
Wingspan: 31.70 m
Length: 19.47 m
Powered by: 2 14-cylinder Pratt & Whitney R-1930-92, each 895 kW (1217 hp)
Max. take-off weight: 16,063 kg
Maximum speed: 180 mph
Range: 2545 miles
Ceiling: 4481 m
Crew: 7–9
Weaponry: 3 MG 7.62 mm, 2 MG 12.7 mm, up to 2200 kg external bomb load, alternatively 2 Mk 13-2 torpedoes of 983 kg each

Dornier Do R4 Superwal

Four-engine passenger flying boat (maiden flight September 1926). A twin-engine version of the aircraft was also built, the Do R2. Customers could choose from various engines, which they had to supply themselves. The Wale and Superwale also flew for the postal services.

Type: Dornier Do R4
Country of origin: Germany
Use: passenger flying boat
Wingspan: 28.60 m
Length: 24.60 m
Powered by: 4 Gnôme-Rhône Jupiter VI, each 318 kW (517 hp)
Max. take-off weight: 14,000 kg

Cruising speed: 120 mph
Range: 930 miles
Ceiling: 2000 m
Passengers: 19 + 4 Crew

Dornier Do X

Twelve-engine passenger flying boat (maiden flight 12.7.1929). The Do X was by far the biggest aircraft of its day. On 5.11.1930, the Do X took off on a round-the-world introductory flight that lasted until 24.5.1932. Commercially the Do X was a failure. Only three were built, two for Italy. The German Do X lost its tail section during a landing on 9.5.1933, was taken apart and never rebuilt. The fate of the Italian versions is not known.

Type: Dornier Do X
Country of origin: USA
Use: passenger flying boat
Wingspan: 48.05 m
Length: 40.05 m
Powered by: 12 V-12-cylinder Curtiss GV-1750 Conquerors, each 485 kW (660 hp) take-off power
Max. take-off weight: 56,000 kg
Cruising speed: 120 mph
Range: 1055–1740 miles
Ceiling: 3200 m
Passengers: 66–100

Dornier Do 24

Three-engine flying boat that was used for marine reconnaissance and sea rescues (maiden flight 5.7.1937). In 1982 a Do 24 was converted into a Do 24 ATT (Amphibischer Technologie Träger = amphibious technology carrier) and given new wings, turboprop engines and a retractable landing gear.

Type: Dornier Do 24 ATT
Country of origin: Germany
Use: flying boat
Wingspan: 27.27 m; Length: 21.95 m

Powered by: 3 Pratt & Whitney Canada PT6A-45, each 827 kW (1125 hp)
Max. take-off weight: 14,000 kg (from land), 12,000 kg (from water)
Maximum speed: 215 mph
Weaponry: 2 MG 7.92 mm, 1 MK 20 mm (only on Do-24 T)

Dornier Do 26 Seeadler

Four-engine flying boat with folding wings and fold-up floats (maiden flight 21.5.1938). Four diesel engines in tandem nacelles, each with two pusher and tractor sets. The Do 26, originally planned as a transatlantic mail carrier, was built for the Luftwaffe as a reconnaissance aircraft.

Type: Dornier Do 26 V-1 A
Country of origin: Germany
Use: reconnaissance flying boat
Wingspan: 30.00 m
Length: 24.60 m
Powered by: 4 Jumo 205E diesel engines, each 442 kW (600 hp)
Max. take-off weight: 20,000 kg

Maximum speed: 210 mph
Range: 5600 miles
Ceiling: 4800 m
Crew: 4
Weaponry: 4 MG-151 20 mm

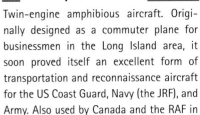

Grumman G-21/JRF Goose

Twin-engine amphibious aircraft. Originally designed as a commuter plane for businessmen in the Long Island area, it soon proved itself an excellent form of transportation and reconnaissance aircraft for the US Coast Guard, Navy (the JRF), and Army. Also used by Canada and the RAF in WWII.

Type: Grumman G-21A/JRF
Country of origin: USA
Use: amphibious aircraft
Wingspan: 14.94 m
Length: 11.68 m
Powered by: 2 Pratt & Whitney Wasp Junior SB-2, each 340 kW (462 hp)
Max. take-off weight: 3600 kg
Maximum speed: 200 mph
Range: 640 miles
Ceiling: 6400 m
Crew: 6–7

Grumman HU-16 Albatross

Twin-engine amphibian (maiden flight prototype 1947). Following the success of the Grumman Goose, the US Navy pushed for the construction of a bigger amphibious aircraft. It was used for sea patrols and rescues, reconnaissance flights and fighting submarines. By 1954, 459 units were built, and were in service in the USA and 16 other countries.

Type: Grumman HU-16
Country of origin: USA
Use: amphibious aircraft
Wingspan: 29.46 m; Length: 19.15 m
Powered by: 2 Wright R-1820-76A or 76B Cyclone, each 1062 kW (1444 hp)
Max. take-off weight: 17,000 kg
Maximum speed: 235 mph
Range: 3280 miles
Ceiling: 6550 m
Crew: 3–6
Weaponry: up to 2350 kg external weapon load

Heinkel He 60

Single-engine biplane reconnaissance seaplane (maiden flight 1933). The aircraft was designed to be catapulted from *Reichsmarine* warships and used for sea reconnaissance. The crew sat one behind the other in two open seats.

Type: Heinkel He 60
Country of origin: Germany
Use: Ship aircraft
Wingspan: 13.50 m
Length: 11.50 m
Powered by: 1 BMW VI 6.0 ZU, 440 kW (600 hp) take-off power

Max. take-off weight: 3500 kg
Cruising speed: 135 mph
Range: max. 590 miles
Ceiling: 5000 m
Crew: 2
Weaponry: 2 MG 7.9 mm

Hughes H-4 Hercules

Eight-engine heavy transport aircraft made of wood that was developed and built between 1942 and 1947 (maiden flight 2.11.1947). The Hughes H-4 Hercules remains to this day the aircraft with the widest wingspan and biggest wing area (1062.80 m²) of any aircraft ever built. In 1942 the US Navy held a competition for a transport aircraft that would take American soldiers to Europe without exposing them to the risk of submarines. Due to wartime priorities, the aircraft could not be made of metal and so was made almost entirely from birch. The aircraft was finished too late for its intended use. Because the flying boat remained in the ground effect on its one and only flight, critics still question its flying abilities to this day.

Type: Hughes H-4
Country of origin: USA
Use: transport flying boat
Wingspan: 97.51 m
Powered by: 8 Pratt & Whitney R4360-4A 28-cylinder radial engines, each 2240 kW (3040 hp)
Length: 66.74 m
Max. take-off weight: 181,500 kg
Maximum speed: 235 mph (planned)
Range: 3000 miles (planned)
Ceiling: 6370 m (planned)
Passengers: bis 750 + 18 crew

Kawanishi H8K

Four-engine all-metal flying boat for military use (maiden flight 1940). The flying boat was used for long-distance reconnaissance flights and transportation. It was notable for its very high load capacity, and had considerable power reserves. Technically it was superior to the Allies' large flying boats such as the Sunderland and Coronado. However it was not easy to fly, and indeed was only ever handled by experienced pilots. Various engines were used during the period of its construction (to 1945). The weaponry was also reinforced during the war. In various versions 162 series craft were constructed. The last modification, the H8K-4, never went into series production.

Type: Kawanishi H8K
Country of origin: Japan
Use: flying boat
Wingspan: 37.80 m
Length: 28.80 m

Powered by: 4 Mitsubishi MK4B Kasei 12, each 1103 kW (1500 hp)
Max. take-off weight: 32,000 kg
Maximum speed: 290 mph
Range: 3000 miles
Ceiling: 6800 m
Crew: 9
Weaponry: up to 5 MK 20 mm, 4 MG7.7 mm, 2 800 kg torpedoes, 8 250 kg bombs or 16 60 kg bombs

Martin M 130

Four-engine high-wing commercial flying boat (1932). The so-called China Clipper flew the Pacific routes from the west coast of America via Hawaii to east Asia. Initially used for mail services, from 1936 it was also used as a passenger aircraft (48 seats by day, 18 beds for night-time flights).

Type: Martin M 130
Country of origin: USA
Use: commercial flying boat
Wingspan: 39.62 m
Length: 27.62 m
Powered by: 4 Pratt & Whitney R-1830 Twin Wasp, each 618 kW (840 hp)
Max. take-off weight: 23,580 kg
Cruising speed: 163 mph
Range: 3200 miles
Ceiling: 5200 m
Passengers: 46–48

Martin Mars

Four-engine flying boat for civilian and military use (maiden flight 23.6.1942). It held up to 15.8 t freight, the JRM II version up to 31 t. On a record-setting flight, the M 170 JRM flew 263 passengers. The Martin Mars was the world's biggest flying boat to go into series production. Two converted Martin Mars remain in service today for fighting forest fires in Canada.

Type: Martin M 170
Country of origin: USA
Use: transport flying boat
Wingspan: 61.00 m
Length: 35.70 m
Powered by: 4 Pratt & Whitney R-4360-4T Wasp Major, each 2240 kW (3045 hp)
Max. take-off weight: 74,800 kg
Maximum speed: 215 mph
Range: 5000 miles
Ceiling: 4450 m
Crew: 4

Martin P5M Marlin

Twin-engine shoulder-wing heavy amphibious aircraft (maiden flight 30.5.1948). Series production (1366 units) began in 1951. The aircraft was used by the US Navy (including in submarine defence) and the Coast Guard, but also flew for the French marine, where it replaced the Sunderland. The US Navy used the final version of the SP-5 in Vietnam.

Type: Martin P5M-2S (SP-5B)
Country of origin: USA
Use: patrol and bomber aircraft
Wingspan: 36.00 m
Length: 30.60 m
Powered by: 2 Wright R-3350-30WA, each 2423 kW (3295 hp)
Max. take-off weight: 38,550 kg
Maximum speed: 250 mph
Range: 3100 miles
Ceiling: 7300 m
Crew: 8
Weaponry: 4 980 kg torpedoes or 4 900 kg bombs, 8 450 kg mines or 16 230 kg bombs or 16 150 kg depth charges

Piaggio P.136

Twin-engine amphibious aircraft with high folding wings and two pressure-screw power plants incorporated in the wing at the point of the bend (maiden flight 1948). This arrangement was the best one when operating from water with a full load. A special version, the Royal Gull, was devel-oped for the American market; approx. 40 units were sold to the USA and Canada.

Type: Piaggio P.136 L2
Country of origin: Italy
Use: amphibious aircraft
Wingspan: 13.51 m
Length: 10.79 m
Powered by: 2 Avco Lycoming GSO-480, each 346 hp (255 kW)
Max. take-off weight: 2995 kg
Maximum speed: 210 mph
Range: approx. 900 miles
Ceiling: 7800 m
Passengers: 4 + 1 pilot

Rohrbach Rocco

Twin-engine flying boat with a strongly tapered body and a high crossover bow, braced all-metal shoulder deck with supporting floats on the side (1926/7). The flying boat flew Baltic Sea routes from Travemünde.

Type: Rohrbach Ro V
Country of origin: Germany
Use: commercial flying boat
Wingspan: 26.00 m
Length: 19.30 m
Powered by: 2 Rolls-Royce Condor, each 480 kW (652 hp)
Max. take-off weight: 2360 kg
Cruising speed: 105 mph
Range: 1500 miles
Ceiling: 3150 m
Passengers: 10

Saunders Roe Princess

Twin-engine commercial flying boat (maiden flight August 1952). Eight of its ten engines were coupled, with pairs of them operating one propeller. Three units were built in total; the last Princess was broken up in 1967.

Type: Saunders Roe SR.45
Country of origin: Great Britain
Use: commercial flying boat
Wingspan: 66.90 m
Length: 42.00 m
Powered by: 10 Bristol Proteus 600 turbo-prop engines, 2386 kW (3245 WPS)

Max. take-off weight: 156,490 kg
Maximum speed: 360 mph
Range: 5760 miles
Ceiling: 11,300 m
Passengers: 105

Short S-23 Empire

Four-engine flying boat (maiden flight 4.6.1936). A total of 31 were built and used as mail and commercial aircraft on routes to Egypt, India, east Africa, South Africa, Malaysia, Hong Kong and Australia. The S-25 Sunderland flying boats were based on the Empire class aircraft.

Type: Short S-23
Country of origin: Great Britain
Use: commercial flying boat
Wingspan: 34.75 m; Length: 26.82 m
Powered by: 4 Bristol Pegasus XC radial engines, each 686 kW (920 hp)
Max. take-off weight: 18,370 kg
Maximum speed: 200 mph
Range: 765 miles
Ceiling: 6095 m
Passengers: 24 + 5 crew

Short S-25 Sunderland

Four-engine multi-purpose flying boat for long distances (1937), cantilevered all-metal shoulder deck with conventional rudder; the military version of the commercial S-23 Empire aircraft. Its uses: maritime reconnaissance, submarine defence, transport and sea rescues. Some of the 721 units that had been built by October 1945 were in service in Great Britain and other countries until 1958.

Type: Short S-25 Mk.V
Country of origin: Great Britain
Use: multi-purpose flying boat
Wingspan: 34.36 m
Length: 26.01 m
Powered by: 4 Pratt & Whitney R-1830 Twin Wasp radial engines, each 895 kW (1217 hp)
Max. take-off weight: 29,482 kg
Maximum speed: 215 mph
Range: 3000 miles; Ceiling: 6250 m
Crew: 7–9 (max. 10)
Weaponry: up to 10 MG 12.7 mm and 1800–2250 kg bombs or water bombs inside

Sikorsky S-40

Four-engine commercial flying boat (maiden flight early 1930), high wing with a maze of struts. Originally designed as an amphibious aircraft, it was later used as a flying boat, which meant the unladen mass could be reduced and the load increased. The S-40 flying boat was in service with PanAm (maiden flight of first PanAm aircraft 19.11.1931; Charles Lindbergh was in command).

Type: Sikorsky S-40
Country of origin: USA
Use: commercial flying boat
Wingspan: 34.80 m
Length: 23.40 m
Powered by: 4 Pratt & Whitney R-1690 Hornet, each 425 kW (580 hp)
Max. take-off weight: 6260 kg
Cruising speed: 115 mph
Range: 595 miles
Ceiling: 5500 m
Crew: 40 + 4 crew

Chetverikov MDR-6

Twin-engine high-wing amphibious aircraft (maiden flight December 1937). The aircraft easily stood up to a competitor's design by Beriev. Fifty series aircraft were produced and used for long-distance reconnaissance purposes. Further developed as the MDR-6B with a revised body and rudder (version 6B-5, see illustration) from the end of 1940, but never went into series production.

Type: Chetverikov MDR-6A
Country of origin: Soviet Union
Use: amphibious aircraft
Wingspan: 19.50 m; Length: 14.68 m

Powered by: 2 Klimov M-63, each 821 kW (1116 hp)
Max. take-off weight: 7200 kg
Maximum speed: 225 mph
Range: 1645 miles; Ceiling: 9000 m
Crew: 4
Weaponry: 1 MG 7.62 mm, 1 MG 12.7 mm, up to 1000 kg bombs

Bombers

Bombers

Air-borne vehicles can be used to carry out military attacks far beyond enemy lines. However, at the beginning of WWI it was still not clear just what an aircraft could do or handle. whereas airships, by contrast, seemed ideal for carrying large bomb loads. This attitude soon changed when Germany's airships suffered massive losses over Great Britain. Warring parties built increasingly large and heavy bomber aircraft in order to reach military destinations as well as attacking the infrastructure of a country. Bombers not only used their equipment against weapons and weapon carriers, but also against the armourers – and the blacksmiths and their families. Since then, the doctrine for the use of these aircraft has changed as often as the character of aerial warfare.

AEG G.IV

Twin-engine bomber, fabric-covered biplane in wood construction. Despite its rugged construction with a steel body, this early bomber was easy to fly and ideal for short-range tactical attacks. The G.IV went into series production at the end of 1916, and large numbers were sent to the front in 1917. Several units went into civilian use after the cease-fire in 1918.

Type: AEG G.IV
Country of origin: Germany
Use: bomber
Wingspan: 18.40 m
Length: 9.70 m
Powered by: 2 6-cylinder Mercedes D IVa, each 191 kW (260 hp) take-off power
Max. take-off weight: 3630 kg
Maximum speed: 105 mph
Range: 400 miles
Ceiling: 4500 m
Crew: 3
Weaponry: 2 MG 7.9 mm and 400 kg bombs externally

Airco DH.9

Single-engine bomber (maiden flight 1917), which was a development of the DH.4. It was intended for precision attacks on German towns and industrial complexes. Frequent engine problems meant it was often impossible for whole squadrons to fly, and yet some 2100 units were produced by the end of WWI. After De Havilland acquired some divisions of Airco in 1920, that company continued to produce the DH.9.

Type: Airco DH.9
Country of origin: Great Britain
Use: bomber
Wingspan: 12.82 m
Length: 9.27 m
Powered by: 1 Armstrong Siddeley Puma mit 172 kW (234 PS)
Max. take-off weight: 1508 kg
Maximum speed: 110 mph
Period of use: approx. 6 hours
Ceiling: 4725 m
Crew: 2
Weaponry: 3 MG 7.7 mm, up to 460 kg bomb load

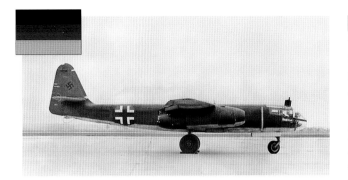

Arado Ar 234 Blitz

Twin-jet all-metal bomber (maiden flight 15.6.1943); the world's first jet-engine bomber. First used as a long-range reconnaissance aircraft at the end of WWII, then as a bomber. The external bomb racks reduced the speed to such an extent that the Allied forces' fighters were able to catch the Ar 234.

Type: Arado Ar 234 B-2
Country of origin: Germany
Use: bomber
Wingspan: 14.40 m
Length: 12.60 m
Powered by: 2 Jumo 004B Orcan, each 28.4 kN (2900 kp) thrust
Max. take-off weight: 10,000 kg
Maximum speed: 460 mph
Range: up to 685 miles
Ceiling: 10,000 m
Crew: 2
Weaponry: 2 MK 151 20 mm, 2 MK 108 30 mm, up to 2000 kg bombs externally

Avro 683 Lancaster

Four-engine mid-wing transport aircraft, the result of the Manchester Project (maiden flight prototype 9.1.1941). From 1942 the aircraft was in use specifically on bombing missions, and particularly for night-time attacks on German towns. During the course of WWII, the Lancaster dropped more than 600,000 tonnes of bombs. The last of the 7377 Lancasters built was decommissioned in 1954.

Type: Avro 683 Lancaster 1
Country of origin: Great Britain
Use: bomber
Wingspan: 31.09 m
Length: 21.13 m
Powered by: 4 Rolls-Royce Merlin 24s, each 955 kW (1298 hp)
Max. take-off weight: 24,000 kg
Maximum speed: 290 mph
Range: 1660 miles
Ceiling: 7470 m
Crew: 7
Weaponry: 8–10 MG 7.7 mm, up to 6350 kg bomb load

Avro 694 Lincoln

Four-engine long-range bomber (maiden flight 9.6.1944). The Lincoln was based on the Avro Lancaster, but was no longer used in WWII. A number of special versions were built for various purposes. The Lincoln was replaced by the Canberra in the late 1950s.

Type: Avro 694
Country of origin: Great Britain
Use: Strategic bomber
Wingspan: 36.58 m
Length: 23.86 m
Powered by: 4 Rolls-Royce Merlin 85, each 1310 kW (1780 hp)
Max. take-off weight: 34,020 kg
Maximum speed: 295 mph
Ceiling: 9295 m
Range: 2930 miles
Crew: 7
Weaponry: 7 MG 12.7 mm, 6350 kg bombs

Boeing B-17 Flying Fortress

Four-engine mid-wing bomber (maiden flight prototype 28.7.1935). It first saw active service in 1941, and quickly became the most important US bomber of WWII. The Flying Fortress had strong defence weaponry, and could continue flying even with severe damage. A chin turret was added in 1942 for use in head-on attacks.

Type: Boeing B-17
Country of origin: USA
Use: bomber
Wingspan: 31.67 m
Length: 22.83 m
Powered by: 4 Wright R-1820-97, each 640 kW (870 hp)
Max. take-off weight: 29,484 kg
Maximum speed: 290 mph
Range: 3750 miles
Ceiling: 10,850 m
Crew: 9
Weaponry: up to 13 MG, 4354 kg bomb load

Boeing B-29 Superfortress

Four-engine mid-wing strategic bomber (maiden flight prototype 21.9.1942). From 1944 the B-29 was used primarily against targets in Japan, and also for mining sea areas. Its defence weaponry consisted of remote-controlled weapon towers. As well as being produced by Boeing, Bell and Martin were also involved. It was a B-29 that dropped the atomic bombs over Hiroshima and Nagasaki.

Type: Boeing B-29
Country of origin: USA
Use: bomber
Wingspan: 43.01 m; Length: 30.18 m
Powered by: 4 Wright R-3550, each 1640 kW (2230 hp)
Max. take-off weight: 47,627 kg
Maximum speed: 360 mph
Range: 5830 miles
Ceiling: 9708 m
Crew: 10
Weaponry: 12 MG, MK 20 mm, 9070 kg bomb load

Boeing B-47 Stratojet

Six-jet shoulder-wing strategic bomber with swept wings (maiden flight prototype 17.12.1947). The Stratojet was intended to replace the fast-ageing propeller war designs. Series production commenced in June 1950. The USAF used Stratojets as strategic atomic weapon carriers. There were also versions for reconnaissance and electronic warfare. By 1957 some 1800 aircraft in a number of variations had been manufactured.

Type: Boeing B-47
Country of origin: USA
Use: bomber
Wingspan: 35.36 m
Length: 33.48 m
Powered by: 6 General Electric J47-GE-25, each 26.7 kN (2722 kp) static thrust
Max. take-off weight: 93,760 kg
Maximum speed: 600 mph
Range: 4000 miles
Ceiling: 11,980 m
Crew: 3
Weaponry: 2 MK 20 mm (rear), up to 9070 kg conventional bombs and nuclear weapons

Boeing B-52 Stratofortress

Eight-jet shoulder-wing strategic bomber with swept wings in a slightly negative V-position (maiden flight prototype 15.4.1952). The B-52 was based on a USAAF catalogue of requirements dating back to 1945. Strategic bombers should be able to operate independently of any foreign bases. Turboprops were originally planned, but in the end eight turbojets were housed in four twin nacelles and the wings given a marked swing (35°); facilities for in-flight refuelling were also incorporated. The wing profile is so thin that the main engine is housed in the body. Over 50 years, various versions were adapted to suit continuously changing purposes. The B-52 was used for blanket bombing in the Vietnam War, later for guided missiles, and for precision attacks in Iraq and Afghanistan. In 2005, 94 of the total of 744 units constructed (version H) were still in use.

Type: Boeing B-52 G
Country of origin: USA
Use: strategic long-range bomber
Wingspan: 56.39 m
Length: 48.03 m
Powered by: 8 Pratt & Whitney J57-P-43-W, each 56.9 kN (5080 kp) static thrust
Max. take-off weight: 221,357 kg
Maximum speed: 590 mph
Range: approx. 8700 miles
Ceiling: 15,150 m
Crew: 6
Weaponry: 4 MG 12.7 mm in the automatic rear stand, and up to 22,680 kg internal weapon load

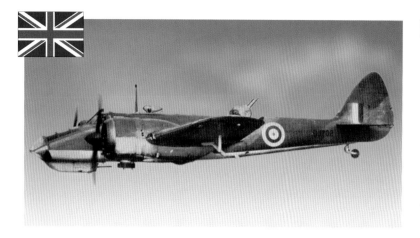

Bristol Blenheim

Twin-engine mid-wing bomber aircraft (maiden flight prototype 25.6.1936). Originally commissioned as a 6- to 8-seater civilian aircraft by Lord Rothermere, owner of the *Daily Mail*, the Blenheim was developed into a bomber shortly before the outbreak of WWII because it was faster than most other fighters. As the result of continued losses over the course of the war, it was then used as a night-time fighter aircraft.

Type: Bristol Typee 142M Blenheim IF
Country of origin: Great Britain
Use: bomber
Wingspan: 17.17 m
Length: 12.16 m
Powered by: 2 Bristol Mercury VIII, each 626 kW (850 hp)
Max. take-off weight: 5534 kg
Maximum speed: 275 mph at 4570 m
Range: 1050 miles
Ceiling: 7500 m
Crew: 3
Weaponry: 1 K 303 cannon, 4 MG, 545 kg bombs internally, 145 kg externally

Bristol Beaufort

Twin-engine mid-wing bomber (maiden flight prototype 15.10.1938); standard torpedo bomber of the RAF from 1940 to 1943. In 1942 all Beaufort units were deployed to the Mediterranean and the Indian Ocean. The Beaufort was also used as a reconnaissance aircraft and for laying mines.

Type: Bristol Typee 152 Mk.I
Country of origin: Great Britain
Use: bomber
Wingspan: 17.63 m
Length: 13.46 m
Powered by: 2 Bristol Taurus VI, each 843 kW (1146 hp)
Max. take-off weight: 9630 kg
Maximum speed: 265 mph
Range: 1055 miles
Ceiling: 5030 m
Crew: 4
Weaponry: 4 MG 7.7 mm, 907 kg bombs or 1 torpedo

Consolidated B-24 Liberator

Four-engine mid-wing bomber with a double lateral rudder (maiden flight prototype 29.12.1939). Valued for its tremendous range, the Liberator was used primarily in the Pacific theatre. The USAF flew the B-24 as a daytime bomber (the RAF used it primarily at night).

Type: Consolidated B-24 Liberator
Country of origin: USA
Use: bomber
Wingspan: 33.53 m
Length: 20.24 m
Powered by: 4 Pratt & Whitney R-1830, each 883 kW (1200 hp)
Max. take-off weight: 25,401 kg
Maximum speed: 300 mph
Range: 2850 miles
Ceiling: 8530 m
Crew: 12
Weaponry: 11 MG 12.7 mm, up to 3630 kg bomb load

Convair B-36 Peacemaker

American six-engine shoulder-wing bomber, powered by thrust propellers (maiden flight 8.8.1946). The B-36 was developed during WWII with the aim of attacking Germany directly from the USA. Commissioned in 1948, the aircraft was at the time the biggest bomber ever built. However, the B-36 also required much maintenance and was extremely expensive to operate.

Type: Convair B-36 B
Country of origin: USA
Use: bomber
Wingspan: 70.10 m
Length: 49.40 m
Powered by: 6 Pratt & Whitney R-4360-41, each 2610 kW (3549 hp)
Max. take-off weight: 185,975 kg
Maximum speed: 410 mph
Range: 6800 miles
Ceiling: 12,160 m
Crew: 15
Weaponry: 12 MK 20 mm, up to 38,958 kg conventional or nuclear bombs

Convair B-58 Hustler

American four-jet-engine mid-wing bomber with delta wings (maiden flight 11.11.1956). The West's first supersonic bomber set 19 international records. Only 116 serial versions of the B-58 were built; because of accident rate and high operating costs, it was taken out of commission in 1969.

Type: Convair B-58 A
Country of origin: USA
Use: bomber
Wingspan: 17.32 m
Length: 29.49 m
Powered by: 4 General Electric J79-GE-1 turbojets, each 69.4 kN (7077 kp) thrust
Max. take-off weight: 73,935 kg

Maximum speed: 1370 mph
Range: 5125 miles
Ceiling: 19,000 m
Crew: 3
Weaponry: 1 20 mm cannon in the rear, up to 8820 kg nuclear or conventional bomb load

Curtiss A-18

Twin-engine lightweight mid-wing bomber (maiden flight 17.7.1935); a complete reconstruction that followed the types A-8 and A-12. The 13 units that were built were briefly in service with the 3rd Attack Group in Barksdale Field, Louisiana, but the aircraft was replaced by more modern aircraft before the outbreak of WWII without ever having been in active service.

Type: Curtiss A-18
Country of origin: USA
Use: bomber
Wingspan: 18.13 m
Length: 12.90 m
Powered by: 2 Wright R-1820-47, each 440 kW (598 hp)
Max. take-off weight: 5750 kg
Maximum speed: 240 mph
Range: 1600 miles
Ceiling: 9120 m
Crew: 2
Weaponry: 5 MG 7.62 mm, 297 kg internal bomb load

Curtiss SB2C (A-25) Helldiver

Single-engine low-wing dive-bomber (maiden flight 18.12.1940). The Navy version (SB2C) was carrier based, and had folding wings. The first Helldiver did not join the Pacific theatre until November 1943. The version for the USAAC (A-25; see ill.) was not constructed in the quantity originally planned.

Type: Curtiss SB2C (A-25)
Country of origin: USA
Use: dive-bomber
Wingspan: 15.2 m
Powered by: 1 Wright R-2600-20, 1285 kW (1747 hp)
Length: 10.80 m
Max. take-off weight: 7550 kg
Maximum speed: 295 mph

Range: max. 1155 miles
Ceiling: 8400 m
Crew: 2
Weaponry: 4 MG 12.7 mm or 2 MK 20 mm, twin MG in rear, 1,900 kg bomb internally, bombs or rockets externally

Dassault Mirage IV

French twin-jet bomber (maiden flight prototype 17.6.1959, and series version 7.12.1963). The Mirage IV is similar to the Mirage II in construction and features, but it also has the specific requirements for a bomber that were intended to make France an independent atomic power. When the Mirage IV was commissioned in 1964, it was the first European aircraft to be able to fly Mach 2 continuously. In the mid-1980s, 18 units were modified as the IV P that could carry a 150 kt atomic missile. The last Mirage was decommissioned in 2005.

Type: Dassault Mirage IV A
Country of origin: France
Use: bomber
Wingspan: 23.50 m
Length: 11.84 m
Powered by: 2 SNECMA Atar 9 K turbo-fans, each 68.65 kN (7000 kp) thrust
Max. take-off weight: 33,475 kg
Maximum speed: 1455 mph
(Mach 2.2)
Range: 770 miles
Ceiling: 18,000 m
Crew: 1
Weaponry: 1 60 kt atomic bomb or 7260 kg conventional bombs

De Havilland DH.98 Mosquito

Twin-engine mid-wing all-wood bomber (maiden flight prototype 25.11.1940). In 1942 its range and speed made the Mosquito a versatile multi-role aircraft. In 27 different versions, 7781 units were produced.

Type: De Havilland DH.98 Mk.IV
Country of origin: Great Britain
Use: bomber
Wingspan: 16.51 m
Length: 12.55 m
Powered by: 2 Rolls-Royce Merlin XXV, each 919 kW (1250 hp)
Max. take-off weight: 9735 kg
Maximum speed: 385 mph
Range: 1990 miles
Ceiling: 10,300 m
Crew: 2
Weaponry: up to 4 MG and approx. 1800 kg bombs

Dornier Do 17

Twin-engine shoulder-wing bomber with a double lateral rudder (maiden flight 23.11.1934). The aircraft was produced in series before and at the outbreak of WWII. Of the various versions, the Do 17 Z was built in greatest quantity with a total of 500 units. It was used less as a fighter from around 1940, and its successor the Dornier Do 217 was produced in series instead.

Type: Dornier Do 17 Z-2
Country of origin: Germany
Use: bomber
Wingspan: 18.00 m
Length: 15.79 m
Powered by: 2 Bramo 323 P radial engines, each 735 kW (1000 hp)
Max. take-off weight: 8590 kg
Maximum speed: 255 mph
Range: 720 miles
Ceiling: 8200 m
Crew: 4
Weaponry: up to 6 MG 7.9 mm and 1000 kg bombs

Dornier Do 217

Twin-engine shoulder-wing bomber with a twin lateral rudder based on the Do 17, but with greatly improved plating and defence weapons (maiden flight August 1938). In service as a standard heavy night bomber of the Luftwaffe from 1941, the Do 217 had the greatest load-bearing capacity of its time. Some 1905 units were built in various versions up to June 1944, many as night fighters.

Type: Dornier Do 217 E-2
Country of origin: Germany
Use: bomber
Wingspan: 19.15 m
Length: 17.30 m
Powered by: 2 BMW 801 A, each 1177 kW (1600 hp)
Max. take-off weight: 16,465 kg
Maximum speed: 515 mph
Range: 2300 miles
Ceiling: 9000 m
Crew: 4
Weaponry: 6 MG, up to 4000 kg bombs

Dornier Do 215

Twin-engine shoulder-wing bomber aircraft (maiden flight of prototype 1938); developed on from the Do 17 Z with better engines. Intended for export, it was no longer delivered following the outbreak of the war. Just under 100 units were built, and used by the Luftwaffe mainly for reconnaissance and night bombings.

Type: Dornier Do 215 A-1
Country of origin: Germany
Use: bomber
Wingspan: 18.00 m
Length: 15.80 m

Powered by: 2 Daimler Benz DB 601 A, each 809 kW (1100 hp)
Max. take-off weight: 8800 kg
Maximum speed: 290 mph
Range: 1520 miles

Ceiling: 9400 m
Crew: 4
Weaponry: 3–4 MG 7.9 mm, up to 1000 kg bomb load (alternatively 3 cameras)

Douglas SBD Dauntless

Single-engine carrier-based bomber (maiden flight prototype June 1935). The Dauntless was the standard dive-bomber of the US Navy in the 1940s, and played an important part in helping America to success in the major Pacific battles of WWII. Almost 6000 units were built by the end of 1944. There was also a different version for the US Army, which was known as the A-24 Banshee.

Type: Douglas SBD-6
Country of origin: USA
Use: bomber
Wingspan: 12.65 m
Length: 10.06 m
Powered by: 1 air-cooled 9-cylinder Wright R-1820-66 Cyclone radial engine, 1007 kW (1369 hp)
Max. take-off weight: 4318 kg
Maximum speed: 255 mph
Range: 775 miles
Ceiling: 7680 m
Crew: 2
Weaponry: 2 MG 12.7 mm, 2 MG 7.62 mm, up to 730 kg bomb load

Douglas TBD Devastator

Single-engine bomber (maiden flight 15.4.1935). The Devastator was the US Navy's first all-metal aircraft. From June 1937, 114 units were stationed on large aircraft carriers. After only 41 Devastators returned to their carriers from the Battle of Midway, the aircraft was no longer used in combat.

Type: Douglas TBD 1
Country of origin: USA
Use: bomber
Wingspan: 15.24 m
Length: 10.67 m
Powered by: 1 Pratt & Whitney R-1830-64 14-cylinder Double Wasp, 625 kW (850 hp)
Max. take-off weight: 4624 kg
Maximum speed: 205 mph
Range: 415 miles
Ceiling: 6005 m
Crew: 3
Weaponry: 2 MG 7.62 mm, 454 kg bombs or torpedoes

Douglas B-18

Twin-engine mid-wing bomber that was developed from the civilian Douglas DC-2. In 1935 it was successful in competition with the Martin 146 and Boeing 299 (forerunners of the 4-engine B-17). The first order was for 133 units, and a further 217 were ordered later; however, by 1942 the aircraft was no longer being used as a bomber but as a transporter and submarine fighter.

Type: Douglas B-18
Country of origin: USA
Use: bomber
Wingspan: 27.28 m
Length: 17.63 m
Powered by: 2 Wright R 1850-53 Cyclone 9, 745 kW (1014 hp)
Max. take-off weight: 12,550 kg
Maximum speed: 215 mph
Range: 1200 miles
Ceiling: 7285 m
Crew: 6
Weaponry: 3 MG 7.62 mm, 2040 kg internal bomb load

Douglas A-26 Invader

Lightweight twin-engine bomber, developed to a USAAF specification of 1940 to provide support for troops (maiden flight 1942); in series production from 1944. The Invader was the fastest US bomber in WWII; it also saw active service in the Korean War and in Vietnam. Some of the total of 1355 units built are still being used today in fire-fighting.

Type: Douglas A-26
Country of origin: USA
Use: bomber
Wingspan: 21.34 m
Length: 15.62 m
Powered by: 2 Pratt & Whitney R-2800-27 or -79, each 1490 kW (2028 hp)
Max. take-off weight: 15 876 kg
Maximum speed: 355 mph
Range: max. 1390 miles
Ceiling: 6735 m
Crew: 3
Weaponry: 10 MG 12.7 mm, 1814 kg bomb load

Douglas A-1 Skyraider

Single-engine low-wing bomber and low-level attack aircraft (maiden flight 18.8.1945). The aircraft was originally developed as a carrier-based bomber, and was used in the Korean and Indo-China wars. More than one-fifth of the 3180 units produced were still being used by various air forces in 1966.

Type: Douglas A-1H
Country of origin: USA
Use: low-level attack aircraft
Wingspan: 15.24 m
Length: 11.94 m
Powered by: 1 Wright R-3550-26WD Cyclone, 2013 kW (2737 hp)
Max. take-off weight: 11,340 kg
Maximum speed: 310 mph
Range: 3045 miles
Ceiling: 7590 m
Crew: 1
Weaponry: 4 MK 20 mm, 2948 kg external weapon load

English Electric (BAC) Canberra

British twin-jet bomber (maiden flight prototype 13.5.1949. Developed from 1944 as a replacement for the De Havilland Mosquito and commissioned in 1951. A US version, the Martin B-57, was produced under licence; it was used in the Vietnam War and remained in service until 1983. The Canberra was exported to more than 15 countries on four continents. Over 1300 aircraft were produced in total, and they were also used for reconnaissance and low-level attacks.

Type: English Electric Canberra B-2
Country of origin: Great Britain
Use: bomber
Wingspan: 19.49 m
Length: 19.96 m
Powered by: 2 Rolls-Royce Avon 101 turbojets, each 28.9 kN (2948 kp) thrust
Max. take-off weight: 21,185 kg
Maximum speed: 570 mph
Range: 2655 miles
Ceiling: 14,630 m
Crew: 3
Weaponry: 4 MG, 2700 kg bombs

Fairchild Republic A-10

Twin-jet fighter aircraft (maiden flight prototype 11.5.1972). Its ability to fly low and slow and with absolute precision mean that the Thunderbolt II can be used against any ground targets – including tanks. Decommissioning had started, but was stopped in 1991.

Type: Fairchild Republic A-10
Country of origin: USA
Use: close air support
Wingspan: 17.53 m
Length: 16.26 m
Powered by: 2 General Electric TF34-100 turbofans, each 403 kN (4110 kp) thrust
Max. take-off weight: 23,636 kg

Maximum speed: 440 mph
Range: 2455 miles
Ceiling: 10,600 m
Crew: 1
Weaponry: MK 30 mm, 8 underwing and 3 underfuselage pylon stations for approx. 7200 kg bombs and missiles

Fairey Swordfish

Single-engine biplane bomber (maiden flight prototype TSR.I in March 1933, TSR.II on 17.4.1934, Swordfish on 31.12.1935). Originally developed privately in 1933 as a submarine fighter, then in series production from November 1934; from 1938 the British Royal Navy's standard torpedo bomber. About 2390 units were constructed in various versions, some of which were also used for reconnaissance purposes.

Type: Fairey Swordfish Mk.II
Country of origin: Great Britain
Use: bomber
Wingspan: 13.87 m
Length: 10.87 m
Powered by: 1 Bristol Pegasus XXX, 552 kW (750 hp)
Max. take-off weight: 3406 kg
Maximum speed: 140 mph
Range: 1030 miles
Ceiling: 3260 m
Crew: 3
Weaponry: 2 MG 7.7 mm, torpedo of 730 kg

Fairey Battle

Single-engine low-wing bomber with a conventional rudder (maiden flight prototype 10.3.1936); commissioned in 1937. Use was halted early in WWII following several losses resulting from poor performance; the aircraft was later used for training purposes. Around 2300 units were produced in several versions.

Type: Fairey Battle Mk.I
Country of origin: Great Britain
Use: bomber
Wingspan: 16.46 m
Length: 15.87 m
Powered by: 1 Rolls-Royce Merlin Mk.I, 758 kW (1030 hp)
Max. take-off weight: 4895 kg
Maximum speed: 240 mph
Range: 1050 miles
Ceiling: 7160 m
Crew: 3
Weaponry: 2 MG 7.7 mm, 500 kg bombs

FIAT BR.20 Cicogna

Twin-engine low-wing bomber with a double lateral rudder (maiden flight prototype 10.2.1936). Became the Italian air force's standard bomber in 1936, when it was also used in the Spanish Civil War. The Cicogna soon proved outdated in WWII.

Type: FIAT BR.20 Cicogna
Country of origin: Italien
Use: bomber
Wingspan: 21.60 m
Length: 16.10 m
Powered by: 2 FIAT A. 80 RC.41, each 735 kW (1000 hp)
Max. take-off weight: 9900 kg
Maximum speed: 270 mph
Range: 1865 miles
Ceiling: 9000 m
Crew: 5
Weaponry: 1 MG 12.7 mm, 2 MG 7.7 mm and 1600 kg bomb load

Grumman TBF Avenger

Single-engine carrier-based bomber, cantilevered mid-wing with a conventional rudder (maiden flight 1.8.1941). Shortly after the USA joined the war, this three-seater aircraft became the Navy's standard torpedo bomber and saw its first active service in the Battle of Midway against the Japanese. What proved to be extremely advantageous was that bombs and/or torpedoes were completely contained inside the body. Many units were also supplied to other powers and flew, for instance, for the Royal Navy (see illustration) in operations over the Atlantic and in the Pacific theatre, and for the New Zealand Air Force. The follow-on version, the TBM-3, carried missiles on underwing racks. After the war the Avenger remained in use for a while as a reconnaissance, supply and rescue aircraft.

Type: Grumman TBF
Country of origin: USA
Use: bomber
Wingspan: 16.51 m
Length: 12.48 m
Powered by: 1 Wright R-2600-2 Cyclone, 1267 kW (1700 hp)

Max. take-off weight: 8278 kg
Maximum speed: 275 mph
Range: 2685 miles
Ceiling: 9200 m
Crew: 3

Weaponry: 3 MG 12.7 mm, 1 MG 7.62 mm, 1 torpedo, missiles on underwing racks

Grumman A-6 Intruder

Twin-engine carrier-based bomber (maiden flight 19.4.1960) that has been in active service on aircraft carriers of the US Navy since 1963. The US Marine Corps also flew the A-6 from its coastal bases. Intruders were used in the Vietnam War. After 1996 the Intruder was replaced by the F/A-18 versions E and F; the EA-6B Prowler for electronic warfare remains in service.

Type: Grumman A-6
Country of origin: USA
Use: bomber
Wingspan: 16.20 m
Length: 16.60 m
Powered by: 2 Pratt & Whitney J52-P8B, each 41 kN (4180 kp) thrust
Max. take-off weight: 27,496 kg
Maximum speed: 650 mph
Range: 1075 miles
Ceiling: 12,400 m
Crew: 2
Weaponry: 5 external load racks, each 1633 kg weapon load (bombs, laser-guided bombs, AGM-12 Bullpup etc.; nuclear weapons B57 and B61)

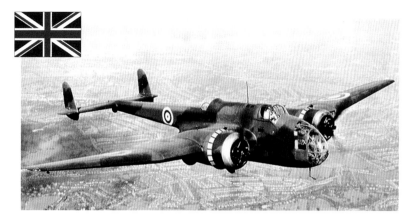

Handley Page H.P.52 Hampden

Twin-engine bomber, cantilevered mid-wing with a double lateral rudder (maiden flight prototype 21.6.1938). This aircraft was involved in the first British bomb attack on Berlin and in the first so-called 1000-bomber attacks on Cologne. Some of the total of 1430 units built were supplied to the USSR; other Hampdens flew in Australia, New Zealand and Sweden.

Type: Handley Page H.P.52 Mk.I
Country of origin: Great Britain
Use: bomber
Wingspan: 21.08 m
Length: 16.33 m
Powered by: 2 Bristol Pegasus XVIII, each 710 kW (965 hp) take-off power
Max. take-off weight: 9526 kg
Maximum speed: 265 mph
Range: 900–2000 miles
Ceiling: 6900 m
Crew: 4
Weaponry: 5 MG 7.7 mm, 1800 kg bombs

Handley Page H.P.57 Halifax

Four-engine bomber, cantilevered mid-wing with a double lateral rudder (maiden flight 25.10.1938); the first series aircraft flew in October 1940, and formed the backbone of Britain's strategic bomber forces. The Mk.II (H.P.59 from July 1941) had an additional tower on the back, which meant it had a stronger defence weaponry. The Mk.III (H.P.61) appeared in August 1943 with more powerful engines and a longer wingspan. By 1956 some 6168 aircraft of various versions had been manufactured.

Type: Handley Page H.P.57
Country of origin: Great Britain
Use: bomber
Wingspan: 31.75 m
Length: 21.82 m

Powered by: 4 Bristol Hercules XVI, each 1230 kW (1672 hp)
Max. take-off weight: 29,484 kg
Maximum speed: 310 mph
Range: 1260 miles

Ceiling: 7315 m
Crew: 7
Weaponry: 9 MG 7.7 mm, 5890 kg bomb load

Handley Page (BAe) H.P.80 Victor

Twin-jet bomber, cantilevered mid-wing with a T-rudder (maiden flight 22.12.1952). This aircraft was one of the three British 'V-bombers'; the others were the Vickers 667 Valiant and the Avro 698 Vulcan. As its altitude performance was unsatisfactory, it was converted into a low-level bomber and given low-flying radar systems. The improved Victor B-2 went into service in 1962. Once it had finished its service as a bomber, some units were used as tankers.

Type: Handley Page (BAe) H.P.80 Victor B-2
Country of origin: Great Britain
Use: bomber
Wingspan: 36.80 m
Length: 34.95 m
Powered by: 4 Rolls-Royce Conway 201 mit je 87,9 kN (8963 kp)
Max. take-off weight: 79,450 kg
Maximum speed: 635 mph
Range: 4575 miles
Ceiling: 18,300 m
Crew: 5
Weaponry: bombs and missiles

Heinkel He 70 F

Single-engine multi-role cantilevered aircraft for military use. Apart from the weaponry and glazing of the cockpit, the aircraft was the same as its civilian counterpart (maiden flight 1.12.1932). It was used primarily as a lightweight bomber, but also as a long-range reconnaissance and liaison aircraft – including with the Legion Condor of Spain.

Type: Heinkel He 70 F-2
Country of origin: Germany
Use: bomber
Wingspan: 14.80 m; **Length:** 12.00 m
Powered by: 1 BMW VI 7.3, 533 kW (750 hp)
Max. take-off weight: 3460 kg
Maximum speed: 225 mph
Range: 1130 miles
Ceiling: 5500 m
Crew: 2–5
Weaponry: 1 MG 7.9 mm (facing to the rear), 300 kg of bombs

Heinkel He 111

Twin-engine bomber, cantilevered low-wing aircraft, based on the He 70 and originally a civilian development commissioned by Lufthansa (maiden flight 1935). After trials with various engines, more than 1000 bombers had been built by the outbreak of WWII – and tested in Spain by the Legion Condor. By the autumn of 1944 over 7000 units had been completed. The He 111 was one of the German Luftwaffe's standard bombers.

Type: Heinkel He 111 P-4
Country of origin: Germany
Use: bomber
Wingspan: 22.50 m
Length: 16.40 m
Powered by: 2 Daimler Benz DB 601 A-1, each 809 kW (1100 hp)
Max. take-off weight: 13,500 kg
Maximum speed: 240 mph
Range: 745–1490 miles
Ceiling: 8000 m
Crew: 5
Weaponry: 5 MG 7.92 mm, 2 MG 13 mm, 2000 kg bombs internally

Heinkel He 177 Greif

Four-engine heavy bomber, cantilevered mid-wing aircraft (maiden flight 19.11.1939). It was powered by two double engines, each of which operated one four-blade propeller. The first series aircraft (A-1) were not at all reliable; 1942 saw the slightly extended series A-3, and in 1943 greater quantities of the A-5.

Type: Heinkel He 177 A-5
Country of origin: Germany
Use: bomber
Wingspan: 31.44 m
Length: 20.40 m
Powered by: 2 Daimler-Benz DB 610A/B twin engines, each 2200 kW (2990 hp)
Max. take-off weight: 31,000 kg
Maximum speed: 300 mph
Range: 3420 miles
Ceiling: 8000 m
Crew: 6
Weaponry: 2 MK 20 mm, 3 MG 7.92 mm, 3 MG 13 mm, 1000 kg bombs internally, two glider bombs

Henschel Hs 129

Twin-engine bomber, cantilevered low-wing (maiden flight prototype 25.5.1939; series production since 1940). The aircraft was armoured and heavily armed, but unpowered at first, and the armoury meant it was of limited use for its intended purpose: to provide support for troops. Subsequent versions had stronger engines, and the B-3 was equipped specifically for fighting tanks.

Type: Henschel Hs 129 B-1
Country of origin: Germany
Use: bomber, fighter
Wingspan: 14.20 m; Length: 9.75 m
Powered by: 2 Gnôme-Rhône 14M, each 522 kW (710 hp)
Max. take-off weight: 5250 kg
Maximum speed: 250 mph
Range: 350 miles
Ceiling: 9000 m
Crew: 1
Weaponry: 2 MG 20 mm, 2 MG 7.92 mm, 450 kg bombs

Ilyushin Il-2 3M Shturmovik

Single-engine armoured fighter (single-, later twin-seater), cantilevered low-wing (maiden flight 30.12.1939). The armoury of the front of the body protected the engine, pilots, fuel tank and aerial gunner (on the twin-seater version), and could withstand even direct fire from 20 mm cannons. An improved version was produced – the Il-10.

Type: Ilyushin Il-2 3M
Country of origin: Soviet Union
Use: close support aircraft
Wingspan: 14.60 m
Length: 11.65 m
Powered by: 1 Mikulin AM-38F, 1282 kW (1720 hp)
Max. take-off weight: 6360 kg
Maximum speed: 410 mph
Range: 765 miles
Ceiling: 4525 m
Crew: 2
Weaponry: 2 MK 23 mm, 1 MG 7.62 mm, 1 MG 12.7 mm, up to 600 kg bombs, 4–8 missiles

Ilyushin Il-4

Twin-engine low-wing bomber (maiden flight June 1939); developed from the DB-3 with a completely new aerodynamic nose. Like its predecessor, the Il-4 was also designed as a long-range bomber. The aircraft was all-metal, but wooden components were also used during the war because of material shortages. Over 5250 aircraft of every version of the Il-4 were produced (including the Il-4T torpedo bomber).

Type: Ilyushin Il-4
Country of origin: Soviet Union
Use: bomber
Wingspan: 21.44 m
Length: 14.76 m
Powered by: 2 Tumanski M-88B, each 810 kW (1100 hp)
Max. take-off weight: 10,055 kg
Maximum speed: 265 mph
Range: 2360 miles
Ceiling: 9700 m
Crew: 3–4
Weaponry: 2 MG 7.62 mm, 1 MG 12.7 mm, up to 2500 kg bombs

Ilyushin Il-28

Twin-jet cantilevered shoulder-wing bomber (maiden flight prototype 8.7.1948). The aircraft was designed as a tactical bomber; several versions were built (including the Il-28T torpedo version), and it was widespread through the pro-Soviet states.

Type: Ilyushin Il-28
Country of origin: Soviet Union
Use: bomber
Wingspan: 21.45 m
Length: 17.65 m
Powered by: 2 Klimov VK-1, each with 26.5 kN (2700 kp) thrust
Max. take-off weight: 23,200 kg
Maximum speed: 560 mph
Range: 1355 miles
Ceiling: 12,500 m
Crew: 3
Weaponry: 2 MK 23 mm each in the nose and rear stand; up to 3000 kg bombs

Junkers Ju 86

Twin-engine low-wing bomber with a double lateral rudder (maiden flight proto-type 4.11.1934). The bomber was the result of the civilian development of a high-speed passenger aircraft for Lufthansa. Despite having better engines, the Ju 86 was not able to prove itself against the Heinkel He 111, and was used primarily as a high-altitude reconnaissance aircraft.

Type: Junkers Ju 86 D-1
Country of origin: Germany
Use: bomber
Wingspan: 22.50 m
Length: 17.87 m
Powered by: 2 Jumo 205 C-4, each 447 kW (600 hp)
Max. take-off weight: 8060 kg
Maximum speed: 200 mph
Range: 932 miles
Ceiling: 5900 m
Crew: 4
Weaponry: 3 MG 7.92 mm, up to 1000 kg bombs internally

Junkers Ju 87

Single-engine dive-bomber, three-part gull wings and a fixed undercarriage (maiden flight 17.9.1935). From the B-2 version onwards, the aircraft had automatic pull-up dive brakes to ensure it recovered from its attack dive. There were wailing sirens in the undercarriage panelling (known as the 'Trumpets of Jericho') that were intended to reinforce the psycho-logical effects of attack.

Type: Junkers Ju 87 B-1 (1938)
Country of origin: Germany
Use: dive-bomber
Wingspan: 13.80 m
Length: 11.00 m
Powered by: 1 Junkers-Jumo 211 Da engine, 882 kW (1200 hp)
Max. take-off weight: 4250 kg
Maximum speed: 235 mph
Range: 370 miles
Ceiling: 8000 m
Crew: 2
Weaponry: 2 MG 7.92 mm forward guns, 1 MG 7.92 mm rear gun, 1 500 kg bomb or 1 250 kg bomb and 4 50 kg bombs

Junkers Ju 88

Twin-engine mid-wing bomber (maiden flight prototype 21.12.1936). The aircraft was made suitable for dive-bombing on the orders of the RLM in 1937 (with automatic pull-up brakes). The Ju 88 was in service throughout WWII in many different versions (including as a bomber, reconnaissance aircraft and night fighter). A total of approx. 15,000 units were built.

Type: Junkers Ju 88 A-4
Country of origin: Germany
Use: bomber
Wingspan: 20.08 m
Length: 14.40 m
Powered by: 2 Junkers Jumo 211 J, each 1045 kW (1420 hp)
Max. take-off weight: 14,000 kg
Maximum speed: 290 mph
Range: max. 1700 miles
Ceiling: 8200 m
Crew: 4
Weaponry: 5 MG 7.92 mm, 1 MG 13 mm, 500 kg bomb load internally, up to 3000 kg bombs on underwing racks

Junkers Ju 188

Twin-engine mid-wing bomber. The aircraft was produced in 1941, based on the operational experiences gained with the Ju 88 and as a further development of the same. The bulbous 'fighting head' was a striking feature. The wings and rudders were also redesigned. From the beginning of series production in the summer of 1943 until the end of the war, a total of 1036 units were built.

Type: Junkers Ju 188 A-2
Country of origin: Germany
Use: bomber
Wingspan: 22.02 m
Length: 14.95 m
Powered by: 2 Junkers Jumo 213 A, each 1287 kW (1750 hp)
Max. take-off weight: 15,000 kg
Maximum speed: 525 mph
Range: 2200 miles
Ceiling: 10,000 m
Crew: 4
Weaponry: 2 MK 20 mm, 2 MG 13 mm, up to 4 MG 7.92 mm, 3000 kg bombs or torpedoes

Lockheed F-117 Nighthawk

Twin-jet bomber in the 'blended wing body' design (low-wing aircraft with a striking swing design to the wings) with Stealth technology – only 5 per cent of the structure is made of metal (maiden flight prototype June 1981). The F-117 flew its first operational sorties in Panama in 1998 and in the Gulf War in 1991. The first one was lost during combat over Yugoslavia in 1999. The aircraft can refuel in-flight, and targets are acquired by the thermal imaging infra-red system; it carries no radar, which lowers emissions and cross-sections. The F-classification is a deliberate misclassification of the bomber, and was included during the development stage.

Type: Lockheed F-117A
Country of origin: USA
Use: bomber
Wingspan: 13.20 m
Length: 20.08 m
Powered by: 2 General Electric F404-F1D2

turbofans, each 48 kN (4895 kp) thrust
Max. take-off weight: 23,814 kg
Maximum speed: 645 mph
Range: 1405 miles
Crew: 1
Weaponry: 2268 kg bombs (laser-guided)

Martin MB

Twin-engine bomber, three-bay covered biplane in wood construction (1918). Passenger (up to 12), freight and postal versions of the so-called Glenn Martin bomber were also built.

Type: Martin MB-1
Country of origin: USA
Use: bomber
Wingspan: 21.80 m
Length: 14.10 m
Powered by: 2 Liberty V-12 313 kW (420 hp)

Max. take-off weight: 5477 kg
Maximum speed: 105 mph
Range: 560–1490 miles
Ceiling: 2590 m
Crew: 2
Weaponry: 4-5 MG, 750 kg bombs or torpedoes

Martin B-26 Marauder

Twin-engine medium-weight shoulder-wing bomber (maiden flight 25.11.1940). The first series version was soon followed by the appearance of the improved and more heavily armed B-26A, which from the spring of 1942 operated from Australia against the Japanese. The B-26B version was also used in Europe from March 1943. The last series version of the B-26G appeared in March 1945, and very many units were also delivered to the RAF.

Type: Martin B-26G
Country of origin: USA
Use: bomber
Wingspan: 21.65 m
Length: 17.12 m
Powered by: 2 Pratt & Whitney RR-2800-43 Double Wasp, each 1412 kW (1920 hp)
Max. take-off weight: 17,320 kg
Maximum speed: 290 mph
Range: 1100 miles
Ceiling: 6040 m
Crew: 7
Weaponry: 11 MG 12.7 mm, 1800 kg bombs

Martin A-30 Baltimore

Twin-engine cantilevered mid-wing bomber (maiden flight prototype 14.6.1941). Although built to the specifications of the USAAF, the aircraft was never flown by the US forces; it was, however, in service with the RAF, the British Fleet Air Arm and the Canadian, Australian and South African air forces. The aircraft was a follow-on to the Martin 167.

Type: Martin A-30 Mk.III
Country of origin: USA
Use: bomber
Wingspan: 18.69 m; Length: 14.78 m
Max. take-off weight: 10,430 kg
Powered by: 2 Wright GR-2600-19 Cyclone, each 1193 kW (1622 hp)
Maximum speed: 300 mph
Range: 950 miles; Ceiling: 7300 m
Crew: 4
Weaponry: 4 forward-firing MG 7.62 mm in the wings, 4 MG 7.62 mm on weapon stands, 900 kg bombs

Mitsubishi G4M Hamaki

Twin-engine cantilevered mid-wing bomber (maiden flight prototype 23.10.1939). Achieving a long range was the primary concern in the construction. Speed and armoury were less important, and as a consequence the aircraft was easy to damage and suffered tremendous losses in the Pacific war.

Type: Mitsubishi G4M Hamaki
Country of origin: Japan
Use: bomber
Wingspan: 24.90 m
Length: 19.60 m
Powered by: 2 Mitsubishi MK4A Kasei, each 1125 kW (1530 hp)
Max. take-off weight: 15,000 kg
Maximum speed: 270 mph
Range: max. 3130 miles
Ceiling: 9000 m
Crew: 7
Weaponry: 2 MK 20 mm, 4 MG 7.7 mm, up to 2200 kg bombs and torpedoes

Mitsubishi Ki-67 Hiryu

Twin-engine medium-weight cantilevered mid-wing bomber aircraft (maiden flight 27.12.1942). The aircraft was the replacement of the Ki-21, and its construction was based on elements of the G4M. The fast, highly manoeuvrable aircraft joined the war in the Pacific theatre in October 1944.

Type: Mitsubishi Ki-67-I
Country of origin: Japan
Use: bomber
Wingspan: 22.40 m
Powered by: 2 Mitsubishi Ha-42-11, each 1417 kW (1900 hp) take-off power
Max. take-off weight: 14,097 kg

Length: 18.70 m
Maximum speed: 340 mph
Range: 2000 miles
Ceiling: 9150 m
Crew: 7
Weaponry: 1 MK 20 mm, 4 MG 12.7 mm, 1600 kg bombs and torpedoes

Myasischev M-4

Four-jet bomber (maiden flight 20.1.1953), cantilevered shoulder-wing, swept wings in a slightly negative V-position, tandem landing gear with supporting wheels on the wing tips. Some 150 units of this strategic bomber and nuclear weapon carrier were built after 1954; some of them have now been scrapped, others 'mothballed'. In 1981 a heavy-transport version with a double lateral tail unit (WMT Atlant) was developed for external loads.

Type: Myasischev M-4
Country of origin: Soviet Union
Use: bomber
Wingspan: 50.48 m
Length: 47.20 m
Powered by: 4 Mikulin AM-3D, each 85.6 kN (8730 kp) thrust
Max. take-off weight: 181,000 kg
Maximum speed: 620 mph
Range: max. 6650 miles
Ceiling: 8200 m
Crew: 6-11
Weaponry: 6-10 MK 23 mm, up to 40,000 kg bombs and missiles

North American B-25 Mitchell

Twin-engine medium-weight bomber, cantilevered mid-wing with gull wings and a double lateral rudder (maiden flight 19.8.1940). The aircraft is widely regarded as one of the most versatile and best-performing bombers of WWII. The B-25's most famous operation (which was later made into a Hollywood movie) was when a small formation of 16 aircraft took off from the Hornet aircraft carrier to attack Tokyo and landed in China (18.4.1942: Doolittle Raid).

Type: North American B-25 J
Country of origin: USA
Use: bomber
Wingspan: 20.60 m
Length: 16.10 m
Powered by: 2 Wright R-2600-92, each 1250 kW (1700 hp)
Max. take-off weight: 15,870 kg
Maximum speed: 275 mph
Range: 2100 miles
Ceiling: 7620 m
Crew: 3–6
Weaponry: 12 MG 12.7 mm, 8 missiles, 1360 kg bomb load

North American B-45 Tornado

Four-jet shoulder-wing bomber (maiden flight in February 1948); the USA's first jet bomber. In 1952 an aerial refuelling B-45 became the first to fly the Pacific non-stop. A total of 142 aircraft were built in three versions. Some flew in combat in the Korean War.

Type: North American B-45C
Country of origin: USA
Use: bomber
Wingspan: 29.26 m
Length: 23.14 m
Powered by: 4 General Electric J47-GE-13, each 26.7 kN (2720 kp) thrust
Max. take-off weight: 51,230 kg
Max. take-off weight: 51,230 kg
Maximum speed: 570 mph
Range: 2530 miles
Ceiling: 12,270 m
Crew: 4
Weaponry: 2 MG 12.7 mm, 9000 kg bombs

Northrop-Grumman B-2 Spirit

Four-jet strategic bomber (maiden flight 17.7.1989). Structurally the B-2 Spirit is a blended wing aircraft. It can be used for many roles, fitted with conventional and atomic weapons, and refuel in-flight. It has stealth properties, enabling it to 'hide' from electromagnetic and infra-red rays (e.g. the jet engines), leaves no condensation trails, the jets are cooled to reduce the infra-red signature, and it has a minimised radar signature (similar to the Hummel). It is the most expensive aircraft ever built to date (estimated price per piece €1.8 billion). Just 21 units were built. Thanks to the aerial refuelling facility, it can fly any distance, anywhere in the world.

Type: Northrop-Grumman B-2
Country of origin: USA
Use: Strategisches bomber
Wingspan: 52.43 m
Length: 21.03 m
Powered by: 4 General Electric F-118-GE-100 turbofans, each 84.53 kN (8620 kp) thrust
Max. take-off weight: 152,635 kg
Maximum speed: 630 mph (at 15,000 m)
Range: 6200–7460 miles (with weapons)
Ceiling: approx. 15,150 m
Crew: 2
Weaponry: up to 18 144 kg weapons in two weapons bays

Petlyakov Pe-2

Twin-engine cantilevered low-wing dive-bomber (trials commenced in 1939). Originally designed as a high-level fighter, it was developed as a dive-bomber after the initial tests, and was used in the thick of various battles during WWII. Over 11,000 units were built.

Type: Petlyakov Pe-2
Country of origin: Soviet Union
Use: dive-bomber
Wingspan: 17.19 m
Length: 12.60 m
Powered by: 2 Klimov WK-105R, each 920 kW (1250 hp)
Max. take-off weight: 8500 kg
Maximum speed: 335 mph
Range: 1200 miles
Ceiling: 8200 m
Crew: 2
Weaponry: 1 MG 12.7 mm, 4 MG 7.62 mm, 1000 kg bomb load

Polikarpov R-5

Single-engine multi-role aircraft, unequal span single-bay biplane in mainly wood construction (1928; series production from 1931). The aircraft was used as a lightweight bomber, to provide support for troops, as a liaison aircraft and lightweight transporter. A civilian version was used for mail. Over 7000 units were built, including 1000 civilian variations.

Type: Polikarpov R-5
Country of origin: Soviet Union
Use: bomber
Wingspan: 15.50 m (top)
Length: 10.56 m
Powered by: 1 M-17 engine, 367 kW (500 hp)
Max. take-off weight: 2955 kg
Maximum speed: 140 mph
Range: 500 miles
Ceiling: 6400 m
Crew: 2
Weaponry: 3 MG 7.62 mm, 500 kg bombs externally

Rockwell B-1 Lancer

Four-jet strategic bomber with swing wings. Designed in the mid-1960s as the successor to the Boeing B-52, North American Rockwell (from 1973 Rockwell International, acquired by Boeing in 1997) stopped work on this aircraft after its maiden flight (B-1A 23.12.1974) in 1977, then continued in 1981 with a completely different profile of use. The modernised B-1 was to fly lower, have a minimised radar signature and fly precision attacks in the lower supersonic range (maiden flight B-1B 18.10.1984).

Type: Rockwell B-1B Lancer
Country of origin: USA
Use: strategic long-range bomber
Wingspan: 41.67 m straight, 23.84 m when swung back
Length: 41.81 m
Powered by: 4 General Electric F-101-GE-102 turbofans, each 136.92 kN (13,960 kp) thrust
Max. take-off weight: 216,365 kg
Maximum speed: 750 mph (low altitude), 825 mph (high altitude)
Range: approx. 7000 miles (without aerial refuelling)
Ceiling: approx. 9100 m
Crew: 4
Weaponry: up to 26,288 kg weapon load in 3 weapons bays

Saab 17

Single-engine lightweight bomber and reconnaissance aircraft (maiden flight May 1940). A total of 322 units in a number of variations (including floats or aeroplane skis) were built with various engine versions. Up to 1944, 132 B 17A were supplied to the Swedish air force. In 1948 the aircraft was officially decommissioned, although it remained in use until 1968.

Type: Saab B 17 A
Country of origin: Sweden
Use: fighter
Wingspan: 13.70 m; **Length:** 9.80 m
Powered by: 1 Pratt & Whitney SC3-G Twin Wasp, 794 kW (1080 hp)
Max. take-off weight: 3790 kg
Maximum speed: 270 mph
Range: 1120 miles
Ceiling: 8700 m
Crew: 2
Weaponry: 2 MK 12.9 mm, 1 MG M22 7.9 mm, 500 kg bombs

Savoia Marchetti SM.79 Sparviero

Triple-engine bomber (maiden flight 2.10.1934). Originally intended as a civilian transport aircraft for eight passengers, it was already designed as a bomber from the second prototype. The SM.79-I types were also used in the Spanish Civil War. Yugoslavia ordered a quantity of 45. Italy joined WWII with approx. 600 Sparviero.

Type: Savoia Marchetti SM.79-II
Country of origin: Italy
Use: bomber
Wingspan: 21.20 m
Length: 16.20 m
Powered by: 3 Piaggio P.XI RC.40, each 746 kW (1000 hp)
Max. take-off weight: 12,500 kg
Maximum speed: 270 mph
Range: 1235 miles (with 2 torpedoes)
Ceiling: 7000 m
Crew: 5
Weaponry: 3 MG 12.7 mm, 2 MG 7.62 mm, 2 450 mm torpedoes with 200 kg warheads

Short S.29 Stirling

Four-engine bomber (maiden flight prototype 14.5.1939). The dimensions of the existing hangars were such that the Stirling's wings had to be as short as possible, which meant that it could not have a particularly high ceiling. The bomb bay could only hold bombs of no more than 907 kg each. It first saw active service on 10.2.1941. Five variations of the aircraft were built, including transport and passenger units.

Type: Short S.29 Mk.III
Country of origin: Great Britain
Use: bomber
Wingspan: 30.20 m
Length: 26.50 m
Powered by: 4 Bristol Hercules VI or XVI, each 1220 kW (1660 hp)
Max. take-off weight: 31,790 kg
Maximum speed: 270 mph
Range: 2000 miles
Ceiling: 5030 m
Crew: 7–8
Weaponry: 8 MG 7.7 mm, 6350 kg bombs in the internal weapons bay

Sikorsky S-23 V Ilya Muromets

Four-engine biplane bomber made of wood (maiden flight 1913). The Ilya Muromets was developed as a heavy bomber from a civilian aircraft. During WWI 73 variations with a range of weapons and engines were built and used by the Russian air force. A single one was lost in combat.

Type: Sikorsky S-23 V
Country of origin: Russia
Use: bomber
Wingspan: 29.80 m
Length: 17.10 m
Powered by: 4 Sunbeam V8, each 110 kW (150 hp)
Max. take-off weight: 7460 kg
Maximum speed: 80 mph
Range: 350 miles
Ceiling: 3200 m
Crew: 4–7
Weaponry: Various MG, 8 100 kg bombs, 16 50 kg bombs or 1 656 kg bomb

Sukhoi Su-2

Single-engine lightweight low-wing bomber, all-metal construction (maiden flight 25.8.1937) – in June 1941 it was the Soviet Union's most modern lightweight bomber, and was initially used as a fighter. Because of heavy losses, the aircraft was taken out of active service in 1942 and used as a training, towing and reconnaissance aircraft.

Type: Sukhoi Su-2
Country of origin: Soviet Union
Use: bomber
Wingspan: 14.30 m
Length: 10.25 m
Powered by: 1 M-88B double-star engine, 735 kW (1000 hp)
Max. take-off weight: 4375 kg
Maximum speed: 285 mph
Range: 740 miles

Ceiling: 8400 m
Crew: 2
Weaponry: 2 fixed and 1 movable MG

SchKAS 7.62 mm, max. 400 kg bombs or missiles RS-82/RS-132

Sukhoi Su-25

Twin-jet close air-support fighter aircraft (maiden flight 22.2.1875); commissioned in 1982. A small pre-series was used in the war in Afghanistan. The Su-25 was designed to work closely with ground troops. Its objective is the targeted destruction of fixed and movable targets (armoured vehicles, helicopters, convoys, bridges, roads etc.).

Type: Sukhoi Su-25K
Country of origin: Soviet Union
Use: close air support
Wingspan: 14.36 m
Length: 15.53 m
Powered by: 2 Tumanski R-195 turbojets, each 44 kN (4487 kp) thrust
Max. take-off weight: 17,600 kg

Maximum speed: 600 mph
Range: max. 775 miles
Ceiling: 7000 m
Crew: 1
Weaponry: 1 MK 30 mm, up to 4400 kg primary weapons (bombs, guided anti-radar missiles and unguided missiles)

Sukhoi T-4 (Su-100)

Four-jet bomber with low delta wings and canards (maiden flight 22.8.1972, project stopped in 1974); the Soviet response to the American XB-70. The most progressive materials and production technologies of the day were used for the T-4. The aircraft was to have fly-by-wire technology. As with Concorde and the Tu-144, the nose of the aircraft could be lowered for take-off and landing. In total ten trials were carried out, but were not sufficient to prove the aircraft's full performance.

Type: Sukhoi T-4
Country of origin: Soviet Union
Use: bomber
Wingspan: 22.00 m; Length: 44.50 m
Powered by: 4 Kolesov RD-36-41, each providing 159.3 kN (16,244 kp) thrust
Max. take-off weight: 135,000 kg
Maximum speed: 2000 mph (projected)
Range: 3730 miles (projected)
Ceiling: 25,000–30,000 m (projected)
Crew: 2
Weaponry: 2 Ch-45 air-to-ground missiles with a range of 1500 km

Tupolev TB-3

Four-engine bomber (also called the ANT-6), cantilevered low-wing, all-metal construction with corrugated metal panels (maiden flight 22.12.1930). The aircraft was notable for its excellent range and load capacity. Some were used as 'flying aircraft carriers', with fighters travelling 'piggy-back' or on underwing racks.

Type: Tupolev TB-3
Country of origin: Soviet Union
Use: bomber
Wingspan: 39.50 m
Length: 24.40 m
Powered by: 4 M-17F engines, each 526 kW (715 hp) take-off power

Max. take-off weight: 17,200 kg
Maximum speed: 110 mph
Range: 840 miles

Ceiling: 3800 m
Crew: 8
Weaponry: 5 MG 7.7 mm, 2000 kg bombs

Tupolev SB-2

Twin-engine cantilevered mid-wing bomber (maiden flight prototype 7.10.1934). The aircraft was faster than most other fighters of its day. In 1936 the SB-2 was used by the Republicans in the Spanish Civil War. In 1943 it was used in active service for the last time.

Type: Tupolev SB-2
Country of origin: Soviet Union
Use: bomber
Wingspan: 20.33 m
Length: 12.27 m
Powered by: 2 Klimov M-100A, each 640 kW (870 hp) take-off power
Max. take-off weight: 5627 kg
Maximum speed: 265 mph
Range: 620 miles
Ceiling: 9500 m
Crew: 3
Weaponry: 3 MG 7.62 mm, 500 kg bomb load

Tupolev Tu-2

Twin-engine medium-weight fighter, cantilevered mid-wing (maiden flight prototype 3.10.1940; maiden flight ANT-58 29.1.1941). It was to be used as a horizontal and dive-bomber, but also for reconnaissance purposes; first used in combat in September 1942. At the beginning of 1943, it was given its final name of Tu-2.

Type: Tupolev Tu-2S
Country of origin: Soviet Union
Use: bomber and dive-bomber
Wingspan: 18.86 m
Length: 13.80 m
Powered by: 2 ASch-82FNW, each 1380 kW (1850 hp)
Max. take-off weight: 11,360 kg
Maximum speed: 340 mph
Range: 870 miles
Ceiling: 9500 m
Crew: 4
Weaponry: 2 MG 20 mm, 3 MG 12.7 mm, up to 4000 kg bombs

Tupolev Tu-16

Twin-engine cantilevered mid-wing bomber (maiden flight prototype 27.4.1952); commissioned in 1955 as a strategic medium-weight bomber. The Tu-16 formed the backbone of the Soviet strategic bomber fleet. The Tu-104 commercial aircraft was developed from the military Tu-16.

Type: Tupolev Tu-16A
Country of origin: Soviet Union
Use: strategic bomber
Wingspan: 32.99 m
Length: 34.80 m
Powered by: 2 Mikulin AM-3M turbojets, each 93.16 kN (9500 kp) thrust
Max. take-off weight: 75,800 kg

Maximum speed: 650 mph
Range: 4475 miles
Ceiling: 12,800 m
Crew: 6
Weaponry: 7 MK 23 mm, up to 9000 kg bombs and missiles

Tupolev Tu-22

Twin-jet cantilevered mid-wing bomber (maiden flight prototype 21.6.1958); the first Soviet supersonic bomber. The high position of the engines is striking. The Tu-22 went into series production in 1961. Although its primary role was ground attack, it was also used for reconnaissance tasks over land and sea.

Type: Tupolev Tu-22B
Country of origin: Soviet Union
Use: bomber
Wingspan: 23.50 m
Length: 41.60 m
Maximum speed: 1510 mph
Powered by: 2 Kolesov RD-7M, each providing 156.9 kN (16,000 kp)
Max. take-off weight: 85,500 kg

Range: 3510 miles
Ceiling: 14,700 m
Crew: 3
Weaponry: 1 MK 23 mm, up to 24,500 kg bombs or 1 9000 kg bomb or atomic bomb

Tupolev Tu-22M

Twin-jet bomber, developed from 1966 as the successor to the Tu-22, but an independent new construction with swing wings. After the prototypes and pre-series, the Tu-22M-2 finally met all the requirements; the further developed Tu-22M-3 was regarded as a strategic weapon. Over 280 units of all versions were built. Many remain in service with various air and naval forces.

Type: Tupolev Tu-22M-3
Country of origin: Soviet Union
Use: bomber
Wingspan: 23.30–34.28 m
Length: 42.46 m
Powered by: 2 Kusnezov/KKBM NK-25, each 245.2 kN (25,000 kp) thrust
Max. take-off weight: 126,400 kg
Maximum speed: 1430 mph
Range: 4350 miles
Ceiling: 13,300 m
Crew: 4
Weaponry: 1 MK 23 mm, 3 Ch-22M or 10 Ch-15 air-to-ground missiles, or up to 24,000 kg bombs

Tupolev Tu-95

Four-engine bomber, cantilevered mid-wing with swept wings (maiden flight 1954). The aircraft is the only turboprop long-distance bomber with opposing pairs of propellers, and the military counterpart to the Tu-114 passenger aircraft. It was also used as a maritime reconnaissance and submarine fighter (Tu-142) and in electronic warfare.

Type: Tupolev Tu-95MS
Country of origin: Soviet Union
Use: bomber
Wingspan: 50.04 m
Length: 46.90 m
Powered by: 4 Kusnezov NK-12M, each 11,032 kW (15,000 hp)
Max. take-off weight: 188,000 kg
Maximum speed: 515 mph
Range: 6525 miles
Ceiling: 10,500 m
Crew: 7
Weaponry: 2 MK 23 mm (rear turret), 6 Ch-55 missiles internally, up to 10 Ch-55 externally

Tupolev Tu-160

Four-jet low-wing bomber with swing wings and a cruciform rudder (maiden flight prototype 19.12.1981). The aircraft was developed parallel to the Tu-144 commercial aircraft. It was intended as the Soviet counterpart to the Rockwell B-1. In 1987 the aircraft went into commission with the Soviet air forces. By 1994 32 units were delivered.

Type: Tupolev Tu-160
Country of origin: Soviet Union/Russia
Use: bomber
Wingspan: 35.6–55.7 m
Length: 54.10 m
Powered by: 4 Kusnezov NK-321, each 245.2 kN (25,000 kp) thrust
Max. take-off weight: 275,000 kg
Maximum speed: 1370 mph
Range: 7650 miles
Ceiling: 15,000 m
Crew: 4
Weaponry: 12 Ch-55 cruise missiles or 24 Ch-15P missiles or up to 40,000 kg bombs

Vickers Wellington

Twin-engine mid-wing bomber with a conventional rudder (maiden flight prototype 15.6.1936), and the most important British bomber at the outbreak of WWII. By October 1945 well over 11,000 units had been produced; after 1940 the Wellington only flew night attacks (April 1941: first dropping of a Blockbuster aerial mine). It was also used for coastal surveillance and anti-submarine.

Type: Vickers Wellington Mk.I
Country of origin: Great Britain
Use: bomber
Wingspan: 26.26 m
Length: 19.68 m
Powered by: 2 Bristol Hercules VII/XVI, each 1165 kW (1585 hp)
Max. take-off weight: 16,500 kg
Maximum speed: 255 mph
Range: 1320 miles
Ceiling: 7325 m
Crew: 6
Weaponry: 6 MG 7.7 mm or 7.92 mm, 2720 kg bombs

Vickers 667 Valiant

Four-jet shoulder-wing bomber with swept wings (maiden flight 10.8.1951), the first of the three British V-bombers and atom-bomb carriers of the RAF. A total of 107 units were produced, and in 1956 Valiants dropped conventional bombs in Egypt during the Suez crisis. After 1960 most of them were converted to tankers; in 1964 they had to be decommissioned because of material fatigue.

Type: Vickers 667 Valiant Mk.I
Country of origin: Great Britain
Use: bomber
Wingspan: 34.76 m
Length: 32.91 m
Powered by: 4 Rolls-Royce Avon R28, each 44.5 kN (4540 kp) thrust
Max. take-off weight: 63,500 kg
Maximum speed: 565 mph
Range: 4500 miles
Ceiling: 16,400 m
Crew: 5
Weaponry: 1 4540 kg bomb or 20 454 kg bombs

Vultee A-31 Vengeance

Single-engine mid-wing dive-bomber. Built as the Vultee model V-72 initially without a government contract, after the fall of France in 1940 the aircraft went to the RAF as the A-31. Brazil, China, Turkey and the USSR also bought it.

Type: Vultee A-31
Country of origin: USA
Use: dive-bomber
Wingspan: 14.63 m
Length: 12.12 m
Powered by: 1 Wright Cyclone GR-2600-A5B-5, 2279 kW (3100 hp)
Max. take-off weight: 7440 kg
Maximum speed: 280 mph
Range: 2300 miles
Ceiling: 6800 m
Crew: 2
Weaponry: 6 MG 7.62 mm, 2 225 kg bombs internally, 2 113 kg bombs externally

Zeppelin Staaken R VI

Four-engine biplane strategic bomber. The engines were located in two nacelles, each powering one pusher and one tractor set. The Staaken made repeated attacks on London starting in mid-September 1917, the last one being in October 1918. None of the 18 Staaken in commission was shot down.

Type: Zeppelin R VI Staaken
Country of origin: Germany
Use: bomber
Wingspan: 42.20 m
Length: 22.10 m
Powered by: 4 Mercedes D IVa, each 191 kW (260 hp)
Max. take-off weight: 11,824 kg
Maximum speed: 85 mph

Range: 500 miles
Ceiling: 4300 m
Crew: 7
Weaponry: 4–7 MG, 2000 kg bombs

Fighters and fighter bombers

Fighters and fighter bombers

When aeroplanes first became involved in battles in WWI, the need arose for countries to defend their forces against their enemies. So they started flying aircraft that hunted and fought others. Later, fighter aircraft accompanied other aircraft such as bombers, or tried to head off the enemy's bombers. A period of specialisation in closely limited areas of use was followed by the trend for multi-role aircraft. They were to build on from one and the same platform and – in the ideal situation – would be able to change roles during a mission.

Aermacchi MB 339

Single-jet training aircraft with a high level of manoeuvrability and good acceleration (maiden flight 12.8.1976); based on the MB 326 but with a stronger body. It can be used to train pilots for the Tornado or Eurofighter, and also to provide support for troops. In a horrific accident at Ramstein Air Show in 1988, several MB 339s collided with an Italian display team.

Type: Aermacchi MB 339
Country of origin: Italy
Use: Jet trainer
Wingspan: 10.86 m
Length: 10.79 m
Powered by: 1 Rolls-Royce Viper MK632-43, 17.8 kN (1825 kp) thrust
Max. take-off weight: 6350 kg
Maximum speed: 570 mph
Range: 1290 miles
Ceiling: 14,200 m
Crew: 2
Weaponry: 2 30 mm DEFA cannons, up to 1815 kg weapons on 6 underwing racks

Aero L-39 Albatros

Single-jet cantilevered low-wing training aircraft (maiden flight 2.11.1968; prototype 4.11.1968). Designed as the successor to the L-29 Dolphin, from the beginning of series construction in 1972 the L-39 Albatross was the standard training aircraft in the military bloc of the Warsaw Pact and other countries. A total of slightly less than 3000 units were built to specifications that approximated to those of a light fighter aircraft.

Type: Aero L-39
Country of origin: Czechoslovakia
Use: Jet trainer
Wingspan: 9.46 m
Length: 12.13 m
Powered by: 1 Progress AI-25 TL, 168.7 kN (17,200 kp) thrust
Max. take-off weight: 4700 kg
Maximum speed: 465 mph in 5000 m
Range: 520 miles
Ceiling: 11,500 m
Crew: 2
Weaponry: 1 Gryazev-Shipunov GSh-23 twin-barrelled 23 mm automatic cannon; up to 1000 kg weapons on 4 underwing racks

Albatros D.III

Single-engine WWI biplane fighter aircraft; successor to the D.II standard fighter since 1917. Thanks to its advantages in speed and manoeuvrability, in April 1917 alone Baron Manfred von Richthofen shot down 21 other aircraft with the D.III. Replaced by the D.V early in 1918. Slightly under 440 units were built.

Type: Albatros D.III
Country of origin: Germany
Use: fighter
Wingspan: 9.05 m
Length: 7.33 m
Powered by: 1 Mercedes D.IIIa, 130 kW (177 hp)
Max. take-off weight: 886 kg
Maximum speed: 110 mph
Period of operation: approx. 2 h
Ceiling: 5500 m
Crew: 1
Weaponry: 2 MG 7.92 mm LMG 08/15 above the engine

Albatros D.V

Single-engine biplane fighter with a narrower underwing; body made of plywood. Successor to the D.III as a standard fighter; in operation from 1917 until the end of the war. Like the D.III, the D.V had wing problems when diving, which caused many crashes.

Type: Albatros D.V
Country of origin: Germany
Use: fighter
Wingspan: 9.05 m
Length: 7.33 m
Powered by: 1 Mercedes D.IIIa, 130 kW (177 hp)
Max. take-off weight: 957 kg
Maximum speed: 115 mph
Range: 215 miles
Ceiling: 6250 m
Crew: 1
Weaponry: 2 MG 7.92 mm

Arado Ar 68

Single-engine biplane fighter in a mixed construction; the body frame was made of welded steel tube, the wings were a fabric-covered wooden frame (maiden flight 1934). Commissioned in 1936, the aircraft was intended to help establish Germany's air force. Due to its disappointing flying characteristics, it was used mainly as a night-time fighter and training aircraft before finally being decommissioned in 1940.

Type: Arado Ar 68 E
Country of origin: Germany
Use: fighter
Wingspan: 11.58 m
Length: 9.40 m
Powered by: 1 Junkers Jumo 210 Ea, 500 kW (680 hp)
Max. take-off weight: 2020 kg
Maximum speed: 210 mph
Range: 310 miles
Ceiling: 12,800 m
Crew: 1
Weaponry: 2 MG-17 7.92 mm, up to 60 kg external bomb load

Bell P-39 Airacobra

Single-engine low-wing fighter bomber (maiden flight April 1939); not particularly successful in the USA because of various faults and performance deficiencies. However, 9584 Airacobras were manufactured by August 1944, of which roughly half were sent to the USSR, where they were extremely popular close air support aircraft.

Type: Bell P-39 Q
Country of origin: USA
Use: fighter bomber
Wingspan: 10.36 m
Length: 9.18 m
Powered by: 1 12-cylinder Allison V-1710-85, 1044 kW (1420 hp)
Max. take-off weight: 3750 kg
Maximum speed: 380 mph
Range: up to 1245 miles
Ceiling: 10,600 m
Crew: 1
Weaponry: 1 37 mm cannon, 4 MG 12.7 mm, approx. 230 kg external bomb load

Bell P-59 Airacomet

Twin-jet fighter aircraft (maiden flight 1.10.1942). The US Air Force commissioned the P-59, its first-ever jet aircraft, under conditions of the highest secrecy. Delivery of the series aircraft began in the autumn of 1944, but only 66 of the 100 units ordered were built. The P-59 was used mainly as a training aircraft and test aircraft for later jets.

Type: Bell P-59 B
Country of origin: USA
Use: fighter
Wingspan: 13.47 m
Length: 11.62 m
Powered by: 2 General Electric 1-16s, each 8.98 kN (907 kp) thrust
Max. take-off weight: 6214 kg
Maximum speed: 410 mph
Range: 400 miles
Ceiling: 14,080 m
Crew: 1
Weaponry: 1 M4 37 mm cannon, 3 MG 12.7 mm

Blohm & Voss BV 40

Unmotorised military glider (maiden flight May 1944); developed by the German Luftwaffe as a potential solution to the shortage of raw materials and fuel. The gliders were to be towed to above the intercept altitude of enemy bombers, which they would then fight as they glided. The project was stopped just a few months after the maiden flight.

Type: Blohm & Voss BV 40
Country of origin: Germany
Use: Glider
Wingspan: 7.90 m
Length: 5.70 m
Max. take-off weight: 950 kg
Maximum speed: 560 mph
Ceiling: 6000 m
Crew: 1
Weaponry: 2 30 mm MK 108 cannons

Boeing P-12

Single-engine fighter biplane, modification of the Navy's F4B for the US Army Flying Corps (maiden flight 6.5.1929). The USAAC was also interested in it, and took delivery of the slightly modified version in 1932. It remained in service until it was replaced by the P-26.

Type: Boeing P-12
Country of origin: USA
Use: fighter
Wingspan: 9.14 m
Length: 6.20 m
Powered by: 1 Pratt & Whitney R-1340-17, 373 kW (507 hp)
Max. take-off weight: 1220 kg
Maximum speed: 190 mph
Range: 570 miles
Ceiling: 8380 m
Crew: 1
Weaponry: 2 MG 7.62 mm or 1 MG 7.62 mm and 1 MG 12.7 mm, up to 110 kg bombs

Boulton-Paul Defiant

Single-engine low-wing fighter, all-metal construction (maiden flight prototype 11.8.1937); won in a competition against the Hawker Hotspur and scored initial successes in battle, but was then later used mainly as a night fighter because of weaknesses in the weaponry. The Defiant was also later used as training aircraft. Over 1000 units were built.

Type: Boulton-Paul Defiant Mk.I
Country of origin: Great Britain
Use: fighter
Wingspan: 11.99 m
Length: 10.77 m
Powered by: 1 Rolls-Royce Merlin III, 768 kW (1044 hp)
Max. take-off weight: 3821 kg
Maximum speed: 315 mph
Range: 465 miles
Ceiling: 9250 m
Crew: 2
Weaponry: 4 MG Browning 7.62 mm in a dorsal tunnel behind the cockpit

Bristol Beaufighter

Twin-engine heavy fighter (maiden flight prototype 17.7.1939). The Beaufighter became increasingly important with the outbreak of WWII because of its speed and firepower. By the end of the war, a total of 5564 units had been built in several versions. The Beaufighter was also used as a night fighter and fighter bomber against targets at sea, and as a torpedo bomber.

Type: Bristol 156 Beaufighter T.F.X
Country of origin: Great Britain
Use: fighter
Wingspan: 17.64 m
Length: 12.59 m
Powered by: 2 Bristol Hercules XVII, each 1286 kW (1748 hp)
Max. take-off weight: 11,520 kg
Maximum speed: 320 mph at 3000 m altitude
Range: 1750 miles
Ceiling: 5790 m
Crew: 2
Weaponry: 4 20 mm cannon, 7 MG, alternatively 8 missiles, torpedoes

BAe/McDonnell Douglas Harrier II

Single-engine jet bomber with STOVL abilities (maiden flight AV-8 B: 5.11.1981; BAe Harrier GR Mk.5: 30.4.1985). The Harrier II was produced by BAe Systems and McDonnell Douglas (now part of Boeing). It has been modernised several times since the 1980s. It is used on Spanish and Italian aircraft carriers, as well as American and British ones.

Type: AV-8 B Harrier II plus
Country of origin: USA, Great Britain
Use: fighter bomber
Wingspan: 9.25 m; **Length:** 14.12 m
Max. take-off weight: 14,061 kg

Powered by: Rolls-Royce-Pegasus 11-61 F408-RR-408, 105 kN (10,707 kp) thrust
Maximum speed: 660 mph
Range: 1105 miles
Ceiling: 15,240 m
Crew: 1
Weaponry: 2 MK 30 mm, AIM-9 Sidewinder and AGM-65 Maverick missiles

British Aerospace BAe Hawk T 1

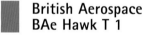

Single-jet fighter aircraft (maiden flight 1974). Initially planned as the replacement for the Folland Gnat, and from 1968 developed by Hawker-Siddeley as a supersonic jet, the trainer was renamed the Hawk in 1973 and commissioned in 1976. The Red Arrows aerobatic team uses the Hawk in its displays.

Type: British Aerospace BAe Hawk T 1
Country of origin: Great Britain
Use: Jet trainer
Wingspan: 9.39 m
Length: 11.96 m
Powered by: 1 Rolls-Royce Turbomeca Adour Mk.151, 23.75 kN (2422 kp) thrust
Max. take-off weight: 8340 kg
Maximum speed: 645 mph
Range: 1490 miles
Ceiling: 15,250 m
Crew: 2
Weaponry: 1 Aden 20 mm cannon, 2 AIM-9 Sidewinder, 3084 kg external bomb load

CASA C-101 Aviojet

Spanish single-jet multi-role aircraft (maiden flight 27.6.1977); developed and built in co-operation with Northrop and MBB from 1974 until 1997. Thanks to the modular construction, the Aviojet can easily be converted from a training to a fighting aircraft.

Type: CASA C-101
Country of origin: Spain
Use: multi-role aircraft
Wingspan: 10.60 m
Length: 12.25 m
Powered by: 1 Garrett TFE731-2-25, 15.6 kN (1590 kp) thrust
Max. take-off weight: 5600 kg
Maximum speed: 425 mph
Range: 300 miles
Ceiling: 13,700 m
Crew: 2
Weaponry: 1 30 mm DEFA cannon, 1000 kg weapons on 4 underwing racks

Convair F-102 Delta Dagger

Single-jet fighter, cantilevered mid-wing with five-sparred delta wings (maiden flight 24.10.1953); the world's first all-weather supersonic jet. On-board electronics and radar guided the aircraft in the right direction for battle and initiated the complex fire-control system. However, its actual performance fell short of expectations. The necessary technical improvements were finally realised on its successor, the Delta Dart.

Type: Convair F-102
Country of origin: USA
Use: fighter
Wingspan: 11.62 m
Length: 20.84 m
Powered by: 1 Pratt & Whitney J57 P-23, 76.54 kN (7800 kp) thrust
Max. take-off weight: 14,300 kg
Maximum speed: 825 mph
Range: 1350 miles
Ceiling: 16,460 m
Crew: 1
Weaponry: 6 guided missiles, 24 unguided 70 mm missiles

Convair F-106 Delta Dart

Single-jet fighter, cantilevered mid-wing (maiden flight 26.12.1956); developed as an improvement of the F-102 Delta Dagger to outperform Soviet supersonic bombers in altitude and speed. The aircraft could fly in all weathers. It remained in service for more than 28 years and still holds the world speed record for single-engine jets (1525.965 mph) today. The last of the 340 units built was decommissioned in 1988.

Type: Convair F-106 A
Country of origin: USA
Use: fighter
Wingspan: 11.67 m; Length: 21.56 m
Powered by: 1 Pratt & Whitney J57 P-17, 109 kN (11,115 kp) thrust
Max. take-off weight: 17,350 kg
Maximum speed: 1525 mph
Range: 2670 miles
Ceiling: 17,400 m
Crew: 1
Weaponry: 1 M61 Vulcan 20 mm cannon, 1 AIR 2A or AIR-2B atomic bomb, 4 missiles

Curtiss F9C Sparrowhawk

Single-engine metal-framed fighter biplane (maiden flight 14.4.1932). The F9C had air hooks and was assigned to the military airship USS *Akron* as an escort; the seven units built remained in service until the *Akron* went down at sea in 1933. The Sparrowhawk's new carrier airship, the USS *Macon*, shared the same fate as its predecessor in 1935.

Type: Curtiss XF9C-1
Country of origin: USA
Use: fighter
Wingspan: 7.75 m
Length: 6.13 m
Powered by: 1 Wright R-975-E3 Whirlwind, 321 kW (436 hp)
Max. take-off weight: 1256 kg
Maximum speed: 155 mph at 1220 m altitude
Range: 350 miles
Ceiling: 5850 m
Crew: 1
Weaponry: 2 7.62 mm Browning MG

Curtiss P-40E Warhawk

Single-engine close air support and fighter bomber; originally developed as a fighter, it was already overpowered by its opponents in 1940 whilst in service with the RAF. The RAF and USAAF therefore used it for close support for their ground troops. The P-40 proved itself against the Japanese aircraft used in the Chinese theatre of war.

Type: Curtiss P-40E
Country of origin: USA
Use: fighter bomber
Wingspan: 11.38 m
Length: 10.16 m
Powered by: 1 Allison V-1710-99, 882 kW (1200 hp)
Max. take-off weight: 3780 kg
Maximum speed: 345 mph
Range: 7845 miles
Ceiling: 9450 m
Crew: 1
Weaponry: 6 MG 12.7 mm, 3 227 kg bombs

Dassault Super Etendard

Single-jet carrier-borne fighter bomber (maiden flight 21.5.1958). The Super Etendard was commissioned by the French navy in 1978. However, it was also used by the Argentineans in the Falklands conflict, and sank two British ships (one of which was HMS *Sheffield*) with two Exocet missiles.

Type: Dassault-Bréguet Super Etendard
Country of origin: France
Use: fighter bomber
Wingspan: 9.60 m
Length: 14.31 m
Powered by: 1 SNECMA Atar 9K50, 49 kN (5000 kp) thrust

Max. take-off weight: 12,000 kg
Maximum speed: 745 mph
Range: 510 miles
Ceiling: 13,700 m
Crew: 1
Weaponry: 2 DEFA 552A 30 mm cannon, up to 2100 kg bomb load or Exocet missiles

Dassault Mirage F1

Single-jet fighter bomber (maiden flight 23.12.1966). Developed from the Mirage III, she had the edge over her predecessor in range and manoeuvrability. She remained the French air force's standard fighter aircraft until the advent of the Mirage 2000.

Type: Dassault-Bréguet Mirage F1C
Country of origin: France
Use: fighter bomber
Wingspan: 8.40 m
Length: 15.00 m
Powered by: 1 SNECMA Atar 9K50, 49 kN (5000 kp) thrust
Max. take-off weight: 16,200 kg
Maximum speed: 1465 mph
Range: 520 miles
Ceiling: 20,000 m
Crew: 1
Weaponry: 2 MK 30 mm, 2 missiles, up to 4000 kg external bomb load

Dassault Mirage 2000

Single-jet fighter bomber, low delta wings (maiden flight 10.3.1978). With a highly developed 'fly-by-wire' system, the aircraft became the standard fighter of the French air force in 1975. In line with Dassault's tried-and-tested strategy, numerous versions were constructed, and it was configured for export.

Type: Dassault-Bréguet Mirage 2000
Country of origin: France
Use: fighter bomber
Wingspan: 9.00 m; Length: 15.33 m

Powered by: 1 SNECMA M53-5, 88.26 kN (9000 kp) thrust
Max. take-off weight: 15,000 kg
Maximum speed: 1520 mph
Range: 435 miles; Ceiling: 16,460 m
Crew: 1
Weaponry: 2 MK 30 mm, 6300 kg bombs

Dassault Rafale

Twin-jet multi-role fighter aircraft (maiden flight prototype 4.7.1986). The Rafale is the most up-to-date fighter of the Armée de l'Air, and from 2006 was to replace almost all older models of the naval and air forces in various versions.

Type: Dassault-Bréguet Rafale A
Country of origin: France
Use: fighter
Wingspan: 11.20 m
Length: 15.80 m
Powered by: 2 General Electric GE F404-GE-100, each producing 69.8 kN (7120 kp) thrust
Max. take-off weight: 20,000 kg
Maximum speed: 1320 mph
Range: 1150 to 2300 miles
Ceiling: 19,810 m
Crew: 1
Weaponry: 1 MK 30 mm, 6000 kg bombs

Dassault/Dornier Alpha-Jet

Twin-jet fighter used as a trainer (France) and light fighter aircraft (Germany); maiden flight 1973. The German versions had the latest technology for active service; the second seat of the trainer version could be replaced by additional electronics.

Type: Dassault/Dornier Alpha-Jet A
Country of origin: France, Germany
Use: fighter bomber
Wingspan: 9.11 m
Length: 12.46 m
Powered by: 2 SNECMA/Turboméca Larzac 04-C20 turbofans, each producing 14.12 kN (1440 kp) thrust
Max. take-off weight: 8000 kg
Maximum speed: 620 mph
Range: 1825 miles (with additional tanks)
Ceiling: 14,630 m
Crew: 2
Weaponry: 1 27 mm cannon, up to 2500 kg external bomb load

De Havilland DH.100 Vampire

Single-jet fighter bomber with a double tail unit (maiden flight 20.9.1943). Its most striking feature was the gondola-shaped body with the double tail unit supports. In service from 1946, it was too late for use in WWII. It was in service with the Swiss air force in 1949.

Type: De Havilland DH.100
Country of origin: Great Britain
Use: fighter bomber
Wingspan: 11.58 m
Length: 9.37 m
Powered by: 1 De Havilland Goblin 3, 14.9 kN (1520 kp) thrust
Max. take-off weight: 5620 kg
Maximum speed: 545 mph
Range: max. 1180 miles
Ceiling: 13,000 m
Crew: 1
Weaponry: 4 MK 20 mm, 8 27 kg bombs or 2 454 kg bombs

Dornier Do 335 Pfeil

Twin-engine fighter aircraft (maiden flight prototype 26.10.1943). Designed as a multi-role aircraft, the Do 335 had one engine on the nose and one on the rear (push–pull configuration in tandem), which made it the fastest series-produced piston engine-powered aircraft in the world. By the end of the war in 1945, 37 units had been made in various versions, although they never got beyond test flights.

Type: Dornier Do 335 A-1
Country of origin: Germany
Use: fighter
Wingspan: 13.80 m
Length: 13.90 m
Powered by: 2 Daimler-Benz DB 603A, each 1287 kW (1750 hp)
Max. take-off weight: 9510 kg
Maximum speed: 480 mph
Range: 1335 miles
Ceiling: 11,500 m
Crew: 1
Weaponry: 1 MK 103 30 mm, 2 MG 151, 1000 kg bombs

Douglas A-1 Skyraider

Single-engine low-wing fighter bomber (maiden flight 18.3.1945); was intended to replace the Dauntless as a torpedo bomber for the US Navy, but in fact was not used in WWII. However, the Skyraider underwent 50 modifications and proved to be extremely successful in Korea and Vietnam. By February 1957, 3180 units were produced.

Type: Douglas A-1J
Country of origin: USA
Use: fighter bomber
Wingspan: 15.47 m
Length: 11.84 m
Powered by: 1 Wright R 3350-26WB Cyclone, 2243 kW (3050 hp)
Max. take-off weight: 11,340 kg
Maximum speed: 320 mph
Range: 1555 miles
Ceiling: 7800 m
Crew: 1
Weaponry: 4 20 mm cannon, 3630 kg external weapon load

Douglas A-3 Skywarrior

Twin-jet carrier-borne fighter bomber (maiden flight 28.10.1952). The aircraft was developed as an atomic weapons carrier. The first series version went into service in 1956. It was then completely overhauled and flew as the B-66. The Skywarrior was the longest-serving carrier aircraft of the US Navy (until 1974).

Type: Douglas A-3B
Country of origin: USA
Use: fighter bomber
Wingspan: 22.10 m
Length: 23.27 m
Powered by: 2 Pratt & Whitney J57-P-10, each providing 46.7 kN (4760 kp) thrust without an afterburner, and 55.2 kN (5630 kp) with an afterburner
Max. take-off weight: 37,195 kg
Maximum speed: 610 mph
Range: max. 2895 miles
Ceiling: 12,500 m
Crew: 2
Weaponry: 4 x 907 kg or 12 x 454 kg or 24 x 227 kg bombs in a weapons shaft; atom bombs are also carried

Douglas A-4 Skyhawk

Single-jet fighter bomber, low delta wings; originally planned as a carrier-borne nuclear bomber (maiden flight 22.6.1954). In 1954 the Skyhawk set the world speed record. A total of 2960 Skyhawks were produced to 1980, some of which remain in service with the military forces of a number of small countries.

Type: Douglas A-4 Skyhawk II
Country of origin: USA
Use: fighter bomber
Wingspan: 8.38 m
Length: 12.27 m
Powered by: 1 Pratt & Whitney J52-P-8A turbojet, 40.5 kN (4130 kp) thrust
Max. take-off weight: 11 113 kg
Maximum speed: 675 mph
Range: max. 2050 miles
Ceiling: 14,500 m
Crew: 1
Weaponry: 2 MK 20 mm, 3720 kg external weapon load

Embraer AMX

Single-jet lightweight fighter bomber co-developed between Brazil and Italy. The aircraft was used for armed reconnaissance and ground support.

Type: Embraer AMX
Country of origin: Brazil, Italy
Use: fighter
Wingspan: 9.97 m
Length: 13.24 m
Powered by: 1 Rolls-Royce Spey Mk. 807, 49 kN (5000 kp) thrust
Max. take-off weight: 13,000 kg
Maximum speed: 585 mph
Range: 2070 miles
Ceiling: 13,500 m
Crew: 1
Weaponry: 1 MK 20 mm, 2 MK 30 mm, 3800 kg bombs, missiles (e.g. Sidewinder)

English Electric Lightning

Twin-jet mid-wing fighter with stacked engines (maiden flight 4.4.1954); the first British fighter to fly at twice the speed of sound in horizontal flight. Despite its much-appreciated flying characteristics, it was decided that the range and weaponry were not sufficient.

Type: English Electric P-1 F.2A
Country of origin: Great Britain
Use: fighter
Wingspan: 10.60 m
Length: 16.25 m
Powered by: 2 Rolls-Royce Avon 211 R, each producing 73.94 kN (7540 kp) thrust (with afterburner)

Max. take-off weight: 17,554 kg
Maximum speed: 1270 mph
Range: 375 miles
Ceiling: 18,300 m
Crew: 2
Weaponry: up to 4 30 mm ADEN cannon, 2 guided or 48 unguided missiles

Eurofighter Typhoon

Twin-jet canard delta-wing fighter aircraft (maiden flight 29.3.1994). Launched in 1983 as a collaboration between the five European NATO countries Germany, France, Great Britain, Italy and Spain. In the late 1990s 620 aircraft were commissioned. Since 2002, the Eurofighter has been gradually replacing the F-4 Phantom II, the MiG-29 and the Tornado.

Type: Eurofighter Typehoon
Country of origin: EU
Use: fighter
Wingspan: 10.95 m
Length: 15.96 m
Powered by: 2 EJ200 turbofans, each with 90 kN (9166 kp) thrust
Max. take-off weight: 23,500 kg
Maximum speed: 1325 mph
Range: 870 miles
Ceiling: 18,300 m
Crew: 2
Weaponry: 1 x 27 mm cannon, 15 external racks for mid- and short-range guided missiles

FIAT CR.32 Chirri

Single-engine 1½-wing fighter (maiden flight 28.4.1933), first used in the Spanish Civil War and later in WWII. By May 1939, 1052 units were in service with the Italian air force. However, from 1942 the CR.32 was used more and more for training purposes and night-time sorties since she was no longer a match for enemy aircraft.

Type: FIAT CR.32
Country of origin: Italy
Use: fighter
Wingspan: 9.50 m
Length: 7.45 m
Powered by: 1 12-cylinder FIAT A 30 RA Vee in-line engine, 441 kW (600 hp)
Max. take-off weight: 1850 kg
Maximum speed: 235 mph
Range: 425 miles
Ceiling: 8800 m
Crew: 1
Weaponry: 2 MG 7.7 mm

FIAT G.91

Single-jet low-wing fighter bomber (maiden flight prototype 1956); the first jet aircraft also to be built in Germany after WWII, and for almost 30 years the Luftwaffe's most important light air support and reconnaissance aircraft. A two-seat training version was also built.

Type: FIAT G.91 R3
Country of origin: Italy
Use: fighter bomber
Wingspan: 8.53 m
Length: 10.06 m
Powered by: 1 Bristol Siddeley Orpheus 801 turbojet, 22.3 kN (2270 kp) thrust
Max. take-off weight: 5670 kg
Maximum speed: 670 mph
Range: 1150 miles
Ceiling: 13,100 m
Crew: 1
Weaponry: 2 MK 30 mm DEFA, rockets or bombs on 4 underwing racks

Focke-Wulf Fw 190

Single-engine low-wing fighter aircraft (maiden flight 13.5.1939). When it was first used in battle in 1941, the Fw 190 was not only superior to the Me 109, but also to most Allied fighters. By the end of the war, some 20,000 units had been built in various versions, roughly two-thirds as fighters and night fighters, and one-third as fighter bombers and for close air support. A number of others were used as torpedo bombers, for long-range reconnaissance or two-seater trainers. After the war, 64 type A-8 units were built in France and flown as the NC 900.

Type: Focke-Wulf Fw 190 A-8
Country of origin: Germany
Use: fighter
Wingspan: 10.50 m
Length: 8.95 m
Powered by: 1 BMW 801 D, 1300 kW (1770 hp)
Max. take-off weight: 4400 kg
Maximum speed: 410 mph
Range: 495 miles
Ceiling: 10,350 m
Crew: 1
Weaponry: 2 MG 131 12 mm, 4 MG 151 20 mm

Focke-Wulf Ta 152

Single-engine low-wing fighter (maiden flight autumn 1944), developed from 1943 as a high-altitude fighter and further development of the Fw 190 D as defence against the Allied forces' high-performance high-altitude bombers. However, the version with an excellent flight performance and weaponry was not achieved until early 1945 – by which time it was too late for the Luftwaffe. In several versions, 150 units were produced.

Type: Focke-Wulf Ta 152 H-1
Country of origin: Germany
Use: fighter
Wingspan: 14.44 m
Length: 10.71 m
Powered by: 1 Junkers Jumo 213 E-1, 1288 kW (1751 hp)
Max. take-off weight: 4750 kg
Maximum speed: 470 mph
Range: up to 930 miles
Ceiling: 14,800 m
Crew: 1
Weaponry: 1 MK 108 30 mm, 2 MG 151 20 mm

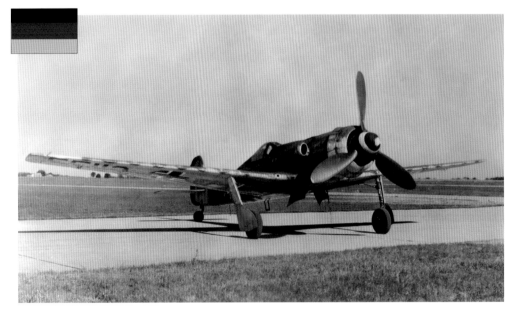

Fokker Dr.I

Single-engine triple-wing fighter aircraft
(maiden flight July 1917). Developed from
1916 in Schwerin by Fokker of Holland;
around 350 units were built. By the end of
WWI it was obvious that triple-deckers were
generally inferior to biplanes. On 21 April
1918, Manfred von Richthofen – the 'Red
Baron' – was shot down in a Fokker Dr.I.

Type: Fokker Dr.I
Country of origin: Germany
Use: fighter
Wingspan: 7.20 m
Length: 8.80 m
Max. take-off weight: 670 kg
Powered by: 1 Oberursel UR II 9-cylinder
rotary engine, 81 kW (110 hp)

Maximum speed: 115 mph
Range: 155 miles
Ceiling: 6000 m
Crew: 1
Weaponry: 2 LMG 08/15 Spandau 7.92 mm

Fokker D.21

Single-engine low-wing fighter aircraft (in service
1938–1940). When Germany attacked The Netherlands in
May 1940, 28 of these aircraft were ready for battle: 5
were destroyed on the ground, 11 in combat. Fokker also
delivered a number of D.21s to Finland, where they were
used in the winter war against the Soviet Union.

Type: Fokker D.21
Country of origin: Netherlands
Use: fighter
Wingspan: 11.01 m
Length: 8.20 m
Powered by: 1 Bristol Mercury VIII, 610 kW (830 hp)
Max. take-off weight: 2050 kg
Maximum speed: 285 mph (at 5100 m)
Radius of use: 580 miles
Ceiling: 11,350 m
Crew: 1
Weaponry: 4 MG in the wings

General Dynamics F-111

Twin-jet shoulder-wing fighter bomber with swing wings (maiden flight 21.12.1964). Developed from the TFX programme (for multi-role fighters, tactical bombers); the world's first operational swing-wing aircraft. Since the Navy and Air Force had different requirements, some versions suffered losses and technical problems in the early stages. Despite that, a total of 563 units were built.

Type: General Dynamics F-111 A
Country of origin: USA
Use: fighter bomber
Wingspan: 9.76 m/19.40 m
Length: 22.40 m
Powered by: 2 Pratt & Whitney TF30-P-100, each producing 111.6 kN (11,385 kp) thrust
Max. take-off weight: 41,500 kg
Maximum speed: 1650 mph
Range: 3800 miles
Ceiling: 17,600 m
Crew: 2
Weaponry: 1 MK 20 mm, 13,600 kg weapons on 8 racks

General Dynamics F-16 Fighting Falcon

Single-jet mid-wing fighter bomber with delta wings and straight trailing edges (maiden flight prototype 13.12.1973, series 7.8.1978); its excellent manoeuvrability and flying properties made it one of the most successful fighters of all times. Over 8000 F-16s were produced in more than ten versions and exported to some 20 countries.

Type: General Dynamics F-16 A
Country of origin: USA
Use: fighter bomber
Wingspan: 9.45 m; Length: 14.52 m
Max. take-off weight: 16,050 k

Powered by: 1 Pratt & Whitney F100-PW 200, 106 kN (10,810 kp) thrust
Maximum speed: 1335 mph
Radius of use: 775 miles
Ceiling: 15,240 m
Crew: 1
Weaponry: 1 MK 20 mm, 5440 kg bombs externally or 2–6 AIM-9 Sidewinder missiles

Gloster Meteor

Twin-jet fighter and fighter bomber, can-tilevered low-wing (maiden flight proto-type 5.3.1943); first British jet-engine fighter aircraft, used in WWII mid-1944 (e.g. against German V1 flying bombs). Its construction left the Gloster Meteor underpowered and offering poor visibility.

Despite that, she set a number of speed records after the war.

Type: Gloster G.41
Country of origin: Great Britain
Use: fighter/fighter bomber
Wingspan: 13.11 m;
Length: 12.57 m

,

Powered by: 2 Rolls-Royce W.2B turbojets each producing 7.6 kN (770 kp) thrust
Max. take-off weight: 6257 kg
Maximum speed: 415 mph
Range: 1340 miles
Ceiling: 12,190 m
Crew: 1
Weaponry: 4 MG Hispano 20 mm

Grumman F6F Hellcat

Single-engine mid-wing fighter aircraft (maiden flight prototype July 1942). Planned before the attack on Pearl Harbor, then developed at speed as the successor to the Wild-cat and commissioned mid-1943 as a carrier-borne fighter bomber. The aircraft was extremely versatile in use: air combat, ground support, reconnaissance and patrol flight, and night-time operations. Around 12,500 units were built, some of which remained in service until the late 1950s.

Type: Grumman F6F-5
Country of origin: USA
Use: fighter
Wingspan: 13.06 m
Length: 10.24 m
Powered by: 1 Pratt & Whitney R-2800-10W, 1450 kW (1973 hp)
Max. take-off weight: 6990 kg
Maximum speed: 380 mph
Range: 1530 miles
Ceiling: 11,370 m
Crew: 1
Weaponry: 6 MG 12.7 mm, approx. 900 kg bombs or missiles

Grumman F9F Panther

Single-jet cantilevered mid-wing fighter bomber (maiden flight prototype 24.11.1947). Commissioned by the US Navy in 1949, the F9F was one of the most important US fighters in the Korean War. Some 1300 units were built, including the F9F-6 Cougar with back-swept wings and various others. Some units remained in operation until the 1960s.

Type: Grumman F9F-6
Country of origin: USA
Use: fighter bomber
Wingspan: 10.52 m
Length: 13.54 m
Powered by: 1 Pratt & Whitney J48-P-8A turbojet, 37.8 kN (3856 kp) thrust
Max. take-off weight: 9352 kg
Maximum speed: 650 mph
Range: 1000 miles
Ceiling: 13,600 m
Crew: 1
Weaponry: 4 MK 20 mm and 900 kg bombs or missiles

Grumman F-14 Tomcat

Twin-jet mid-wing fighter bomber with swing wings and a double lateral tail unit (maiden flight prototype 21.12.1970). The winner of a 1969 Navy competition, the Tomcat soon found itself in the role of an air dominance fighter, reconnaissance and patrol aircraft in countless international operations. During its time of service, it was the most important carrier-borne fighter aircraft of the US armed forces.

Decommissioning of older units began in 2004. At the end of the 1970s, 80 units were delivered to Iran, where they remain in service today.

Type: Grumman F-14 A
Country of origin: USA
Use: fighter bomber
Wingspan: 19.54 m
Length: 19.10 m
Powered by: 2 Pratt & Whitney TF-30P-412A turbofans, each producing 91.2 kN (9300 kp) thrust
Max. take-off weight: 33,724 kg
Maximum speed: 1585 mph
Range: 1530 miles
Ceiling: 20,000 m
Crew: 2
Weaponry: 1 MK 20 mm, 6500 kg weapons externally (e.g. Phoenix, Sidewinder and Sparrow missiles)

Hawker Hurricane

Single-engine cantilevered low-wing fighter aircraft (maiden flight prototype 6.11.1935). Together with the Spitfire, this aircraft formed the backbone of Britain's air defence against German attacks at the beginning of WWII. After 1942, the Hurricanes were modified as ground support and attack aircraft. Over 14,000 units were delivered in various versions, used by the RAF and exported to numerous countries.

Type: Hawker Hurricane
Country of origin: Great Britain
Use: fighter
Wingspan: 12.20 m
Length: 9.98 m
Powered by: 1 Rolls-Royce Merlin XX mit 940 kW (1280 PS)
Max. take-off weight: 3740 kg
Maximum speed: 335 mph
Range: 1320 miles
Ceiling: 11,000 m
Crew: 1
Weaponry: 12 MG 7.7 mm, 2 bombs or 8 missiles

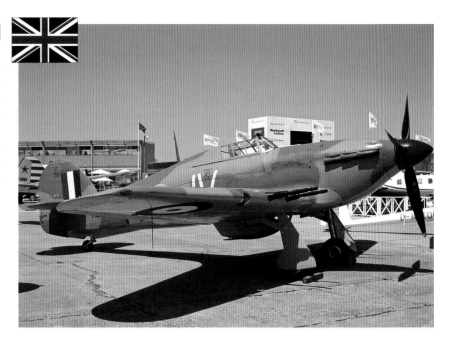

Hawker Tempest

Single-engine low-wing fighter aircraft (maiden flight 2.9.1942); a further development of the Hawker Typhoon. The Tempest developed a superior speed at low and medium altitudes. The aircraft was used against the Fi 103 (V-1) cruise missile, and later against the Me 262. A total of almost 1400 Hawker Tempests were built.

Type: Hawker Tempest Mk.V
Country of origin: Great Britain
Use: fighter
Wingspan: 12.50 m
Length: 10.26 m
Powered by: 1 Napier Sabre IIB, 1780 kW (2420 hp)
Max. take-off weight: 6142 kg

Maximum speed: 430 mph
Range: 1520 miles
Ceiling: 11,000 m
Crew: 1
Weaponry: 4 MK 20 mm

Heinkel He 51

Single-engine biplane fighter (pre-series from May 1933). The aircraft was the crossover point between the era of the fighters of WWII and completely new constructions such as the Messerschmitt Bf 109. Even while in service with the Legion Condor, it was obvious that the aircraft could no longer fulfil its role as a fighter, and so it was used as a ground attack aircraft.

Type: Heinkel He 51
Country of origin: Germany
Use: fighter
Wingspan: 11.00 m
Length: 8.40 m
Powered by: 1 BMW VI-7.3-Z, 550 kW (750 hp)
Max. take-off weight: 1900 kg
Maximum speed: 195 mph
Range: 435 miles
Ceiling: 7500 m
Crew: 1
Weaponry: 2 MG 7.92 mm, bombs on underwing racks

Heinkel He 100

Single-engine cantilevered low-wing fighter with a conventional rudder (maiden flight V1 22.1.1938). Although Heinkel's design of the He 112 came after Messerschmitt's Bf 109 in the competition for the German standard fighter, he had a new high-speed fighter developed that went on to set the world speed record. However, the Luftwaffe abided by its decision for the Messerschmitt, so despite its good flying performance the He 100 did not go into series production.

Type: Heinkel He 100
Country of origin: Germany
Use: fighter
Wingspan: 9.42 m
Length: 8.17 m
Powered by: 1 Daimler-Benz DB 601 M, 865 kW (1175 hp)
Max. take-off weight: 2500 kg
Maximum speed: 415 mph
Range: 620 miles
Ceiling: 11,000 m
Crew: 1
Weaponry: 1 MK 20 mm, 2 MG 7.92 mm

Heinkel He 219 Uhu

Twin-engine shoulder-wing fighter with a double lateral rudder (maiden flight prototype 15.11.1942). From 1943 the aircraft was used as a night fighter, and it was clear that its flying abilities far exceeded those of the Ju 188 in that role. A lighter version with a supercharged engine was able to intercept the fast and high-flying Mosquito.

Type: Heinkel He 219
Country of origin: Germany
Use: night fighter
Wingspan: 18.53 m
Length: 15.55 m
Powered by: 2 DB 603A/G, each with 1287/1434 kW (1750/1900 hp) take-off power
Max. take-off weight: 16,500 kg
Maximum speed: 380 mph
Range: 960–1245 miles
Ceiling: 9400–12,700 m
Crew: 2
Weaponry: 6 MK 20 mm

Heinkel He 280

Twin-jet low-wing fighter with a double tail unit (maiden flight 30.3.1941); in initial trials with the first German jet fighter there were problems with the tail unit and fuel consumption. Seven prototypes were built, and the Jumo 004 and BMW 003 jet engines were trialled. In September 1942, Luftwaffe command removed the aircraft from its assembly list in favour of the Me 262.

Type: Heinkel He 280
Country of origin: Germany
Use: fighter
Wingspan: 12.20 m
Length: 10.40 m
Powered by: 2 Heinkel He S 8 A, each producing 5.9 kN (600 kp) thrust
Max. take-off weight: 4125 kg
Maximum speed: 510 mph
Range: 600 miles
Ceiling: 11,500 m
Crew: 1
Weaponry: 3 MG 20 mm

Hunting P-84 Jet Provost (BAC 145)

Light single-jet trainer aircraft, cantilevered low-wing (maiden flight 26.6.1954). The aircraft was developed from the Provost with a piston engine. The Mk.4 was fully aerobatic; the Mk.5 was fitted with the latest electronics and had a pressurised cabin. The Jet Provost was the RAF's standard trainer until the end of the 1980s.

Type: Hunting P-84
Country of origin: Great Britain
Use: fighter, jet trainer
Wingspan: 10.77 m
Length: 10.36 m
Powered by: 1 Bristol Siddeley Viper Mk 202, 11.1 kN (1134 kp) thrust
Max. take-off weight: 4173 kg
Maximum speed: 440 mph
Range: 900 miles
Ceiling: 11,180 m
Crew: 2
Weaponry: 2 MG, rockets, bombs (max. 1724 kg on external racks)

Jakovlev Jak-1

Single-engine low-wing fighter aircraft (maiden flight prototype 13.1.1940). In 1941 the aircraft was used for the air defence of Moscow. The steel tube/wood construction was improved during series production as the result of experiences gained in action. The cockpit of the Jak-1M was encased in steel sheet, and it had more powerful weapons.

Type: Jakovlev Jak-1M
Country of origin: Soviet Union
Use: fighter
Wingspan: 10.00 m
Length: 8.47 m
Powered by: 1 Klimov WK-105PF, 912 kW (1240 hp) take-off power
Max. take-off weight: 2600 kg
Maximum speed: 380 mph (in 3200 m)
Range: 440 miles
Ceiling: 10,770 m
Crew: 1
Weaponry: 1 MK 20 mm, 1 MG 12.7 mm, 2 100 kg bombs externally or 4 82 mm RS-82 missiles

Jakovlev Jak-3

Single-engine low-wing fighter (maiden flight and beginning of series production 1943); developed from the Jak-1. Experiences gained with its predecessor were incorporated in its construction. The rear body section was kept lower in order to give the pilot a clearer all-round view. By the end of the war, 4500 units of this aircraft had been manufactured in a number of variations.

Type: Jakovlev Jak-3
Country of origin: Soviet Union
Use: fighter
Wingspan: 16.68 m
Length: 11.23 m
Powered by: 1 Klimov WK-105PF-2, 913 kW (1241 hp)
Max. take-off weight: 2650 kg
Maximum speed: 405 mph (in 3100 m)
Range: 560 miles
Ceiling: 10,700 m
Crew: 1–2
Weaponry: 1 MG 20 mm, 2 MG 12.7 mm, 2 100 kg bombs

Jakovlev Jak-9

Single-engine low-wing fighter aircraft (maiden flight 1942). The aircraft was based on the Jak-1, and incorporated the experience gained with the Jak-3 and Jak-7. By the end of the war more than 14,500 units had been built in various versions (including for fighting tanks with 45 mm cannon).

Type: Jakovlev Jak-9
Country of origin: Soviet Union
Use: fighter
Wingspan: 9.74 m
Length: 8.55 m
Powered by: 1 Klimov WK-107A, 1250 kW (1700 hp)
Max. take-off weight: 3260 kg
Maximum speed: 430 mph
Range: 545 miles
Ceiling: 10,500 m
Crew: 1
Weaponry: 1 MG 23 mm, 2 MG 12.7 mm, 2 100 kg bombs externally

Jakovlev Jak-38

Single-jet multi-role VTOL aircraft (first hovered on 22.9.1970; first complete flight with double transition 25.2.1972). The aircraft was based on the Jak-36. The operational version was stationed on Kiev-class aircraft carriers. Since 1981, a modernised version with more powerful engines, the Jak-38M, has been developed.

Type: Jakovlev Jak-38M
Country of origin: Soviet Union
Use: fighter bomber
Wingspan: 7.32 m
Length: 16.37 m
Powered by: 1 R-28W-300, 69.6 kN (7000 kp), 2 RD-38 lift fans, each producing 31.9 kN (3250 kp)
Max. take-off weight: 11,700 kg
Maximum speed: 630 mph
Range: 425 miles
Ceiling: 12,000 m
Crew: 1
Weaponry: 2000 kg externally on short take-off, 600 kg on vertical take-off

Junkers J 10

Single-engine low-wing fighter, all-metal construction (maiden flight 4.5.1918). A total of 44 units were constructed in series production, but only eight of them had been completed by the end of the war. The J 10 all-metal aircraft was particularly popular with pilots on the front because of its firing and weather resistance.

Type: Junkers J 10-1
Country of origin: Germany
Use: close air support, reconnaissance
Wingspan: 12.02 m
Length: 7.90
Powered by: 1 Mercedes D IIIa, 118 kW (160 hp)
Max. take-off weight: 1135 kg
Maximum speed: 120 mph
Range: 235 miles
Ceiling: 5000 m
Crew: 2
Weaponry: 1 MG, small bombs and hand grenades for throwing

Kawanishi N1K-J Shiden

Single-engine low-wing fighter aircraft (27.12.1942); a land-based version of the N1K aircraft carrier. After the loss of the Japanese carriers, the aircraft was considered one of Japan's most important fighters; it was highly effective against the American fighters, but it was late into operation and, with just some 1000 built, there were not enough of them for it to have a major effect on the outcome of any battles.

Type: Kawanishi N1K-J
Country of origin: Japan
Use: fighter
Wingspan: 12.00 m
Length: 8.89 m
Powered by: 1 NK9N Homare-21, 1324 kW (1800 hp)
Max. take-off weight: 4321 kg
Maximum speed: 355 mph
Range: 870 miles
Ceiling: 12,500 m
Crew: 1
Weaponry: 2 MG 20 mm, 2 MG 7.7 mm, 500 kg bombs

Lavochkin La-7

Single-engine low-wing fighter aircraft, wood construction, wings with metal struts; developed from the La-5 (trialled in the spring of 1944). Prototypes were fitted with rocket engines on the rear or additional jets under the wings.

Type: Lavochkin La-7
Country of origin: Soviet Union
Use: fighter
Wingspan: 9.80 m
Length: 8.60 m
Powered by: 1 ASch FNW, 1360 kW (1850 hp)

Max. take-off weight: 3400 kg
Maximum speed: 415 mph
Range: 395 miles
Ceiling: 11,000 m
Crew: 1
Weaponry: 2–3 MK SchWAK 20 mm, 150 kg bombs or RS-82 missiles

Lockheed P-38 Lightning

Twin-engine fighter aircraft (maiden flight prototype 27.1.1939); body nacelle between twin booms; double tail unit connected by a high rudder section. Initially used as an interceptor and escort fighter, later versions flew as fighter bombers, ground support and scouts for bomber squadrons.

Type: Lockheed P-38L
Country of origin: USA
Use: fighter bomber
Wingspan: 15.88 m
Length: 11.55 m
Powered by: 2 Allison V-1710-111, each 1085 kW (1475 hp)

Max. take-off weight: 7950 kg
Maximum speed: 395 mph
Range: 2250 miles
Ceiling: 13,390 m
Crew: 1
Weaponry: 4 MG 12.7 mm, 1 MG 20 mm, up to 1820 kg bombs or missiles

Lockheed F-80 Shooting Star

Single-engine cantilevered low-wing fighter with a conventional rudder (maiden flight 9.1.1944). The F-80 was the first jet-powered fighter aircraft to go into operation with the USAF. On 19 June 1947 it set a world record of 623.82 mph. In November 1950 the F-80 was the first American aircraft to be in direct combat with Chinese MiG-15 of Soviet construction.

Type: Lockheed F-80
Country of origin: USA
Use: fighter
Wingspan: 11.81 m
Length: 10.49 m
Powered by: 1 Allison J33-A-35, 24 kN (2450 kp) thrust
Max. take-off weight: 7646 kg
Maximum speed: 600 mph
Range: 825 miles
Ceiling: 14,265 m
Crew: 1
Weaponry: 6 MG 12.7 mm, 2 454 kg bombs or missiles

Lockheed F-104 Starfighter

Single-jet cantilevered mid-wing fighter with a T-rudder (maiden flight 28.2.1954). The aircraft was based on experience gained in the Korean War. The further development called the F-104G Super Starfighter (maiden flight 5.10.1960) was a multi-role fighter aircraft (interceptor, reconnaissance, fighter bomber).

Type: Lockheed F-104
Country of origin: USA
Use: fighter
Wingspan: 13.56 m
Length: 18.87 m
Powered by: 1 General Electric J79-GE-11A, 47.5 kN (4850 kp) thrust
Max. take-off weight: 13,170 kg
Maximum speed: 1145 mph
Range: 1080 miles
Ceiling: 15,240 m
Crew: 1
Weaponry: 1 20 mm cannon, 2 air-to-air missiles, 1814 kg bombs

Lockheed Martin F-35

Single-jet STOVL fighter currently under development by nine countries (production of test units commenced 13.7.2004). The Joint Strike Fighter (JSF) was to have air supremacy from the first act of war, and be used in ground battles for additional support. Three basic versions are in development: a) the conventional take-off and landing variant (F-35A); b) the STOVL variant for small aircraft carriers and aircraft-carrying cruisers (F-35B), and c) a carrier-based version with a longer range and folding wings (F-35C).

Type: Lockheed Martin XF-35A/B
Country of origin: USA
Use: fighter and fighter bomber
Wingspan: 10.67 m; Length: 15.37 m
Powered by: 1 Pratt & Whitney F135 turbofan, 179 kN (18,250 kp) max. thrust
Max. take-off weight: 30,000 kg
Maximum speed: 1200 mph
Range: 685 miles (F-35B: 515 miles)
Ceiling: 15,240 m
Crew: 1
Weaponry: 1 20 mm or 27 mm cannon (F-35A only), 4 air-to-air missiles

Macchi MC.200

Single-engine low-wing fighter aircraft with a conventional rudder (maiden flight prototype 24.12.1937). Despite its manoeuvrability, poor engine performance and firing ability made it inferior to other fighters. The high cockpit was initially closed on the prototypes, but then left open on the series versions at the pilots' request.

Type: Macchi MC.200
Country of origin: Italy
Use: fighter
Wingspan: 10.58 m
Length: 8.19 m
Powered by: 1 FIAT-A.74-RC 38 radial engine, 649 kW (840 hp)
Max. take-off weight: 2590 kg
Maximum speed: 310 mph
Range: 540 miles
Ceiling: 8900 m
Crew: 1
Weaponry: 2 MG 12.7 mm (cowling), later 2 additional MG 7.7 mm

McDonnell F-101 Voodoo

Twin-jet mid-wing fighter with a T-rudder (maiden flight 29.9.1954). Originally commissioned as an escort fighter, its role was soon increased to cover those of a typical multi-role aircraft that was also intended as a fighter bomber and atomic weapon carrier. When series production first commenced, it was the fastest aircraft of its day.

Type: McDonnell F-101
Country of origin: USA
Use: fighter and fighter bomber
Wingspan: 12.09 m
Length: 20.54 m
Max. take-off weight: 21,170 kg
Powered by: 2 Pratt & Whitney J57-P-55, each producing 53.35 kN (5440 kp) thrust
Maximum speed: 1220 mph
Range: 1555 miles

Ceiling: 15,850 m
Crew: 2
Weaponry: 4 MK 20 mm, up to 15 missiles (e.g. AIM-4E Super Falcon, AIR-2A Genie)

McDonnell Douglas F-4 Phantom II

Twin-jet cantilevered low-wing fighter with a conventional rudder (maiden flight 27.5.1958). The aircraft was initially planned as an all-weather interceptor, but was also used for ground support and reconnaissance. Over the course of its construction period, the aircraft underwent many modifications and modernisation programmes. It has participated in almost every military conflict since 1960. By October 1979, 5059 units (plus Japanese licensed versions) had been built.

Type: McDonnell Douglas F-4
Country of origin: USA
Use: fighter/fighter bomber
Wingspan: 11.78 m
Length: 19.18 m
Powered by: 2 General Electric J79-GE-17, each producing 79.6 kN (8120 kp) thrust with afterburners
Max. take-off weight: 26,300 kg
Maximum speed: 1500 mph (fighter)
Range: 1365 miles
Ceiling: 18,180 m
Crew: 2
Weaponry: MK 20 mm, missiles on 9 underwing stations, as a fighter bomber 5625 kg bombs externally

McDonnell Douglas F-15 Eagle

Twin-jet mid-wing fighter with a double lateral rudder (maiden flight prototype 27.7.1972). The aircraft was designed primarily as an air dominance fighter; thanks to modern electronics, the crew can detect, follow and fight enemy aircraft in their own or enemy air space. The weaponry (guided and cluster bombs, laser-guided missiles etc.) means it can also be used as a fighter bomber. A second-stage satellite defence missile has even been launched from an Eagle.

Type: McDonnell Douglas F-15A
Country of origin: USA
Use: fighter
Wingspan: 16.68 m
Length: 11.23 m
Max. take-off weight: 25,000 kg
Powered by: 2 Pratt & Whitney F100-PW-100 turbofans, each producing 112.1 kN (11 430 kp) thrust with afterburners
Maximum speed: 1650 mph (in 11,000 m)
Range: 2795 miles
Ceiling: 20,400 m
Crew: 2
Weaponry: 1 Gatling-MK 20 mm, 8 missiles (4 Sidewinders, 4 Sparrows or 8 AIM-120 AMRAAM) externally

McDonnell Douglas F-18 Hornet

Twin-jet mid-wing fighter bomber with a double tail unit and swing wings (maiden flight 18.11.1978). The aircraft appealed to the military for its reliability (it even withstood direct hits from ground-to-air missiles) and versatility. It is easy to convert from an air dominance fighter to ground support aircraft – if necessary even while in operation. The A and C versions are single-seaters; the B and D two-seaters (one pilot and one weapons systems officer).

Type: McDonnell F-18D
Country of origin: USA
Use: fighter and fighter bomber
Wingspan: 11.43 m
Length: 17.07 m
Powered by: 2 General Electric F404/402-GE-400 turbofans, each producing 79.16 kN (8070 kp) thrust
Max. take-off weight: 25,400 kg
Maximum speed: 1190 mph
Range: 2300 miles (with additional tanks)
Ceiling: 15,240 m
Crew: 2
Weaponry: 1 MK Gatling 20 mm, missiles (Sidewinder, Sparrow, AMRAAM, Harpoon, HARM, Shrike, SLAM, Maverick and other weapons)

Messerschmitt Bf 109 (Me 109)

Single-engine cantilevered low-wing fighter, all-metal construction, fabric-covered rudder (maiden flight September 1935). In a competition against the designs of several other companies, Messerschmitt's version won (it was based on his work in the Bavarian aircraft works), and it became the standard fighter of the German Luftwaffe as an air dominance fighter, escort and interceptor, and as a fighter bomber. In total, more than 33,000 units (including several under licence) were built in many versions; during WWII, and as the result of operational requirements and experiences, it underwent constant improvements and adaptations. Of all versions 70 per cent were produced in the series G (major series from 1943).

Type: Messerschmitt Bf 109 G-10
Country of origin: Germany
Use: fighter
Wingspan: 9.97 m
Length: 8.95 m
Powered by: 1 DB 605 B with max. 1085 kW (1475 hp)
Max. take-off weight: 3500 kg
Maximum speed: 425 mph (in 7000 m)
Range: 350 miles
Ceiling: 12,500 m
Crew: 1
Weaponry: 2 MG 13 mm, 1 MK 20 mm or 30 mm (fired through the propeller), other barrelled weapons, missiles and bombs (50, 250 or 500 kg) on underwing racks

Messerschmitt Bf 110 (Me 110)

Twin-engine transport aircraft, cantilevered low-wing with elevator and double lateral unit on the body (maiden flight 12.5.1936). The aircraft was intended to accompany bomber squadrons as a so-called destroyer. However, it soon became evident in the air battle over England that the Me 110 was too immobile for this task (loss of over 200 units). From the end of 1940, amended versions were built as fighter bombers, reconnaissance aircraft and night-time fighters; from 1943 almost only night-time fighters (with 'Lichtenstein' radar and *schräge Musik* – upward-firing cannon).

Type: Messerschmitt Bf 110
Country of origin: Germany
Use: night fighter
Wingspan: 16.29 m
Length: 12.68 m
Powered by: 2 Daimler-Benz DB 605 B, each 1085 kW (1475 hp)
Max. take-off weight: 9800 kg
Maximum speed: 365 mph
Range: max. 530 miles
Ceiling: 8000 m
Crew: 3
Weaponry: 4 MG 7.92 mm, 2 MK 20 mm, 1 twin MG 7.92 mm in the turret (from 2 MG FF/M as *schräge Musik*)

Messerschmitt Me 163 Komet

Single-jet rocket-powered fighter, cantilevered mid-wing, tail unit without elevator (first glider flight in spring 1941, powered flight trials in summer 1941). On 2 October 1941 the prototype reached a speed of 623 mph in horizontal flight. In summer 1944 a fighter was fitted with the new rocket engines and used against American B-17s. Although 9 aircraft were shot down, the aircraft was not successful as 14 losses were suffered.

Type: Messerschmitt Me 163 B-1a
Country of origin: Germany
Use: fighter
Wingspan: 9.30 m
Length: 5.70 m
Powered by: 1 Walter HWK 109-509 A-2, 15.7 kN (1600 kp) thrust
Max. take-off weight: 4310 kg
Maximum speed: 595 mph
Range: 50–600 miles
Ceiling: 12,000 m
Crew: 1
Weaponry: 2 MK 30 mm

Messerschmitt Me 262

Twin-jet cantilevered low-wing fighter (maiden flight 17.7.1942, maiden flight with piston engine 18.4.1941). Hitler himself banned the use of the Me 262 as a fighter; instead the aircraft had to be used as a 'Blitzbomber', as the result of which it lost its advantage of speed over the Allied fighters. Further, the aircraft was put into operation without undergoing sufficient testing, so it suffered numerous losses. In 1945 most of the 1433 Me 262s produced ceased flying because of a fuel shortage. The jet fighter offensive feared by the Allies never occurred.

Type: Messerschmitt Me 262 A-1a
Country of origin: Germany
Use: fighter
Wingspan: 12.65 m
Length: 10.60 m
Powered by: 2 Junkers Jumo 004 B, each providing 8.8 kN (900 kp) thrust
Max. take-off weight: 6775 kg
Maximum speed: 540 mph (in 6000 m)
Range: 650 miles
Ceiling: 11,400 m
Crew: 1
Weaponry: 4 MK 108 30 mm

Mikoyan/Gurevich MiG-3

Single-engine fighter, cantilevered low wing (series production from 1941); further development of the MiG-1. The body was a little longer, and the range increased by the addition of a fuel tank. However, the speed at lower and medium operational heights remained too low, so the MiG-3 was used primarily as a high-altitude fighter.

Type: Mikoyan/Gurevich MiG-3
Country of origin: Soviet Union
Use: fighter
Wingspan: 10.20 m; Length: 8.26 m
Powered by: 1 Mikulin AM-35A, 1007 kW (1350 hp)
Max. take-off weight: 3350 kg
Maximum speed: 400 mph
Range: 745 miles
Ceiling: 12,000 m
Crew: 1
Weaponry: 1 MG 12.7 mm, 2 MG 7.62 mm, 200 kg bombs or 6 RS-82 missiles

Mikoyan/Gurevich MiG-19

Twin-jet fighter, cantilevered mid-wing (maiden flight 16.5.1951), further development of the MiG-17 with two jet engines that could be used as an all-weather fighter and fighter bomber. The aircraft was flown by the armed forces of 25 countries (in operation with the NVA from 1959 to 1967). MiG-19 interceptors were used in the Vietnam War.

Type: Mikoyan/Gurevich MiG-19
Country of origin: Soviet Union
Use: fighter
Wingspan: 9.20 m; Length: 12.60 m
Powered by: 2 Tumanski WP-6, each producing 31.9 kN (3250 kp) thrust
Max. take-off weight: 8700 kg
Maximum speed: 900 mph
Range: max. 850 miles; Ceiling: 17,500 m
Crew: 1
Weaponry: 3 MK 30 mm, guided and unguided missiles or 1000 kg bombs on 4 underwing racks

Mikoyan/Gurevich MiG-23

Single-jet fighter, cantilevered shoulder wing with swing wings (maiden flight 1967). The aircraft was used as an interceptor and air dominance fighter, and as a fighter bomber. Thanks to the improved slow-flying properties (swing wings), it was able to use very short runways. In various versions, 25 air forces used the MiG-23, and it was produced under licence in India. There are significant technical differences between the fighter-bomber version (MiG-23BN, also MiG-27) and the fighters.

Type: Mikoyan/Gurevich MiG-23
Country of origin: Soviet Union
Use: fighter
Wingspan: 7.77–13.96 m
Length: 16.70 m
Powered by: 1 Tumanski R-29-300 jet engine, 112.8 kN (11,500 kp) thrust
Max. take-off weight: 18,800 kg
Maximum speed: 1395 mph
Range: max. 1505 miles
Ceiling: 18,200 m
Crew: 1
Weaponry: 1 MK 23 mm on the fuselage on a movable carriage; guided air-to-air missiles (R-3S, R-60, R-23T, R-23R etc.)

Mikoyan/Gurevich MiG-29

Twin-jet fighter, cantilevered mid-wing with arrow-shaped trapeze wings (maiden flight prototype 6.10.1977). The aircraft was designed as the counterpart to the American F-15 and F-16 fighters, and was intended to be used as an air-dominance fighter by armed forces on the front. When taking off from field runways, the jet intakes – which were positioned low down on the aircraft – could be closed to prevent foreign bodies from being drawn in. The MiG-29 is extremely manoeuvrable, and is able to execute the so-called 'cobra' manoeuvre in close aerial combat. The aircraft has modern target and weapons-guiding technology (front windscreen projector, helmet mounted display, laser and infra-red finders etc.); it is still being constructed today and is exported into many countries. The MiG-29K served on the Russian navy's aircraft carrier *Admiral Kuznetsov*.

Type: Mikoyan/Gurevich MiG-29
Country of origin: Soviet Union, Russia
Use: fighter
Wingspan: 11.36 m
Length: 17.32 m
Powered by: 2 Tumanski R-33D turbofans, each producing 86.4 kN (8810 kp) thrust with afterburners
Max. take-off weight: 21,000 kg
Maximum speed: 1510 mph
Range: max. 1800 miles
Ceiling: 18,000 m
Crew: 1–2
Weaponry: 1 MK 30 mm, guided and unguided missiles, up to 3500 kg bombs on up to 6 underwing racks

Mikoyan/Gurevich MiG-31

Twin-jet fighter, cantilevered shoulder wing (maiden flight 16.9.1975) that can be used to intercept strategic bombers, cruise missiles and stealth bombers and was developed from the MiG-25. It was the first Soviet aircraft to use digital technology to guide weapons. Series production began in 1979, and around 500 units were produced.

Type: Mikoyan/Gurevich MiG-31
Country of origin: Soviet Union
Use: fighter
Wingspan: 13.46 m
Length: 22.69 m
Powered by: 2 Soloviev D-30F-6 Perm, each producing 151.9 kN (15,500 kp) thrust
Max. take-off weight: 46,200 kg
Maximum speed: 1865 mph
Range: max. 2050 miles
Ceiling: 24,400 m
Crew: 2
Weaponry: 1 MK 23 mm, up to 6 R-33 air-to-air missiles, others on underwing racks

Mikoyan/Gurevich MiG-33

Twin-jet fighter, cantilevered mid-wing, modernised version of the MiG-29 (official name MiG-29M). The manufacturer uses the name MiG-33 for potential buyers from abroad. The cell was completely overhauled, based on the carrier-borne MiG-29K. The size of the air intakes was increased, and they were given better protection against foreign bodies.

Type: Mikoyan/Gurevich MiG-33
Country of origin: Russia
Use: fighter
Wingspan: 11.40 m
Length: 17.30 m
Powered by: 2 RD-33K turbojets, each producing 81.4 kN (8300 kp) thrust
Max. take-off weight: 15,300 kg
Maximum speed: 1520 mph
Range: 930 miles
Ceiling: 18,000 m
Crew: 1
Weaponry: 1 MK 30 mm, air-to-air missiles (AA-10, AA-11, AA-12) and others, or bombs to a total weight of 4500 kg

Mitsubishi A5M

Single-engine cantilevered low-wing fighter with a conventional rudder and open cockpit (maiden flight 4.2.1934). The version A5M4 was used as a fighter on the aircraft carriers of Japan's imperial navy. It was also used as a light bomber. The aircraft first saw active service in China. At the time of the attack on Pearl Harbor, only a few of the more than 880 aircraft of this type were stationed on aircraft carriers.

Type: Mitsubishi A5M
Country of origin: Japan
Use: fighter
Wingspan: 11.00 m
Length: 7.57 m
Powered by: 1 Kotobuki 41 radial engine, 523 kW (710 hp)
Max. take-off weight: 1670 kg
Maximum speed: 275 mph
Range: 745 miles
Ceiling: 9800 m
Crew: 1
Weaponry: 2 MG 7.7 mm, 2 30 kg bombs

Mitsubishi A6M

Single-engine cantilevered low-wing fighter with a conventional rudder (maiden flight 1.4.1939). The aircraft was the result of a tender by the Japanese navy for a carrier-borne fighter as the successor to the A5M4. The official allied code-name Zeke was never actually able to gain the advantage over the popular name Zero. Zeros formed the backbone in the attack on Pearl Harbor. More than 11,000 aircraft were constructed.

Type: Mitsubishi A6M5b
Country of origin: Japan
Use: fighter
Wingspan: 12.00 m
Length: 9.07 m
Powered by: 1 Nakajima Sakae 21, 830 kW (1128 hp)
Max. take-off weight: 2940 kg
Maximum speed: 350 mph
Range: 970 miles
Ceiling: 10,700 m
Crew: 1
Weaponry: 2 MG 20 mm, 1 MG 12.7 mm, 1 MG 7.7 mm, up to 318 kg bombs

Mitsubishi J2M Raiden

Single-engine cantilevered low-wing fighter aircraft (maiden flight 20.3.1942) that was intended to be an interceptor. A number of faults were revealed in trials, and it proved impossible to rectify them completely. In various versions, 476 aircraft were built. From September 1944 the Raiden was used in battles for the Philippines and the main Japanese islands.

Type: Mitsubishi J2M3
Country of origin: Japan
Use: fighter
Wingspan: 10.82 m
Length: 9.95 m
Powered by: 1 Mitsubishi MK-4R-A Kasei 23a, 1340 kW (1820 hp)
Max. take-off weight: 3945 kg
Maximum speed: 370 mph
Range: max. 655 miles
Ceiling: 11,700 m
Crew: 1
Weaponry: 4 MK 20 mm, 2 x 60 kg bombs

Mitsubishi F-1

Twin-jet fighter bomber, cantilevered shoulder wing, based on the design of the SEPECAT Jaguar, initially as a two-seater jet trainer T-2 (maiden flight prototype 20.7.1971); built as a single-seated multi-role aircraft for the Japanese defence forces in 1975 (maiden flight 3.6.1975) intended primarily for ground support and use against targets at sea.

Type: Mitsubishi F-1
Country of origin: Japan
Use: fighter bomber
Wingspan: 7.88 m; Length: 17.86 m
Powered by: 2 Ishikawajima-Harisma TF40- IHI-801, each producing 3249 kN (3313 kp) thrust
Max. take-off weight: 13,674 kg
Maximum speed: 1055 mph
Range: 685 miles; Ceiling: 15,240 m
Crew: 1 (T-2: 2)
Weaponry: 1 MK 20 mm, 2722 kg weapons on 6 underwing racks

Morane-Saulnier Type N

Single-engine mid-wing fighter (1913). The aircraft was used at the beginning of WWI for the interception of enemy reconnaissance and fighter aircraft. Aviation pioneer Roland Garros fitted an MG to the cowling that fired through the propeller circuit. The propeller blades were armoured in metal in order to prevent damage from accidental hits. Armed in this manner, the Morane-Saulnier became the first fighter aircraft in history. Because of the unusual shape of the propeller hub, the pilots of the Royal Flying Corps – who also flew the aircraft – nicknamed it the 'Bullet'.

Type: Morane-Saulnier Type N
Country of origin: France
Use: fighter
Wingspan: 8.30 m
Length: 6.70 m
Powered by: 1 Le Rhône 9J radial engine, 82 kW (110 hp)
Max. take-off weight: 510 kg
Maximum speed: 105 mph
Period of operation: 1 hr 30 mins
Ceiling: 4000 m
Crew: 1
Weaponry: 1 MG 7.7 mm or 1 MG 7.9 mm

Nakajima Ki-84 Hayate

Single-engine cantilevered low-wing fighter (maiden flight April 1943). This versatile aircraft was used by the Japanese army as an interceptor and night bomber, a dive bomber and in ground support. The Ki-84 was lighter and more manoeuvrable than its Allied opponents, and had better climbing abilities. It was still in use in July 1945 instead of the less powerful Ki-45 for the air defence of Tokyo.

Type: Nakajima Ki-84
Country of origin: Japan
Use: fighter
Wingspan: 11.23 m
Length: 9.92 m
Powered by: 1 Nakajima Homare Ha-45 model 11, 1417 kW (1926 hp)
Max. take-off weight: 3890 kg
Maximum speed: 390 mph
Range: max. 1340 miles
Ceiling: 10,500 m
Crew: 1
Weaponry: 4 MK 20 mm, 2 x 250 kg bombs

Nieuport 17

Single-engine single-bay biplane (maiden flight January 1916). The aircraft was armed with a synchronised MG that fired through the propeller circuit. Small unguided missiles were also attached to the wing braces and used to set fire to captive balloons and airships. Large numbers of the aircraft were used in the Battle of the Somme and the battles on the Isonzo.

Type: Nieuport 17
Country of origin: France
Use: fighter
Wingspan: 8.20 m
Length: 5.80 m
Powered by: 1 Le Rhône JB, 81 kW (110 hp)
Max. take-off weight: 560 kg
Maximum speed: 100 mph
Range: 155 miles
Ceiling: 5300 m
Crew: 1
Weaponry: 1 MG 7.7 mm

North American P-51 Mustang

Single-engine cantilevered low-wing fighter (maiden flight prototype 26.10.1940). The aircraft was used in WWII (versions P-51B onwards had a new engine) from December 1943 as a long-range escort fighter for the Allied bomber groups, and achieved air dominance over Germany for the Allies. In 1947 it was reclassified from P-51 (for 'pursuit') to F-51 ('fighter').

Type: North American P-51D
Country of origin: USA
Use: fighter
Wingspan: 11.28 m
Length: 9.82 m
Powered by: 1 Rolls-Royce/Packard-Merlin V-1650-7, 1229 kW (1670 hp)

Max. take-off weight: 5260 kg
Maximum speed: 435 mph
Range: max. 2055 miles
Ceiling: 12,500 m
Crew: 1
Weaponry: 6 MG 12.7 mm, up to 907 kg bomb load or 12.7 mm missiles

North American F-86 Sabre

Single-jet cantilevered low-wing fighter (maiden flight prototype 1.10.1947). Its appearance over Korea put an end to the 'autarchy' of China's Soviet-built MiG-15. The aircraft became the standard fighter aircraft in more than 30 countries. The 86D was configured for the interception of Soviet atomic bombers.

Type: North American F-86D
Country of origin: USA
Use: fighter
Wingspan: 11.28 m
Length: 12.27 m
Powered by: 1 General Electric J47-GE-17B, 33.35 kN (3400 kp) thrust

Max. take-off weight: 7756 kg
Maximum speed: 705 mph
Range: 835 miles
Ceiling: 16,640 m
Crew: 1
Weaponry: 24 air-to-air missiles

North American F-100 Super Sabre

Single-jet low-wing fighter bomber with distinctly swept wings and tail unit (maiden flight 25.5.1953). The Super Sabre aged quickly as a fighter, but in its role as a fighter bomber – with several upgrades – remained in operation until 1970, and was also used in Vietnam.

Type: North American F-100D-75-NA
Country of origin: USA
Use: fighter bomber
Wingspan: 11.82 m
Length: 14.36 m
Powered by: 1 Pratt & Whitney J57-P-21A, 75.4 kN (7689 kp) thrust with afterburner

Max. take-off weight: 15,800 kg
Maximum speed: 865 mph
Range: 600 miles (with no additional tanks)
Ceiling: 14,000 m
Crew: 1
Weaponry: 4 MK 20 mm, 3400 kg external bombs and missiles

Northrop P-61

Twin-engine mid-wing fighter aircraft with a double tail unit (maiden flight prototype May 1942). The aircraft was designed specifically as a night fighter. The first series units still had a gun turret (see illustration) on the central nacelle, but as this affected the stability of the aircraft it was subsequently omitted. The aircraft became the USAF's standard night fighter, but was also used as a fighter bomber and for ground support. Reconnaissance, photographic and liaison versions were also built.

Type: Northrop P-61B
Country of origin: USA
Use: fighter
Wingspan: 20.11 m
Length: 15.09 m
Powered by: 2 Pratt & Whitney R-2800-65 Double Wasp, each 1491 kW (2027 hp)
Max. take-off weight: 17,230 kg
Maximum speed: 365 mph
Range: 2995 miles
Ceiling: 10,640 m
Crew: 2
Weaponry: 4 MK 20 mm, 4 MG 12.7 mm, up to 2900 kg bombs

Northrop F-89 Scorpion

Twin-jet mid-wing fighter (maiden flight prototype 16.8.1948). Its most striking features were the large gun pods on the ends of the wings and the fact that the engines were positioned near the front. USAF squadrons flew this all-weather interceptor from the mid-1950s, and in 1957 it became the first fighter aircraft to be equipped with atomic weapons. From 1957 it was replaced in stages with the Convair F-102. The Scorpions were then used by the Air Force Reserve and National Guard.

Type: Northrop F-89D
Country of origin: USA
Use: fighter
Wingspan: 18.19 m
Length: 16.41 m
Powered by: Allison J35-A-35, 33.4 kN (3400 kp) thrust with afterburner
Max. take-off weight: 19,160 kg
Maximum speed: 635 mph
Range: 1990 miles
Ceiling: 15,000 m
Crew: 2
Weaponry: 1 MG 7.7 mm or 7.92 mm, 104 x 70 mm missiles or 27 missiles and 3 Falcon guided missiles, up to 2720 kg bombs

Northrop F-5 Freedom fighter

Twin-jet cantilevered low-wing fighter (maiden flight 30.7.1959). A light fighter (F-5A single-seat, F-5B twin seat), developed as a replacement jet trainer for the Lockheed T-33 and also available as a training aircraft (T-38 Talon). The aircraft was developed as the F-5E and F, and finally the F-5G (1982). Over 2700 units were produced in the various versions, and it was exported to 30 countries.

Type: Northrop F-5 E
Country of origin: USA
Use: fighter
Wingspan: 8.13 m
Length: 14.45 m
Powered by: 2 General Electric J85-GE-21B, each producing 22.24 kN (2270 kp) thrust with afterburners
Max. take-off weight: 11,190 kg

Maximum speed: 1085 mph
Radius of use: 870 miles
Ceiling: 15,970 m
Crew: 1
Weaponry: 2 MK 20 mm, 3175 kg bombs and missiles (Sparrow, Sidewinder, Maverick) on 7 underwing racks

Panavia Tornado

Twin-jet shoulder-wing reconnaissance aircraft with swing wings (maiden flight 14.8.1974). Developed since 1967 by an international consortium as a Multi-Role Combat Aircraft (MRCA) and a successor to the F-104 Starfighter. Intended as a platform for aircraft with as many roles as possible (ground support, air dominance, use at sea, reconnaissance etc.), with the main focus on its role as a fighter bomber. The Panavia joint venture was founded for production.

Type: Panavia Tornado IDS
Country of origin: EU
Use: fighter bomber
Wingspan: 8.60 m to 13.91 m
Length: 16.72 m
Powered by: 2 Turbo Union RB199-34 Mk.103 or Mk.101, each producing 74.7 kN (7620 kp) thrust

Max. take-off weight: 27,215 kg
Maximum speed: 1400 mph
Range: 1725 miles
Ceiling: 15,000 m
Crew: 2
Weaponry: 2 MK 27 mm, 8165 kg bombs (Sidewinder, Maverick etc.) on 8 underwing racks

Polikarpov I-16

Single-engine cantilevered low-wing fighter, wood construction (maiden flight 21.12.1933). The aircraft is notable for its good combination of speed, manoeuvrability and weaponry. It was used by the Republicans in the Spanish Civil War. This aircraft fired the first missiles in 1939.

Type: Polikarpow I-16 Type 24
Country of origin: Soviet Union
Use: fighter
Wingspan: 8.88 m
Length: 6.04 m
Powered by: 1 M-62 radial engine, 735 kW (1000 hp)
Max. take-off weight: 2060 kg

Maximum speed: 305 mph
Range: 370 miles
Ceiling: 9470 m
Crew: 1
Weaponry: 4 MG 7.62 mm, 200 kg bombs or 6 RS-82 missiles on underwing racks

Republic P-47 Thunderbolt

Single-engine cantilevered mid-wing fighter, all-metal construction (maiden flight 6.5.1941). The Thunderbolt was the heaviest single-engine fighter to be used in WWII. From 1943 the P-47C performed in the European theatre, but its range was inadequate. Thunderbolts were often used as fighter bombers instead of escort fighters. Over 15,600 units (approx. 12,500 of them as version D) were built in the various versions.

Type: Republic P-47D
Country of origin: USA
Use: fighter
Wingspan: 12.42 m
Length: 11.01 m
Powered by: 1 Pratt & Whitney R-2800-59 Double Wasp, each 1865 kW (2535 hp)
Max. take-off weight: 8200 kg
Maximum speed: 427 mph (in 9150 m)
Range: 590 miles
Ceiling: 12,800 m
Crew: 1
Weaponry: 6–8 MG 12.7 mm, up to 1175 kg bombs or 10 missiles

Republic F-84 Thunderjet/Thunderstreak

Single-jet fighter bomber, mid-wing aircraft with a cruciform rudder (maiden flight prototype 28.2.1946), initially with straight wings, then from version 84F with swept wings (Thunderstreak). Up to 1953, 4450 series aircraft were produced and exported to many countries. The aircraft was used in the Korean War, but was no match for the MiG-15. The USAF units were sent to the National Guard or sold to smaller countries in the 1960s, where they remained in service for many years.

Type: Republic F-84F
Country of origin: USA
Use: fighter bomber
Wingspan: 11.13 m
Length: 11.73 m
Powered by: 1 Allison J35, 21.8 kN (2222 kp) thrust
Max. take-off weight: 12,200 kg
Maximum speed: 620 mph
Range: 1485 miles
Ceiling: 13,180 m
Crew: 1
Weaponry: 6 MG 12.7 mm, 8 x 12.7 mm missiles, 900 kg bombs

Republic F-105 Thunderchief

Single-jet mid-wing fighter bomber with a conventional rudder (maiden flight 22.10.1955). As a supersonic fighter bomber, the aircraft was designed to carry both conventional and nuclear weapons. It was used in the Vietnam War.

Type: Republic F-105D
Country of origin: USA
Use: fighter bomber
Wingspan: 10.64 m
Length: 19.58 m
Powered by: 1 Pratt & Whitney J75-P-19W, 118 kN (12,300 kp) thrust with after-burner
Max. take-off weight: 23,835 kg
Maximum speed: 1420 mph
Range: 1500 miles
Ceiling: 15,240 m
Crew: 1
Weaponry: 1 MK M61A1 Vulcan 20 mm, up to 6350 kg weapons

Saab 21

Single-jet twin-tail fighter (1950), the first jet aircraft to be built in Sweden and also the only one to be converted from rear propeller (21A; see illustration) to jet propulsion (21R) and built in series. From 1945 to 1949, a total of 298 units were built with propellers and from 1950 to 1952, 64 others with jet engines. However, the short flying time (46 minutes) and range were problematic.

Type: Saab 21
Country of origin: Sweden
Use: fighter and fighter bomber
Wingspan: 11.60 m
Length: 10.45 m

Powered by: 1 De Havilland Goblin 3, 14.71 kN (1500 kp) thrust
Max. take-off weight: 4990 kg
Maximum speed: 495 mph
Range: 445 miles

Ceiling: 12,000 m
Crew: 1
Weaponry: 1 x 20 mm cannon, 4 MG 13.2 mm, 2000 kg weapons on 6 underwing racks

Saab 37 Viggen

Single-jet low-wing fighter aircraft with large canards positioned upwards (maiden flight 8.2.1967), built as the successor to the Saab 35 Draken. The aircraft was used as a fighter, for ground support and for reconnaissance.

Type: Saab JA 37
Country of origin: Sweden
Use: all-weather interceptor
Wingspan: 10.60 m
Length: 16.40 m
Powered by: 1 Volvo Flygmotor RM8B turbofan, 125 kN (12 750 kp) thrust

Max. take-off weight: 20,500 kg
Maximum speed: 1320 mph
Range: over 620 miles
Ceiling: 15,500 m
Crew: 1
Weaponry: 1 MK 30 mm, missiles on 7 underwing stations, optional bombs

Saab 39 Gripen

Single-jet mid-wing fighter with movable canards (maiden flight 9.12.1988) that was intended to replace the Saab 37 Viggen as a light multi-role aircraft. The Gripen is used as an interceptor and air-dominance fighter and reconnaissance.

Type: Saab JAS 39
Country of origin: Sweden
Use: fighter
Wingspan: 8.40 m
Length: 14.10 m
Powered by: 1 Volvo Flygmotor RM12 turbofan, 80.5 kN (8200 kp) thrust
Max. take-off weight: 14,000 kg
Maximum speed: 1520 mph
Range: over 1865 miles
Ceiling: 18,500 m
Crew: 1
Weaponry: 1 MK 27 mm, 6 air-to-air missiles, other weapons (max. 5000 kg)

Saab 105/Sk 60

Twin-jet shoulder-wing fighter and training aircraft with a T-rudder (maiden flight prototype 29.6.1963). In addition to its primary role as a jet trainer (Sk 60), it is also used as a light fighter and reconnaissance aircraft. The pilot and co-pilot (or student) sit beside each other. The export version Saab 105 XT went to Austria (see illustration).

Type: Saab 105 XT
Country of origin: Sweden
Use: fighter and training aircraft
Wingspan: 9.50 m
Length: 10.50 m
Powered by: 2 General Electric J85-GE-17B, each producing 12.65 kN (1290 kp) thrust
Max. take-off weight: 6500 kg
Maximum speed: 515 mph
Range: 1720 miles (with additional tanks)
Ceiling: 13,700 m
Crew: 2
Weaponry: MK and missiles (max. 2000 kg)

SEPECAT Jaguar

Twin-jet shoulder-wing fighter bomber (maiden flight prototype 8.9.1968); Franco–British joint project. France purchased 200 units as replacements for the F-100 Super Sabre; Great Britain purchased 202 to replace the Hawker Hunter.

Type: SEPECAT Jaguar
Country of origin: France, Great Britain
Use: fighter bomber
Wingspan: 8.69 m
Length: 15.52 m
Powered by: 2 Rolls-Royce/Turboméca Adour Mk811, each producing 37.4 kN (3815 kp) thrust

Max. take-off weight: 15,700 kg
Maximum speed: 1085 mph
Range: 620–870 miles
Ceiling: 15,240 m
Crew: 1
Weaponry: 2 x 30 mm cannon in the rear, 7 underwing racks for up to 4763 kg weapons

SPAD S.VII

Single-engine fighter biplane (maiden flight April 1916). The aircraft – the second series was given more powerful engines – was extremely successful in WWI, not only with the French air force but also with the British, Belgian, Russian and other air forces. The larger two-seat S.XI was developed from the SPAD S.VII.

Type: SPAD S.VII (2. Serie)
Country of origin: France
Use: fighter
Wingspan: 7.82 m
Length: 6.16 m
Powered by: 1 Hispano-Suiza 8Ac-V8 in-line engine, 134 kW (180 hp)
Max. take-off weight: 755 kg
Maximum speed: 120 mph (in 2000 m)
Period of operation: 2 hr 15 mins
Ceiling: 5485 m
Crew: 1
Weaponry: 1 MG 7.7 mm synchronised

SPAD S.XIII

Single-engine fighter biplane (maiden flight prototype 4.4.1917), further development of the S.VII. The circular cooler on the V-engine caused the front section to act like an aircraft with a radial engine. The S.XIII had a greater wingspan and stronger weapons than its predecessor. It remained in service with many air forces (including Poland and Czechoslovakia) for many years after the end of WWI.

Type: SPAD S.XIII
Country of origin: France
Use: fighter
Wingspan: 8.10 m
Length: 6.30 m
Powered by: 1 Hispano-Suiza 8B-V8, 164 kW (220 hp)
Max. take-off weight: 845 kg
Maximum speed: 145 mph
Range: 185 miles
Ceiling: 6650 m
Crew: 1
Weaponry: 2 MG 7.7 mm synchronised

Sukhoi Su-7B

Single-jet mid-wing fighter with swept wings (maiden flight prototype 1955). The aircraft could be fitted with auxiliary rockets to shorten the take-off distance, which was of benefit when operating from field runways. It was used as the standard fighter bomber by the Soviet air forces as an interceptor and ground support aircraft.

It flew in a number of countries as well as the Soviet Union.

Type: Sukhoi Su-7B
Country of origin: Soviet Union
Use: fighter bomber
Wingspan: 8.90 m
Length: 17.38 m
Powered by: 1 Ljulka AL 7 F1, max.

88.2 kN (9000 kp) thrust
Max. take-off weight: 13,500 kg
Maximum speed: 1055 mph
Ceiling: 18,000 m
Range: 900 miles
Crew: 1
Weaponry: 2 MK 30 mm, rockets or bombs on underwing racks

Sukhoi Su-24

Twin-jet shoulder-wing fighter bomber with swing wings (maiden flight of Su-19, 1970). Its course of development led from the two-seat Su-19 and the modified Su-19M to the Su-24 (1974) and Su-24 (1986). The Su-24 was the first Soviet aircraft to be fitted with integrated avionics (bomb sight, weapons computer, navigation system).

Type: Sukhoi Su-24 M
Country of origin: Soviet Union
Use: fighter bomber
Wingspan: 17.64 m/10.50 m
Length: 21.29 m
Powered by: 2 Ljulka AL-21F-3 turbojets, each 110 kN (11,200 kp)
Max. take-off weight: 39,700 kg
Maximum speed: 900 mph
Range: 1555 miles
Ceiling: 12,000 m
Crew: 1
Weaponry: 1 MK 23 mm, 8000 kg external weapon load

Sukhoi Su-30

Twin-jet fighter with a double rudder (maiden flight December 1989), further development of the Su-27. A platform for a family of aircraft that includes air dominance fighters, long-range interceptors and multi-role fighters. The Su-30 has been in service with the Russian armed forces since 1992. Related versions: the Su-32 as a tactical bomber, and the Su-33 as the marine version.

Type: Sukhoi Su-30 MKK
Country of origin: Russland
Use: fighter bomber
Wingspan: 14.70 m; **Length:** 21.94 m
Powered by: 2 Ljulka AL-31F, each producing 122.6 kN (12,440 kp) thrust with afterburners
Maximum speed: 1320 mph
Range: 1865 miles
Ceiling: 17,500 m
Crew: 2
Weaponry: 1 GSch-301 30 mm cannon, weapons payload 6000 kg on 10 underwing racks

Sukhoi Su-33

Twin-jet fighter bomber, special derivation of the Su-27 for carrier-borne use (maiden flight prototype 1985). Tail unit and wings fold in. The Russian navy received the first aircraft in 1994; 24 of them are on what is currently Russia's only aircraft carrier, the *Admiral Kuznetsov* (Su-33 MK: single-seater, Su-33 KUB: twin-seater).

Type: Sukhoi Su-33
Country of origin: Russia
Use: fighter bomber
Wingspan: 14.70 m
Length: 21.19 m
Powered by: : 2 Ljulka AL-31F, each producing 122.6 kN (12,440 kp) thrust with afterburners
Max. take-off weight: 33,000 kg
Maximum speed: 1430 mph
Range: 1865 miles
Ceiling: 17,000 m
Crew: 1–2
Weaponry: 1 GSch-301 30 mm cannon, weapons payload 6500 kg on 12 underwing racks

Supermarine Spitfire

British single-engine cantilevered low-wing fighter (maiden flight prototype 5.3.1936). Over the course of time, the engine performance was doubled, the maximum speed increased by one-third and its climbing performance improved by 80 per cent. The aircraft was particularly popular with pilots because of its manoeuvrability, which is due in no small part to its characteristic elliptic wing geometry.

During the Battle of Britain, the Spitfire and the Hawker Hurricane were the most involved in combat against Germany's Luftwaffe. More than 20,000 Spitfires were built in a total of 24 versions and countless sub-versions.

Type: Supermarine Spitfire Mk.1
Country of origin: Great Britain
Use: fighter
Wingspan: 11.23 m

Length: 9.12 m
Powered by: 1 Rolls-Royce Merlin Mk.2, 758 kW (1030 hp)
Max. take-off weight: 2415 kg
Maximum speed: 355 mph
Range: 500 miles
Ceiling: 10,360 m
Crew: 1
Weaponry: 8 MG 7.7 mm

Tupolev I-4/ANT-5

Single-engine single-bay 1½-wing fighter, all-metal construction (trials commenced in July 1927). Of this aircraft 370 units were built and used in fighter squadrons. From 1934 the I-4 gradually changed over to training purposes.

Type: Tupolev I-4 (ANT-5)
Country of origin: Soviet Union
Use: fighter
Wingspan: 11.40 m (top), 5.70 m (bottom)
Length: 7.28 m
Powered by: 1 M-22 (Gnôme-Rhône GR-9ASB) radial engine, 353 kW (480 hp)
Max. take-off weight: 1430 kg
Maximum speed: 145 mph
Range: 520 miles
Ceiling: 7000 m
Crew: 1
Weaponry: 2 MG 7.62 mm, 4 x 50 kg bombs

Tupolev Tu-128 (Tu-28B)

Twin-jet bomber, cantilevered mid-wing with swept wings (delivered in 1961). The aircraft was designed as a long-range interceptor, and is probably one of the heaviest fighters ever built. The Tu-128M was built from 1971, and was intended for low flying operations (500–1500 m).

Type: Tupolev T-128M
Country of origin: Soviet Union
Use: fighter
Wingspan: 17.53 m
Length: 30.06 m
Powered by: 2 Ljulka AL-7F-2, each producing 99.1 kN (10,105 kp) thrust

Max. take-off weight: 43,260 kg
Maximum speed: 1185 mph
Range: 1530 miles
Ceiling: 15,600 m
Crew: 2
Weaponry: 4 long-range air-to-air missiles, 2 R-4TM and R-4RM missiles

Vought F4U Corsair

Single-engine cantilevered low-wing fighter with folding wings (maiden flight prototype 29.5.1940). Because of changes in the specifications, the Corsair was not delivered until July 1942. Due to the tremendous demand during WWII, Goodyear and Brewster also built the aircraft under licence and with a different name. The aircraft was used by the US Marine Corps and US Navy, mainly in the Pacific theatre. It was used to provide ground support in the Korean War.

Type: Chance Vought F4U-1
Country of origin: USA
Use: fighter
Wingspan: 12.49 m
Length: 9.99 m
Powered by: 1 Pratt & Whitney R-2800-8, 1491 kW (2027 hp)
Max. take-off weight: 6280 kg
Maximum speed: 390 mph
Range: 1070 miles
Ceiling: 11,310 m
Crew: 1
Weaponry: 6 MG M2 12.7 mm, up to 1000 kg bomb load

Vought F7U Cutlass

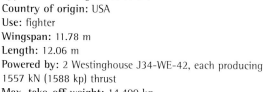

Twin-jet fighter aircraft (maiden flight prototype 29.9.1948). The US armed forces issued a specification in 1945 for the development of a twin-jet fighter with a speed of more than 560 mph at an altitude of around 12,000 m. There were 162 units of the Cutlass built, and it was the first aircraft to break the sound barrier while diving.

Type: Chance Vought 346 F7U-1
Country of origin: USA
Use: fighter
Wingspan: 11.78 m
Length: 12.06 m
Powered by: 2 Westinghouse J34-WE-42, each producing 1557 kN (1588 kp) thrust
Max. take-off weight: 14,400 kg
Maximum speed: 695 mph
Range: 650 miles
Ceiling: 12,200 m
Crew: 1
Weaponry: 4 x 30 mm cannons, 1 bomb or missile

Vought A-7 Corsair II

Single-jet shoulder-wing fighter bomber (maiden flight 27.9.1965). The aircraft was designed as a light, carrier-borne attack aircraft. From the end of 1967 the aircraft was flown by the US Navy in combat over Vietnam. However, it also flew as a land-based aircraft (version 7D for the USAF), and with the air forces of other countries.

Type: Vought A-7D
Country of origin: USA
Use: fighter bomber
Wingspan: 11.81 m
Length: 14.06 m
Powered by: 1 Allison TF41 turbofan, 645 kN (6580 kp) thrust
Max. take-off weight: 19,050 kg
Maximum speed: 700 mph
Range: 715 miles
Ceiling: 12,800 m
Crew: 1
Weaponry: 1 MK M61 20 mm, 4310 kg weapons payload under the fuselage and wings

Westland Whirlwind

Twin-engine low-wing fighter with a cruciform rudder (maiden flight 11.10.1938). The aircraft was designed as a long-range fighter, and was notable for its high speed and strong weaponry. However, it suffered a number of engine problems that could never be entirely rectified. It was used with success against ships in the waters around Great Britain.

Type: Westland Whirlwind
Country of origin: Great Britain
Use: fighter bomber
Wingspan: 13.72 m
Length: 9.83 m
Powered by: 2 Rolls-Royce Peregrine I V-12, each 650 kW (885 hp)
Max. take-off weight: 5175 kg
Maximum speed: 360 mph
Range: 800 miles
Ceiling: 9240 m
Crew: 1
Weaponry: 4 MK 20 mm, 453 kg bombs

Reconnaissance aircraft

Reconnaissance aircraft

Aircraft were first used by the military for reconnaissance purposes. Before that commanders sought out an elevated position for their command posts, from where they kept things under control. Now, though, flying gave them an airborne surveillance point – and one that furthermore was mobile. Although the possible uses and requirements for reconnaissance flights changed throughout the course of military history, the basic principle remains the same: to seek out that which was concealed – be it missile silos, submarines or night-time troop movements – and attack it if necessary. Also, special machines are used as command units (and are in effect flying surveillance points), and to interrupt the opponent's communications by electronic means.

AEG B.I

Single-engine reconnaissance biplane. Precursor to the more successful armed C' designs of AEG. By the end of 1914 the unarmed reconnaissance aircraft was replaced by the improved – although with a somewhat poorer performance – AEG B.II, and was used as a training aircraft until the end of the war.

Type: AEG B.I
Country of origin: Germany
Use: reconnaissance aircraft
Wingspan: 14.50 m

Length: 10.50 m
Powered by: 1 Benz FX in-line engine, 74 kW (100 hp)
Max. take-off weight: 1040 kg
Maximum speed: 70 mph
Ceiling: 2500 m
Crew: 2

Airspeed AS 39 Fleet Shadower

Four-engine reconnaissance aircraft, high-wing strut-braced monoplane (maiden flight on 18.10.1940); taken into operation in 1939 for shadowing enemy fleets. However only a prototype was built since it proved impossible to realise the ambitious specifications for its flying characteristics.

Type: Airspeed AS 39
Country of origin: Great Britain
Use: reconnaissance aircraft
Wingspan: 16.26 m
Length: 12.20 m
Powered by: 4 Niagara V, each 97 kW (132 hp)
Max. take-off weight: 3146 kg
Maximum speed: 125 mph
Range: 620 miles
Ceiling: 4500 m
Crew: 3

Arado Ar 240

Twin-engine multi-role heavy fighter aircraft, cantilevered low wing with an H-tail unit (maiden flight prototype June 1940). Designed as a destroyer, fast bomber and night-time fighter, the Ar 240 was in direct competition to the Me 210 and He 219, but had some very problematic flying characteristics. It was used mainly for reconnaissance purposes along the Channel coast.

Type: Arado Ar 240
Country of origin: Germany
Use: reconnaissance aircraft
Wingspan: 16.59 m
Length: 13.45 m
Powered by: 2 Daimler-Benz DB 603A, 1305 kW (1774 hp)
Max. take-off weight: 10,700 kg
Maximum speed: 415 mph
Range: 1300 miles
Ceiling: 9800 m
Crew: 2
Weaponry: 6 MG151, up to 2000 kg external payload

Avro 500

Single-engine multi-role biplane (maiden flight prototype 3.12.1912); developed from 1911 as a two-seater military aircraft with special requirements for flight duration and load capacity. A total of 21 aircraft were built and used for observation and liaison, light transportation duties and training purposes at the beginning of WWI.

Type: Avro 500 E
Country of origin: Great Britain
Use: multi-role aircraft
Wingspan: 10.97 m
Length: 8.84 m
Powered by: Gnôme rotary engine, 37 kW (50 hp)
Max. take-off weight: 617 kg
Maximum speed: 100 mph
Range: 220 miles
Ceiling: over 1300 m
Crew: 2

Avro 504

Single-engine reconnaissance aircraft (maiden flight July 1913). Occasionally – because of its ceiling – the only effective weapon against German Zeppelins, the Avro 504 was in use until the 1930s, mainly for training purposes. Numerous variants up to and including amphibious aircraft, licensed production and exports to several countries meant that over 10,000 of these aircraft were produced in total.

Type: Avro 504 K
Country of origin: Great Britain
Use: reconnaissance aircraft
Wingspan: 10.97 m
Length: 8.97 m
Powered by: Rhône Clerget 9 B rotary engines, 96 kW (130 hp)
Max. take-off weight: 830 kg
Maximum speed: 105 mph
Range: 150 miles
Ceiling: 5800 m
Crew: 2
Weaponry: 1 MG, 45 kg payload

Avro 555 Bison

Single-engine reconnaissance biplane, fuselage a fabric-covered steel tube frame (maiden flight prototypes 1921, 1922 and 1923). Designed as a reconnaissance aircraft for the Navy for use on aircraft carriers, a low double-figure number of them were built.

Type: Avro 555 Mk.1a Bison
Country of origin: Great Britain
Use: reconnaissance aircraft
Wingspan: 14.02 m
Length: 10.97 m
Powered by: 1 Napier Lion ll, 358 kW (487 hp)
Max. take-off weight: 2631 kg
Maximum speed: 110 mph
Range: 340 miles
Ceiling: 4265 m
Crew: 3
Weaponry: 1 MG 7.7 mm

Blackburn B-26 Botha

Twin-engine reconnaissance aircraft, cantilevered shoulder-wing; intended for maritime reconnaissance and as a torpedo bomber (maiden flight 28.12.1938). Because of problems with the engines, the B-26 – which went into service at the end of 1939 – was taken out of service in 1944. It was last used for training purposes.

Type: Blackburn B-26 Botha Mk.I
Country of origin: Great Britain
Use: reconnaissance aircraft
Wingspan: 17.98 m
Length: 15.58 m
Powered by: 2 Bristol Pegasus X A, each 683 kW (928 hp)
Max. take-off weight: 8369 kg
Maximum speed: 250 mph
Range: 1270 miles
Ceiling: 5335 m
Crew: 4
Weaponry: 3 MG 7.7 mm, approx. 900 kg bombs/water bombs or 1 torpedo

Blériot XI
La Manche/XI-2

Single-engine reconnaissance aircraft. Louis Blériot designed this aircraft in 1908, and became the first person to cross the English Channel on 25 July 1909. The Blériot XI was used in France and Italy for reconnaissance purposes and as an artillery scout in WWI.

Type: Blériot XI-2
Country of origin: France
Use: reconnaissance aircraft
Wingspan: 8.45 m
Length: 10.25 m
Powered by: Gnôme-7B rotary engine, 52 kW (71 hp)
Max. take-off weight: 625 kg
Maximum speed: 66 mph
Period of use: 3 hrs 30 mins
Ceiling: 200 m
Crew: 1

Blohm & Voss BV 142

Four-engine low-wing reconnaissance aircraft with folding wings and twin tail unit (maiden flight 11.10.1938); originally based on the Ha 139 seaplane and designed as a transatlantic aircraft, but work was halted after the construction of four prototypes. The prototypes were converted for war purposes, and taken out of service by 1942.

Type: Blohm & Voss BV 142 V2/U1
Country of origin: Germany
Use: reconnaissance aircraft
Wingspan: 29.35 m
Length: 20.45 m
Powered by: 4 BMW 132H1, each 610 kW (830 hp)

Max. take-off weight: 16,700 kg
Maximum speed: 235 mph
Range: 2735 miles
Ceiling: 6800 m
Crew: 4–5
Weaponry: 5 MG 15 7.9 mm, approx. payload 400 kg

Boeing RC-135

Four-jet reconnaissance aircraft that was based on the C-135. Built in 17 versions and constantly modified since 1964, the RC-135 has seen active service during Operation Desert Storm, on Haiti, in Bosnia and most recently in Iraq.

Type: Boeing RC-135
Country of origin: USA
Use: reconnaissance aircraft
Wingspan: 44.40 m
Length: 46.60 m
Powered by: 4 Turbofans Pratt & Whitney TF33-P-5, each 71 kN (7231 kp) thrust
Max. take-off weight: approx. 152,400 kg
Maximum speed: 600 mph
Range: 4040 miles
Ceiling: 13,400 m
Crew: 5

Boeing E-3 Sentry

Four-jet reconnaissance aircraft based on the Boeing 707-320B, cantilevered low-wing (maiden flight 9.2.1972). This aircraft was the first to carry Boeing's AWACS (Airborne Warning and Control System), and was used by NATO for airspace patrolling and early warning.

Type: Boeing E-3
Country of origin: USA
Use: early warning and control aircraft
Wingspan: 44.42 m
Length: 46.61 m
Max. take-off weight: 151,955 kg

Powered by: 4 Pratt & Whitney TF33-PW-100, each 93.41 kN (9525 kp) thrust
Maximum speed: 590 mph
Period of use: 10 hrs
Ceiling: 9333–11,000 m
Crew: 4 + 13 AWACS specialists

Breguet Atlantic

Twin-engine mid-wing reconnaissance aircraft (maiden flight 21.10.1961), intended by NATO as the successor to the Lockheed P2 V-7; first supplied from 1963. Thanks to many modernisations, the aircraft remains in use to this day. The Atlantic's primary missions are reconnaissance, anti-submarine and anti-surface warfare, although it is also used for search and rescue missions.

Type: Breguet 1150 Atlantic
Country of origin: France
Use: maritime reconnaissance
Wingspan: 36.60 m
Length: 31.80 m
Powered by: 2 Rolls-Royce Tyne RTy20, each 4410 kW (6000 hp)
Max. take-off weight: 43,500 kg
Maximum speed: 405 mph
Range: 6000 miles
Ceiling: 10,000 m
Crew: 12
Weaponry: 1 gun Mk.46; torpedoes, water bombs, mines, missiles and guided missiles

British Aerospace Nimrod

Four-jet low-wing reconnaissance aircraft. (Maiden flight prototype 23.5.1967, MR1 28.6.1968, final version MRA4 26.8.2004.) Developed directly from the world's first jet-engined commercial aircraft, the De Havilland Comet 4C, as a high-performance sea reconnaissance aircraft. It was fitted out with comprehensive radar, sonar and radio technology. It even had a tiny galley for the crew.

Type: British Aerospace Nimrod MR1
Country of origin: Great Britain
Use: reconnaissance aircraft
Wingspan: 35.08 m
Length: 38.63 m
Powered by: 4 Rolls-Royce RB 168-20 Spey Mk.250, each 54 kN (5506 kp) thrust
Max. take-off weight: 87,090 kg
Maximum speed: 575 mph
Range: 5755 miles
Ceiling: 13,040 m
Crew: up to 13
Weaponry: 9 torpedoes or bombs internally; other missiles, guns or sea mines externally

Canadair CL 28 Argus

Four-engine low-wing maritime reconnaissance aircraft (maiden flight 28.3.1957), which – like the Canadair CL 44 civilian version – was based on the Bristol 175 Britannia. The fuselage was completely rebuilt; the rear sensor contained the magnetic search devices for hunting submarines. The plans were for the aircraft to be able to remain airborne at low heights for 24 hours.

Type: Canadair CL 28
Country of origin: Canada
Use: maritime reconnaissance
Wingspan: 43.40 m
Length: 39.30 m
Powered by: 4 Wright R-3350-EA1 Cyclones, each 2535 kW (3446 hp)
Max. take-off weight: 71,214 kg
Maximum speed: 290 mph
Range: 5900 miles
Ceiling: 7620 m
Crew: 15
Weaponry: 3629 kg payload in the fuselage, 1724 kg on external racks

Cessna O-2

Twin-engine reconnaissance aircraft (maiden flight January 1967), powered by thrust propellers on the nose and rear in a push/pull configuration. The military version of the Cessna 337 Skymaster replaced the Cessna O-1 Bird Dog. The Cessna O-2 was in operation as a reconnaissance aircraft in Vietnam and used for range control. The last of the 532 units that were manufactured up to 1970 were in operation with the USAF until the 1980s.

Type: Cessna O-2 A
Country of origin: USA
Use: reconnaissance aircraft
Wingspan: 11.63 m
Length: 9.07 m
Powered by: 2 Continental IO-360-GB, each 157 kW (213 hp)
Max. take-off weight: 2100 kg
Maximum speed: 260 mph
Range: 1420 miles
Ceiling: 9500 m
Crew: 2
Weaponry: MG 7.62 mm, lightweight missiles on 4 underwing racks

Consolidated PB4Y Privateer

Four-engine shoulder-wing reconnaissance aircraft (maiden flight 20.9.1943); Navy version of the B-24 Liberator. The fuselage of the B-24 was extended and made more flak proof. Some of the more than 700 units, which were in operation mainly in the Pacific area, were used for fire-fighting until 2002.

Type: Consolidated PB4Y-2
Country of origin: USA
Use: reconnaissance aircraft
Wingspan: 33.53 m
Length: 22.73 m
Powered by: 4 Pratt & Whitney R-1830-94, each 1007 kW (1369 hp)
Max. take-off weight: 29,480 kg
Maximum speed: 235 mph
Range: 2800 miles
Ceiling: 6310 m
Crew: 11
Weaponry: 12 MG 12.7 mm, up to 5800 kg payload

DFS 228

Single-jet reconnaissance aircraft (maiden flight 1943); prototype developed as a high-altitude level reconnaissance aircraft (with 2 Zeiss infra-red cameras); rocket powered from 1941 to make it supersonic. More than 40 test flights had been carried out by the end of the war (illustration: DFS 228 on Dornier Do-217). The information obtained was to be used in the construction of the DFS 228 V2, but its prototype was destroyed in the spring of 1945.

Type: DFS 228 V1
Country of origin: Germany
Use: reconnaissance aircraft
Wingspan: 17.60 m
Length: 10.59 m
Powered by: 1 Walter HWK 109-509 A-1 rocket engine, 15.7 kN (1600 kp) thrust
Max. take-off weight: 4200 kg
Maximum speed: 560 mph
Range: 650 miles
Ceiling: 10,000 m
Crew: 1

Fieseler Fi 156 Storch

Single-engine multi-role aircraft with STOL characteristics (maiden flight 24.4.1936). Some 2900 units were manufactured between 1937 and 1945, and used primarily as liaison and reconnaissance aircraft. Remained in production after the war in France and Czechoslovakia and/or used as a template for further developments. A small number remain in operation today.

Type: Fieseler Fi 156 C 2
Country of origin: Germany
Use: reconnaissance aircraft
Wingspan: 14.25 m
Length: 9.90 m
Powered by: 1 Argus As 10C-3, 175 kW (238 hp)
Max. take-off weight: 1325 kg
Maximum speed: 110 mph
Range: 290 miles
Ceiling: 5300 m
Passagiere: 2 + 1 pilot
Weaponry: 1 MG 15 7.92 mm

Focke-Wulf Fw 189 Eule

Twin-engine low-wing reconnaissance aircraft with twin tail unit (maiden flight 1938). The aircraft was used for short-range reconnaissance. In line with its purpose, the fuselage – a nacelle positioned on the centre of the wing – is largely glass for all-round visibility; photographic equipment was on board.

Type: Focke-Wulf Fw 189 A-1
Country of origin: Germany
Use: reconnaissance aircraft
Wingspan: 18.40 m
Length: 11.90 m
Powered by: 2 Argus As 410 A-1, each 345 kW (465 hp)
Max. take-off weight: 3950 kg
Maximum speed: 200 mph
Range: 585 miles
Ceiling: 7000 m
Crew: 3
Weaponry: 4 MG 7.92 mm, 4 50 kg bombs

Focke-Wulf Fw 200 Condor

Four-engine reconnaissance aircraft (maiden flight 27.7.1937). Originally designed as a transatlantic commercial aircraft, the Fw 200 was converted at the outbreak of WWII and used for long-range maritime reconnaissance and as a maritime bomber over the North Atlantic to provide convoy support.

Type: Focke-Wulf Fw 200 C-1 Condor
Country of origin: Germany
Use: reconnaissance aircraft
Wingspan: 30.86 m
Length: 23.85 m
Powered by: 4 BMW 132 G, each 735 kW (1000 hp)
Max. take-off weight: 17,000 kg
Maximum speed: 265 mph
Range: 1100 miles
Ceiling: 7500 m
Crew: 4
Weaponry: 2 MG 151 20 mm, 4 MG 15 7.92 mm, up to 5600 kg bombs

Grumman S-2 Tracker

Twin-engine reconnaissance aircraft (maiden flight prototype 4.12.1952). Used from 1954 until the 1970s, mainly for maritime reconnaissance and hunting submarines. After being withdrawn from service, a number of these aircraft were used for fire-fighting purposes. A total of 1186 machines were built in various versions; some were exported and are still in service today.

Type: Grumman S-2 F-1
Country of origin: USA
Use: maritime reconnaissance
Wingspan: 21.23 m
Length: 12.88 m
Powered by: 2 Wright R-1820-82WA Cyclones, each 1137 kW (1546 hp)

Max. take-off weight: 11,900 kg
Maximum speed: 285 mph
Range: 840 miles
Ceiling: 6710 m
Crew: 4
Weaponry: 2180 kg torpedoes, missiles, sea mines

Grumman OV-1 Mohawk

Twin-engine reconnaissance mid-wing aircraft, with triple lateral tail unit, powered by turboprop (maiden flight 14.4.1959); taken into service in 1959 and used until 1996. Initially unarmed, but later equipped with defence missiles as the result of experience gained during the Vietnam War. Between 1957 and 1969 380 aircraft of various versions were manufactured.

Type: Grumman OV-1
Country of origin: USA
Use: reconnaissance aircraft
Wingspan: 14.63 m
Length: 13.69 m
Powered by: 2 Avco Lycoming T53-L-701, each 1044 kW (1420 hp)
Max. take-off weight: 8085 kg
Maximum speed: 305 mph
Range: 1075 miles
Ceiling: 9240 m
Crew: 2

Ilyushin Il-20

Four-engine, low-wing, cantilevered all-metal reconnaissance aircraft. The aircraft was derived from the civilian Il-18. It was used for radar scanning, cartography, intercepting radio traffic and aerial photography. During the Cold War it was often used for patrolling NATO members' sea areas.

Type: Ilyushin Il-20
Country of origin: Soviet Union
Use: reconnaissance aircraft
Wingspan: 37.42 m
Length: 35.90 m
Powered by: 4 Ivchenko AI-20M, each 3126 kW (4250 hp)
Max. take-off weight: 64,000 kg
Maximum speed: 420 mph
Range: 4040 miles
Ceiling: 10,000 m
Crew: 4 + 8

Ilyushin Il-38

Four-engine low-wing maritime reconnaissance aircraft, based on the Il-18 commercial aircraft (in use since 1967/8). The marine version has a longer fuselage, and the search radar is housed in a bulged radome. The wing unit was shifted forward slightly because of the change in the centre of gravity. A later development in 1970 had a take-off weight of 82 tonnes and could carry a load of 9 tonnes.

Type: Ilyushin Il-38
Country of origin: Soviet Union
Use: maritime reconnaissance
Wingspan: 37.40 m
Length: 40.83 m
Powered by: 4 Ivchenko A1-20M, each 3675 kW (5000 hp)
Max. take-off weight: 63,500 kg
Maximum speed: 400 mph
Range: 4500 miles
Ceiling: 8000 m
Crew: 12
Weaponry: water bombs, homing torpedoes, guided weapons on external stations

Ilyushin A-50

Four-jet high-wing reconnaissance aircraft (maiden flight prototypes 1982); based on the Il-76 transport aircraft. It is used primarily for aerial surveillance, but also as an air-borne command centre and relay station for exchanging battle data; can guide its own fighters to enemy objects.

Type: Ilyushin A-50
Country of origin: Soviet Union
Use: reconnaissance aircraft
Wingspan: 50.54 m
Length: 46.59 m
Powered by: 4 Soloviev D-30KP, each 117.7 kN (12,000 kp) thrust
Max. take-off weight: 172,370 kg
Maximum speed: 530 mph
Range: 4535 miles
Service ceiling: 13,000 m
Crew: 15-16
Weaponry: 2 MK 23 mm in the tail, ECM, infra-red and chaffs

Junkers Ju 21

Single-engine high-wing reconnaissance aircraft; successor to the type T 21 made in Dessau (maiden flight there on 12.6.1923) and manufactured in Fili (USSR). It was intended for use as an armed reconnaissance aircraft. The fuel tanks on the outside of the fuselage (see illustration) could be jettisoned in the event of danger. A total of 122 of these aircraft were manufactured in the USSR.

Type: Junkers Ju 21
Country of origin: Soviet Union
Use: reconnaissance aircraft
Wingspan: 10.77 m
Length: 7.30 m
Powered by: 1 BMW IIIa engine, 136 kW (185 hp)
Max. take-off weight: 1135 kg
Maximum speed: 135 mph
Crew: 2

Lockheed PV-2 Harpoon

Twin-engine patrol aircraft, developed in 1943 from the PV-1 Ventura, which in turn is related to the Lockheed model 14 Super Electra through the Bomber A-29. Harpoons were still involved in the battles for the Aleutians at the end of WWII.

Type: Lockheed PV-2H
Country of origin: USA
Use: maritime reconnaissance
Wingspan: 22.82 m
Length: 15.88 m
Powered by: 2 Pratt & Whitney R-2800-31 Double Wasp, each 1491 kW (2027 hp)

Max. take-off weight: 16,300 kg
Maximum speed: 280 mph
Range: 1740 miles
Ceiling: 7280 m
Crew: 6
Weaponry: 9 MG12.7 mm, 1600 kg bombs, water bombs or torpedo

Lockheed P-3 Orion

Four-engine low-wing maritime reconnaissance aircraft (maiden flight second prototype 25.11.1959); the aircraft was developed from the Lockheed L-188 Electra. Whereas the first prototype strongly resembled the original, following the initial tests the fuselage was shortened and the window removed; the search radar was housed in the rear. The aircraft replaced the P-2 Neptune in anti-submarine activities. Series production commenced in 1961; in 1969 the P-3 C was first fitted with the latest electronics of the time. Three aircraft were fitted with rotating radar antennae, and were used by US Customs for coastal patrols. The P-3 F (without data-processing system) was built for maritime reconnaissance and anti-submarine activities.

Type: Lockheed P-3
Country of origin: USA
Use: maritime reconnaissance
Wingspan: 30.37 m
Length: 35.61 m
Powered by: 4 Allison T56-A-14 propeller turbines, each 3645 kW (4955 hp)
Max. take-off weight: 61,000 kg
Maximum speed: 475 mph
Range: 2175–5530 miles
Ceiling: 8625 m
Crew: 10
Weaponry: 9000 kg weapons: 3290 kg inside (water bombs, torpedoes), 5782 kg outside (e.g. AGM-84 Harpoon)

Lockheed U-2

Single-jet mid-wing high-altitude reconnaissance aircraft. Its mission was reconnaissance at altitudes of over 20,000 m, and it was assumed that the aircraft could not be reached by defence missiles or interceptors. The U-2 owes its flight characteristics to a design that is similar to a glider. On 1 May 1960 a U-2 was shot down over the Soviet Union, which led to considerable political complications. Another U-2 was shot down over Cuba.

Type: Lockheed U-2
Country of origin: USA
Use: high-altitude reconnaissance aircraft
Wingspan: 24.38 m
Length: 15.24 m
Powered by: 1 Pratt & Whitney J75 P-13, 66.7 kN (6800 kp) thrust

Max. take-off weight: 7815 kg
Maximum speed: 495 mph
Range: 2880 miles
Ceiling: 21,335 m
Crew: 1

Lockheed SR-71 Blackbird

Twin-jet cantilevered mid-wing reconnaissance aircraft with delta-shaped wings and a twin tail unit; titanium constructed fuselage and wings (maiden flight prototype 16.4.1961). The aircraft was designed for operation at high altitudes and speeds, and set several records. In 1990 32 of them were still in operation.

Type: Lockheed SR-71 A
Country of origin: USA
Use: strategic high-altitude reconnaissance aircraft
Wingspan: 16.94 m
Length: 32.74 m
Powered by: 2 Pratt & Whitney J-58 JT-11, each 151.1 kN (15,408 kp) thrust with after-burner
Max. take-off weight: 77,112 kg
Maximum speed: 2200 mph
Range: 3000 miles (without refuelling)
Ceiling: max. 26,213 m
Crew: 2

Lockheed S-3 Viking

Twin-jet shoulder-wing reconnaissance and fighter aircraft (maiden flight 21.1.1972). Since 1974 the aircraft has replaced the slow, old anti-submarine Grumman S-2 in the US Navy. Wings and tail unit folded down, and the Magnetic Anomaly Detector (MAD) on the rear could be extended as required. Later it was modified and turned into a tanker and transporter.

Type: Lockheed S-3
Country of origin: USA
Use: maritime reconnaissance
Wingspan: 20.93 m
Length: 16.26 m
Max. take-off weight: 23,800 kg
Powered by: 2 GE TF-34-GE-400B, each 41.26 kN (4207 kp)
Maximum speed: 505 mph (sea height)
Range: 2300 miles

Ceiling: 12,200 m
Crew: 1
Weaponry: max. 1780 kg weapons: AGM-84 Harpoon and AGM-65 Maverick; mines, missiles and bombs

Martin P4M Mercator

Twin-engine mid-wing patrol aircraft (maiden flight 20.10.1946). In addition to two radial engines, the aircraft had two jet engines to increase its power on take-off and in battle situations. The jets were also powered by aviation fuel. Despite the problematic propulsion concept, some of the aircraft remained in use until 1960 and were used for electronic surveillance.

Type: Martin R4M-1
Country of origin: USA
Use: patrol aircraft
Wingspan: 34.75 m
Length: 25.5 m

Powered by: 2 Pratt & Whitney R-4360, each 2423 kW (3295 hp), 2 Allison J33-A-23 turbo jets, each 20.4 kN (2080 kp) thrust
Max. take-off weight: 40,088 kg
Maximum speed: 660 mph

Range: 4570 miles
Ceiling: 10,500 m
Crew: 3–4 (max. 9
Weaponry: 4 MG 20 mm, 2 MG 12.7 mm, 2722 kg bombs

McDonnell RF-101 Voodoo

Twin-jet cantilevered mid-wing reconnaissance aircraft (maiden flight prototype May 1954) that was the first supersonic reconnaissance aircraft. The reconnaissance version was developed from the McDonnell F-101. It was unarmed, but had the latest photographic technology of its time. Shots of Soviet missile silos on Cuba were taken from this aircraft in 1962. However, it was also used in Vietnam.

Type: RF-101 Voodoo
Country of origin: USA
Use: reconnaissance aircraft
Wingspan: 12.09 m
Length: 21.11 m
Powered by: 2 Pratt & Whitney J57, each 66.7 kN (6800 kp) thrust with after-burner
Max. take-off weight: 23,100 kg
Maximum speed: 1000 mph
Range: 2060 miles
Ceiling: 13,060 m
Crew: 1

Messerschmitt Bf 161

Twin-engine reconnaissance aircraft, developed from the Bf 110 B. Apart from the rear, which was extended by 1 metre for the photographic equipment, the reconnaissance version was largely the same as the original, as Legion Condor used it. There were three prototypes but no series production.

Type: Messerschmitt Bf 161
Country of origin: Germany
Use: reconnaissance aircraft
Wingspan: 16.25 m
Length: approx. 13.30 m
Powered by: 2 DB 600A, each 706 kW (960 hp)
Crew: 2
Weaponry: 1 MG 15 7.92 mm

Mitsubishi Ki-46-III

Twin-engine cantilevered low-wing reconnaissance aircraft (maiden flight 14.11.1939). The aircraft was originally developed as a long-distance fighter, but after being used for troops was then used as a long-range reconnaissance and training aircraft (crew trainer). The Ki-46-IIIb was used for low-level attacks. The aircraft appealed because of its extraordinarily clever aerodynamic shape.

Type: Mitsubishi Ki-46-III
Country of origin: Japan
Use: reconnaissance aircraft
Wingspan: 14.70 m
Length: 11.00 m
Powered by: 2 double-star Mitsubishi Ha-112-II engines, each 1100 kW (1500 hp)
Max. take-off weight: 5720 kg
Maximum speed: 390 mph (at 6000 m)
Range: 2485 miles
Ceiling: 10,500 m
Crew: 2

Rockwell/North American OV 10 Bronco

Twin-engine shoulder-wing reconnaissance aircraft with twin tail unit (maiden flight prototype 16.7.1965, series version 6.8.1967). The rear is designed as the central nacelle, the engine nacelles are carried in two wing supports, the lateral tail units are connected by a high tail unit. Its purpose is armed reconnaissance, although the Bronco is also used for light freight transport and as an air ambulance.

Type: Rockwell OV-10A
Country of origin: USA
Use: reconnaissance aircraft
Wingspan: 12.20 m
Length: 12.67 m
Powered by: 2 Garret T-76-G10/12, each

525 kW (715 hp)
Max. take-off weight: 6560 kg
Maximum speed: 280 mph
Radius of use: 385 miles
Ceiling: 7300 m
Crew: 2
Weaponry: 4 MG 7.62 mm, 1633 kg weapons on 4 underwing racks

Tupolev R-6 (ANT-7)

Twin-engine, low-wing, cantilevered all-metal reconnaissance aircraft (maiden flight 11.9.1929). Before 1932 45 units of the reconnaissance version of the multi-role ANT-7 were built. After its military service many of the aircraft remained in civilian use. The ANT-7 became famous for Gromov's flight over the North Pole on 5 May 1937.

Type: Tupolev R-6 (ANT-7)
Country of origin: Soviet Union
Use: reconnaissance aircraft
Wingspan: 23.20 m
Length: 15.06 m
Powered by: 2 12-cylinder M-17F in-line engines, each 526 kW (715 hp) take-off power
Max. take-off weight: 6472 kg
Maximum speed: 145 mph
Range: 500 miles
Ceiling: 4900 m
Crew: 3-4
Weaponry: 5 MG 7.62 mm, 500 kg bombs

Military transport aircraft

Military transport aircraft

In some respects, the tasks of military aircraft differ greatly from those of civilian transport; for instance, not much attention is paid to comfort when transporting soldiers or paratroopers. Transport aircraft that are to be used in a battle area are generally armed. In fact, some transport aircraft have been converted into veritable gunships and given a tactical role to provide ground battle support. In some other respects, the boundaries between military and civilian transport are less distinct. It is not really surprising that a particular type of aircraft can be used in both aviation sectors, and large military aircraft are also much used for humanitarian purposes.

Aeritalia G.222

Twin-engine high-wing STOL military transport aircraft (maiden flight 18.7.1970). The individual components were made by various different Italian manufacturers; the final assembly was by Aeritalia in Naples. In several versions (including for export),108 units were produced – mainly for the Italian air force, where the aircraft was introduced for troop services.

Type: Aeritalia G.222
Country of origin: Italy
Use: transport aircraft
Wingspan: 28.70 m
Length: 22.70 m
Powered by: 2 General Electric T-64-GE-P4D, each 2536 kW
Max. take-off weight: 26,500 kg
Maximum speed: 335 mph
Range: 785 to 3070 miles
Ceiling: 7620 m
Crew: 4
Load: 44 people or 8500 kg freight

Airbus A400M

Four-engine military transport aircraft; production commenced in 2005 (maiden flight planned for 2009). The Airbus A400M is intended to meet the increased requirements for military transport: long range, speed and load capacity, spacious and variable interior, and flexibility in use.

Type: Airbus A400M
Country of origin: EU
Use: transport aircraft
Wingspan: 42.40 m
Length: 42.20 m
Powered by: 4 TP400-D6, each 8200 kW (11,150 hp)
Max. take-off weight: 24 000 kg
Maximum speed: 500 mph
Range: max. 5600 miles
Ceiling: 11,300 m
Crew: 4–5
Load: 5500–6300 kg or 39 passengers or 30 paratroopers

Airtech CN-235

Twin-engine multi-role transport aircraft, made by the Spanish aircraft manufacturer Airtech (Aircraft Technology Industries) and a joint project between CASA of Spain and IPTN of Indonesia (maiden flight 11.11.1983). Over 250 units have been built to date. The CN-235MPA is equipped as a marine patrol aircraft with 360° search radar.

Type: Airtech CN-235
Country of origin: Spain
Use: transport aircraft
Wingspan: 25.81 m
Length: 21.35 m
Powered by: 2 General Electric CT7-9C3, each 1397 kW (1900 hp)

Max. take-off weight: 15,800 kg
Maximum speed: 285 mph
Range: 1100 miles
Ceiling: 7620 m
Load: 40 people or 4300 kg freight
Weaponry: 2 AM-39 Exocet missiles or 2 Mk.46 torpedoes (marine version)

Alenia C-27 Spartan

Twin-engine STOL shoulder-wing transport aircraft with conventional tail unit (maiden flight prototype 12.5.1999). The aircraft was developed in co-operation with Lockheed Martin as a further development of the G.222 for short- and medium-range strategic operations such as evacuation and supply flights.

Type: Alenia C-27A
Country of origin: Italy
Use: transport aircraft
Wingspan: 28.70 m
Length: 22.70 m
Powered by: 2 Allison AE2100D3, each 3090 kW (4200 hp)
Max. take-off weight: 30,000 kg
Maximum speed: 350 mph
Range: up to 1560 miles
Ceiling: over 8000 m
Crew: 3
Load: 53 people/42 paratroopers or 10,000 kg freight

Antonov An-12

Four-engine military transport aircraft, shoulder wing with turbo-prop (maiden flight 16.12.1956); originally developed parallel to the An-10 passenger aircraft as a medium-weight standard transport aircraft for the Soviet air forces. The An-12 is basically a counterpart to the American C-130. Since the end of the Cold War, it has also been used for civilian transports. Between 1959 and 1973, some 1250 aircraft were manufactured in series.

Type: Antonov An-12 BP
Country of origin: Soviet Union
Use: transport aircraft
Wingspan: 38.00 m
Length: 33.10 m
Powered by: 4 Ivchenko AI-20M, each 3126 kW (4250 hp)
Max. take-off weight: 61,000 kg
Maximum speed: 480 mph
Range: 2235 miles
Ceiling: 10,200 m
Crew: 5–6
Load: 132 people/90 soldiers or 20,000 kg freight
Weaponry: 2 MK 23 mm

Antonov An-26

Twin-engine transport aircraft, a further development of the An-24 T and An-24 RT types (1967). Large cars can be driven in and out through the large rear cargo ramp. The ramp fits under the body for when paratroopers or loads are being dropped from the air. The aircraft has an on-board crane. It can be converted within 30 minutes for a wide range of uses.

Type: Antonov An-26
Country of origin: Soviet Union
Use: transport aircraft
Wingspan: 29.20 m; **Length:** 23.80 m
Powered by: 2 Ivchenko AI-24WT, each 2103 kW (2860 hp), 1 turbojet RU 10A-30, 7.85 kN (800 kp) thrust
Max. take-off weight: 24,000 kg
Cruising speed: 275 mph
Range: max. 5220 miles; **Ceiling:** 8400 m
Crew: 4–5
Load: 5500–6300 kg or 39 passengers/30 paratroopers

BAC (Vickers) VC-10

Four-jet low-wing tanker and transport aircraft with T-tail unit. Based on the passenger aircraft, the tanker version was more successful and longer lasting than the original version. It was taken into service in 1982. The tankers could fuel two aircraft simultaneously. As recently as 1994, several formerly civilian VC-10s were converted to tankers.

Type: VC-10 C-1K
Country of origin: Great Britain
Use: tanker and transport aircraft
Wingspan: 44.55 m
Length: 48.36 m
Powered by: 4 Conway RCo.43, each 100.1 kN (10,207 kp) thrust
Max. take-off weight: 146,060 kg
Maximum speed: 580 mph
Range: 7200 miles
Ceiling: 11,580 m

Bell/Boeing V-22 Osprey

Twin-engine rotary-wing aircraft for military use; with double tail unit and engines located in rotating nacelles on the ends of the wings (maiden flight prototype 19.3.1989). The aircraft has VTOL properties: it can take off like a helicopter, then continue flying like an aircraft by tilting the rotors by 90°. The critical stage is the transition from hovering to horizontal flight. Following an extensive trial period, series production of the versions for the USAF, Navy and Marine Corps commenced at the end of 2005.

Type: Bell/Boeing V-22
Country of origin: USA
Use: rotary-wing aircraft
Wingspan: 13.97 m
Rotor diameter: 11.58 m
Body length: 17.48 m
Powered by: 2 Rolls-Royce AE 1107C-Liberty, each 4586 kW (6235 hp) on tilting nacelles
Max. take-off weight: 23,495 kg (for VTOL)
Maximum speed: 315 mph
Range: 735 miles
Ceiling: 7925 m
Passengers: 24 soldiers with kit + 2 crew

Boeing C-97 Stratofreighter

Four-engine transport aircraft, cantilevered mid-wing (maiden flight 9.11.1944), military counterpart to the civilian Boeing 377. Based on the technology of the B-29 bomber, the tanker version (KC-97) in particular provided important support in strategic operations. Between 1947 and 1958, 888 aircraft in different versions were built.

Type: Boeing C-97
Country of origin: USA
Use: transport aircraft
Wingspan: 43.07 m
Length: 35.81 m
Powered by: 4 Pratt & Whitney Wasp Major, 2610 kW (3561 hp)
Max. take-off weight: 79,379 kg
Maximum speed: 375 mph
Range: 4300 miles
Ceiling: 10,668 m
Passengers: 96 people with equipment + 4 crew

Boeing C-135 Stratolifter

Four-jet transport aircraft, cantilevered low wing (maiden flight as KC-135 on 31.8.1956); designed as the basic military version parallel to the Boeing 707 for various transport and support tasks. These aircraft are some of the longest serving in the USAF. Of the transport version, 60 units were produced.

Type: Boeing C-135 A (Boeing 717-157)
Country of origin: USA
Use: transport aircraft
Wingspan: 39.90 m
Length: 41.00 m
Powered by: 4 Pratt & Whitney J57-P-59W, each 61.2 kN (6233 kp) thrust
Max. take-off weight: 125,000 kg
Maximum speed: 600 mph
Range: 9200 miles
Ceiling: 10,700 m
Crew: 5
Load: 125 people or 35,000 kg freight

Boeing KC-135 Stratotanker

Four-jet tanker aircraft (maiden flight 31.8.1956); military counterpart to the civilian Boeing 707 – used from Vietnam to Desert Storm. A number of the 732 units built between 1954 and 1965 – frequently modernised – are still in use today.

Type: Boeing KC-135 E
Country of origin: USA
Use: refuelling aircraft
Wingspan: 39.99 m
Length: 41.53 m
Powered by: 4 Pratt & Whitney TF-33-PW-102, each 80 kN (8154 kp) thrust
Max. take-off weight: 148,000 kg
Maximum speed: 530 mph
Range: 1500 miles
Ceiling: 15,300 m
Crew: 4–5
Load: 90.72 tonnes of kerosene

Boeing C-17 Globemaster III

Four-jet multi-role transport aircraft (maiden flight 15.9.1991); in service since 1995, and since then used all over the world for military and humanitarian purposes. Thanks to aerial refuelling, the Globemaster III can reach almost any point on the planet non-stop. Planned to remain in production until 2009.

Type: Boeing C-17 Globemaster III
Country of origin: USA
Use: transport aircraft
Wingspan: 16.79 m
Length: 52.76 m
Powered by: 4 turbofans, Pratt & Whitney F117-PW-100, each 180 kN (18,355 kp)
Max. take-off weight: 265,352 kg
Maximum speed: 500 mph
Range: 2800 miles
Ceiling: 13,716 m
Crew: 3
Load: 102 people with equipment or 70,000 kg freight

CASA C-212 Aviocar

Twin-engine high-wing transport aircraft with fixed landing gear. It is suitable for use on unpaved runways and areas lacking in infrastructure. Instead of freight, it can transport 25 paratroopers or 12 stretchers and 4 doctors. A number of special versions were also built.

Type: CASA C-212-300
Country of origin: Spain
Use: transport aircraft
Wingspan: 20.40 m
Length: 16.20 m
Powered by: 2 Allied Signal TPE 331 10R, each 493 kW (670 hp)
Max. take-off weight: 7700 kg
Cruising speed: 190 mph
Range: max. 1200 miles
Ceiling: 7950 m
Crew: 2
Load: 2870 kg or 25 paratroopers

Curtiss C-46 Commando

This aircraft was very much in the shadow of the famous DC-3/C-47, but in its day the Curtiss Commando was the biggest twin-engine aircraft in the world. Because of its strength and range, the Commando was used primarily in Asia and the Pacific.

Type: Curtiss C-46R
Country of origin: USA
Use: medium-range transport aircraft
Wingspan: 32.92 m
Length: 23.30 m
Powered by: 2 Pratt & Whitney R-2800-34 Double Wasp, each 1566 kW (2130 hp)
Max. take-off weight: 22,680 kg
Maximum speed: 270 mph
Range: 1800 miles
Ceiling: 6700 m
Crew: 3–5
Load: 8200 kg or up to 62 passengers

DFS 230

Unmotorised shoulder-wing transport glider with a fabric-covered steel tube body (maiden flight 1937). Maximum secrecy meant it was extremely successful when war broke out in 1939; during the course of the remainder of the war it was used increasingly for supply and ambulance flights, since its capacity of just nine soldiers proved to be too little. Some 1600 units were built in various versions up to 1944.

Type: DFS 230 A-1
Country of origin: Germany
Use: freight-carrying glider
Wingspan: 21.98 m
Length: 11.24 m
Max. take-off weight: 2100 kg
Crew: 2
Weaponry: 1 MG 7.9 mm
Passengers: 9

Douglas C-47

Twin-engine transport aircraft, military version of the Douglas DC-3 (maiden flight 17.12.1935). The C-47 (it is also known by other names) was the backbone of the US transport fleet in World War 2. Large numbers of the C-47 were also used during the Berlin Airlift.

Type: Douglas C-47
Country of origin: USA
Use: transport aircraft
Wingspan: 29.98 m
Length: 19.66 m
Powered by: 2 Pratt & Whitney R-1830-92 Twin Wasp, each 895 kW (1216 hp)
Max. take-off weight: 13,190 kg

Cruising speed: approx. 175–185 mph
Range: 1340 miles
Ceiling: 7350 m
Crew: 4
Load: up to 3400 kg
Weaponry: 3 MG 7.62 mm Miniguns on the port side (Gunship I on the AC-47)

Douglas C-74 Globemaster

Four-engine transport aircraft, cantilevered low wing (maiden flight 5.9.1945); 50 units were commissioned by the USAAF in 1942 as transatlantic transporters. Because the war ended only 14 units were built, and they remained in use until 1959 (including for the Berlin Air-lift). Experience gained with the C-74 was incorporated in the development of the C-124 Globemaster II.

Type: Douglas C-74
Country of origin: USA
Use: transport aircraft
Wingspan: 37.86 m; Length: 13.34 m

Powered by: 4 Pratt & Whitney R-4360-49, each 2422 kW (3293 hp)
Max. take-off weight: 78,000 kg
Maximum speed: 310 mph
Range: 7770 miles
Ceiling: 6600 m
Crew: 4–5
Load: 125 people or 22,680 kg freight

Douglas C-124 Globemaster II

Four-engine low-wing transport aircraft (maiden flight prototype 27.11.1949). The C-124 Globemaster II was developed from the Douglas C-74 Globemaster, and 448 units were supplied between 1950 and 1955. A between-deck was fitted for troop transports. The C-124 carried out a wide range of transport and supply tasks in south-east Asia. It proved to be economical in operation, and remained in use until 1974.

Type: Douglas C-124 C
Country of origin: USA
Use: transport aircraft
Wingspan: 53.08 m
Length: 39.62 m
Powered by: 4 Pratt & Whitney R-4360-63A Wasp Major, each 2800 kW (3807 hp)
Max. take-off weight: 88,225 kg
Maximum speed: 320 mph
Range: 4025 miles
Ceiling: 5600 m
Crew: 8
Load: 200 people or 31,070 kg freight

Fairchild C-82 Packet

Twin-engine shoulder-wing transport aircraft with twin lateral rudder connected by the tail unit (maiden flight 10.9.1944). Some aircraft were used in the Berlin Airlift. Further development resulted in the C-119.

Type: Fairchild C-82
Country of origin: USA
Use: transport aircraft
Wingspan: 32.31 m
Length: 23.47 m
Powered by: 2 Pratt & Whitney R-2800-85, each 1566 kW (2130 hp)
Max. take-off weight: 24,493 kg
Maximum speed: 250 mph
Range: 2140 miles
Ceiling: 8230 m
Passengers: 41 paratroopers + 5 crew

Fairchild C-119 Flying Boxcar

Twin-engine transport aircraft, high wing with body nacelle and double tail unit (1948); redesign of the C-82 Packet with a more aerodynamic body (cockpit right in the nose) and more powerful engines. A total of 1184 units were constructed in various versions. In the 1960s some units were given an additional jet engine on the body.

Type: Fairchild C-119
Country of origin: USA
Use: transport aircraft
Wingspan: 33.32 m
Length: 26.36 m
Max. take-off weight: 33,780 kg
Powered by: 2 Wright R-3350-85 Duplex Cyclone, each 2610 kW (3550 hp)
Maximum speed: 300 mph (at 5200 m)

Range: 2000–2275 miles
Ceiling: 6700 m
Load: 62 soldiers/35 stretchers or 4500 kg freight

Fairchild AC-119 Gunship III

Twin-engine shoulder-wing fighter aircraft with double tail unit for supporting troops in contact (TIC); derived from the C-119 Flying Boxcar transport aircraft. The aircraft was much used in the Vietnam War to provide support for troops; weapons were typically concentrated on one side of the body as the aircraft circled its destination and fought 'broadsides'.

Type: Fairchild AC-119K
Country of origin: USA
Use: close support aircraft
Wingspan: 33.30 m
Length: 26.36 m
Powered by: 2 Wright R-23350-89W, each 2525 kW (3433 hp), 2 General Electric J85-GE-17 turbojets, each 12.8 kN (1293 kp) thrust
Max. take-off weight: 36,469 kg
Maximum speed: 250 mph
Range: 1980 miles
Crew: 4–8
Weaponry: 2 MK 20 mm, 4 MG 7.62 mm

Fairchild C-123 Provider

Twin-engine shoulder-wing transport aircraft (maiden flight prototype 14.10.1949); later, between 1955 and 1968, fitted with two additional jet engines and renamed the C-123 K. A total of 320 units were built and in service from 1955 to 1979; uses included as a rescue aircraft for the Coast Guard.

Type: Fairchild C-123
Country of origin: USA
Use: transport aircraft
Wingspan: 33.53 m
Length: 23.09 m
Powered by: 2 Pratt & Whitney R-2800-99W, each 1864 kW (2534 hp)

Max. take-off weight: 27,240 kg
Maximum speed: 245 mph
Range: 2100 miles
Ceiling: 7300 m
Crew: 2
Load: 13,000 kg or 62 people

General Aircraft Hamilcar

Unmotorised transport glider, shoulder wing with landing-gear struts (maiden flight prototype 27.3.1942). The Hamilcar was designed as a vehicle and freight transporter with the capacity for a small 7-tonne tank or two Jeeps, specifically for the Normandy Landings. On D-Day alone, around 70 of the total of 412 units produced were used. Some were fitted with two Bristol Mercury 31 engines as an aid to take-off.

Type: General Aircraft GAL 49
Country of origin: Great Britain
Use: freight-carrying glider
Wingspan: 33.53 m
Length: 20.73 m
Max. take-off weight: 16,329 kg
Maximum speed: 150 mph
Range: up to 1680 miles
Crew: 2
Load: 40 people or 8000 kg freight

Junkers Ju 52

Triple-engine cantilevered low-wing all-metal transport aircraft. In addition to the civilian version, military versions of the Ju 52 were already produced and in use before the outbreak of World War II. They were used in the Spanish Civil War of 1936–1939 by the Legion Condor as auxiliary bombers and fighters for night-time operations. They were fitted out with MG stands and racks for dispatching 1500 kg bombs. The Ju 52 formed the backbone of the German Luftwaffe's transport fleet in World War II.

Type: Junkers Ju 52/3m g53
Country of origin: Germany
Use: transport aircraft
Wingspan: 29.95 m
Length: 19.90 m

Powered by: 3 BMW 132 T, each 610 kW (830 hp)
Max. take-off weight: 10,500 kg
Maximum speed: 190 mph
Range: 810 miles
Ceiling: 5500 m
Crew: 3
Weaponry: 1 MG 13 mm (cockpit), 2 MG 7.92 mm in the side windows

Junkers Ju 352

Triple-engine transport aircraft, can-tilevered low wing in a combination of materials, which was necessary because of the lack of strategic raw materials such as aluminium (maiden flight 1.10.1943). By the time a halt was called to the produc-tion of multi-engine aircraft in the autumn of 1944, 44 aircraft had been completed; most of them flew in the wide-span trans-port group of the Air Fleet Reich.

Type: Junkers Ju 352
Country of origin: Germany
Use: transport aircraft
Wingspan: 34.21 m
Length: 24.60 m
Powered by: 3 Bramo 323B-2, each 735 kW (1000 hp)

Max. take-off weight: 19,600 kg
Cruising speed: 150 mph
Range: 1055 miles
Ceiling: 6000 m
Crew: 3
Weaponry: 2 MG 151/20 in a dorsal turret

Junkers Ju 290

Four-engine transport aircraft, can-tilevered low wing with double lateral tail units (maiden flight 16.7.1942). The air-craft was a further development of the civilian Ju 90 for military purposes; the first units were already used for air sup-plies to Stalingrad. The A-5 series aircraft were used as long-range maritime and reconnaissance aircraft and fitted with jet-tison weapons.

Type: Junkers Ju 290 A-5
Country of origin: Germany
Use: transport aircraft, maritime reconnaissance
Wingspan: 42.00 m
Length: 28.64 m
Powered by: 4 BMW 801 D-2, each 1250 kW (1700 hp) take-off power
Max. take-off weight: 44,970 kg
Cruising speed: 225 mph
Range: 3820 miles
Ceiling: 6010 m
Crew: 5-6
Weaponry: 2 dorsal turrets with MG 151, 1 MG 151 in the rear, 2 in side windows, 1 in the front under the nose

Kawasaki C-1

Twin-jet high-wing transport aircraft with swept wings and a T-rudder (maiden flight 12.11.1970). The aircraft were intended to replace the obsolete Curtiss C-46 of the Japanese self-defence forces. Bulky items were loaded through a rear ramp.

Type: Kawasaki C-1A
Country of origin: Japan
Use: transport aircraft
Wingspan: 30.60 m
Length: 29.00 m
Powered by: 2 Pratt & Whitney JT8D-9, each 64.5 kN (7580 kp) thrust
Max. take-off weight: 45,000 kg
Cruising speed: 425 mph
Range: 2080 miles
Ceiling: 12,000 m
Crew: 5
Load: 60 soldiers with all their equipment or 45 paratroopers (max. 11,900 kg)

Lisunov Li-2

Twin-engine low-wing transport aircraft; Soviet licence-built version (since 1938) of the Douglas DC-3. Military versions built in series after 1943. As well as performing transport operations, the Li-2VV (Vojenny Variant) was used as a front bomber.

Type: Lisunov Li-2WW
Country of origin: Soviet Union
Use: transport aircraft
Wingspan: 28.83 m
Length: 19.65 m
Powered by: 2 M-62IR, each 735 kW (1000 hp)

Max. take-off weight: 1535 kg
Maximum speed: 168 mph
Range: 1615 miles
Ceiling: 5600 m
Crew: 1–2
Weaponry: 3 MG 7.62 mm, 1 MG 12.7 mm, 1000–2000 kg bombs or missiles

Lockheed C-130 Hercules

Four-engine transport aircraft (maiden flight prototype 23.8.1954). With over 40 versions (apart from transport, it was used as a tanker, for sea rescue, as a weather and patrol aircraft and for flying fire services), it is one of the most built and most versatile aircraft in the world.

Type: Lockheed C-130 H
Country of origin: USA
Use: transport aircraft
Wingspan: 40.40 m
Length: 29.80 m
Powered by: 4 Allison T56-A-15 propeller turbines with turbo charger, each 3160 kW (4300 hp)

Max. take-off weight: 79,380 kg
Maximum speed: 385 mph
Range: 5045 miles
Ceiling: 8070 m
Crew: 5
Load: 19,350 kg freight or 128 soldiers with equipment/92 paratroopers

Lockheed AC-130

Four-engine fighter aircraft, weapon platform based on the C-130. The transport aircraft were fitted with Minigun machine guns and multi-barrel cannons in order to circuit their targets and fight 'broadsides'.

Type: Lockheed AC-130A
Country of origin: USA
Use: transport aircraft, Gunship
Wingspan: 40.41 m
Length: 29.79 m
Powered by: 4 Allison T56-A-7, each 3020 kW
Max. take-off weight: 70,300 kg
Cruising speed: 365 mph
Range: 1490 miles
Ceiling: 7570 m
Crew: 13
Weaponry: 2 MK 40 mm, 2 MK 20 mm, 4 MG 7.62 mm Minigun (grenade thrower 105 mm on AC-130H, 25 mm gun on AC-130U)

Lockheed C-141 Starlifter

Four-jet transport aircraft (maiden flight 17.12.1963); intended to replace the Douglas DC-124. Bulky items could be loaded via a rear ramp, which could also be used by paratroopers and for freight when the aircraft was airborne. The load capacity of the C-141B (1977) was increased to 42 tonnes.

Type: Lockheed C-141A
Country of origin: USA
Use: transport aircraft
Wingspan: 48.80 m
Length: 44.20 m
Powered by: 4 Pratt & Whitney TF-33P7 mit je 91 kN (9280 kp) Schub
Max. take-off weight: 143,600 kg
Maximum speed: 570 mph
Range: 4080 miles
Ceiling: 10,970 m
Crew: 5
Load: 28,800 kg freight or 155 soldiers with equipment/123 paratroopers/80 stretchers

Lockheed C-5 Galaxy

Four-jet cantilevered shoulder-wing transport aircraft with a T-rudder (maiden flight prototype 30.6.1968); the biggest aircraft in the world until 1982. The cell has two decks that can be used for passengers or freight or a combination of both. Construction was halted in 1972 after eight trial versions and 81 series aircraft. The C-5B with its improved wing unit and avionics, first appeared in 1985 (maiden flight 10.9.1985). Remaining A-series aircraft were refitted with the new wing units.

Type: Lockheed C-5B
Country of origin: USA
Use: transport aircraft
Wingspan: 67.90 m
Length: 75.50 m
Max. take-off weight: 380,000 kg
Powered by: 4 General Electric TF39-GE-1C, each 195 kN (19,880 kp)

Cruising speed: 540 mph
Range: 3730–5970 miles
Ceiling: 11,000 m
Crew: 6
Load: 131,000 kg or 345 soldiers with equipment

Messerschmitt Me 321 Gigant

Unmotorised transport glider, strut braced shoulder wing (maiden flight March 1941). The aircraft was developed in anticipation of operation Sea Lion, the planned invasion of Great Britain, in 1940. It could hold a P IV tank or 200 soldiers with their equipment. As there were initially no suitable towing aircraft, the Me 321 was towed by three Messerschmitt Bf 110 aircraft; if one of the three towing aircraft had a problem on take-off, the whole thing was at risk of crashing. Later, the specially constructed He-111 Z towing aircraft was used.

Type: Messerschmitt Me 321
Country of origin: Germany
Use: freight-carrying glider
Wingspan: 55.00 m
Length: 28.15 m
Max. take-off weight: 34,400 kg
Cruising speed: 110 mph
Crew: 3
Weaponry: 2–4 MG 15

Nord Aviation N 2501 Noratlas

Twin-engine cantilevered high-wing transport aircraft with double tail unit (maiden flight 30.11.1950). The aircraft was intended to replace the Douglas C-47. Thanks to the size of rear tailboard, even large, bulky items could be transported. The Noratlas was used by the air forces of many countries, including as a combat zone transporter and for dropping paratroopers.

Type: Nord Aviation N 2501
Country of origin: France
Use: transport aircraft
Wingspan: 32.50 m
Length: 21.96 m
Powered by: 2 SNECMA Hercules 730, each 1500 kW (2040 hp)
Max. take-off weight: 22,000 kg
Maximum speed: 275 mph
Range: 1555 miles
Ceiling: 7500 m
Crew: 5
Load: 45 passengers or 8458 kg freight

Transall C-160

Twin-engine high-wing military transport aircraft (maiden flight 25.2.1963). The Transall – developed as a Franco–German joint project – has been in service since 1968, much longer than originally planned. Throughout this time, there have been many upgrades and reinforcements. The Transall is to be replaced by the Airbus A400M in 2010.

Type: Transall C-160
Country of origin: Germany, France
Use: transport aircraft
Wingspan: 40.00 m
Length: 32.40 m
Powered by: 2 Rolls-Royce Tyne 20 MK 22, each 4222 kW (5740 hp)
Max. take-off weight: 49,150 kg
Maximum speed: approx. 320 mph
Range: max. 1150 miles
Ceiling: 8230 m
Crew: 5
Load: 16,000 kg or max. 96 people

Index

Glossary

General Aviation (GA) – civilian, generally private air travel (private and commercial flights including SAR helicopters etc.); all civilian air traffic with the exception of scheduled and charter travel by airlines. Includes flight movements that are carried out visually and to the rules of instrument flying, in controlled and uncontrolled air space. Based on the number of aircraft and flight movements (but not the number of passengers or amount of freight), general aviation is the largest sector in civil aviation.

APU – Auxiliary Power Unit = supply unit that usually provides electric power and if required also compressed air or hydraulic pressure for the independent operation of the aircraft's equipment on the ground without the need for the main engines to be in operation.

ATPL-Licence – abbreviation for Airline Transport Pilot's Licence. In the UK, the ATPL is issued by the Civil Aviation Authority and allows the holder to fly aeroplanes and helicopters commercially as a responsible pilot.

BOAC – British Overseas Airways Corporation. Airline that was established in 1937 and which merged with British European Airways in 1974 to create British Airways.

Canards – also known as 'duck wings', or a 'duck' aircraft (based on the French word for

duck), on which the stabiliser is ahead of the main lifting surfaces rather than behind them, as on a conventional aircraft, or where there is an additional small set of wings in front of the main lifting surface.

Cobra manoeuvre – vertical alignment of the nose in vertical ascent with a sudden increase in air resistance; the aircraft is momentarily "upright" in the air before returning to normal horizontal flight; it does not roll or yaw in either direction.

ECM – abbreviation for Electronic Counter Measures; a subsection of electronic warfare which uses the electromagnetic spectrum to prevent, stop or trick an opponent.

EFIS – abbreviation for Electronic Flight Instrument System.

EICAS – abbreviation for Engine Indication and Crew Alerting System; electronic system that is used to monitor the engines.

FAA – abbreviation for Federal Aviation Administration, the aviation authority of the USA.

FAI – Fédération Aéronautique Internationale, international non-state and non-commercial organisation for aviation and space travel that records and checks record performances.

Glascockpit – common name for an electronic flight information system where the displays are shown on screens (hence the name).

High-wing – an aircraft on which the wings are positioned at the top of the body.

Hydrogen power – fuel alternative to kerosene. In 1957, trials were run on a Martin B-57 with hydrogen as fuel.

ICAO – International Civil Aviation Organisation, based in Montreal and founded in 1944 as the result of agreements on international civil aviation.

IFR – flying an aircraft in accordance with Instrument Flight Rules.

Lichtenstein radar – radar system used by German night bombers in WWII after 1942.

Low-wing – an aircraft on which the wings are positioned on the underside of the body.

Mid-wing – an aircraft on which the wings are positioned in the middle of the body.

NVA – abbreviation for 'Nationale Volksarmee'; the armed forces of the GDR (1956–1990).

Parasol high-wing – aircraft on which the wing is over the pilot's seat, like a canopy.

RAF – the Royal Air Force of Great Britain. As well as the RAF, the Royal Navy (Fleet Air Arm) and the Army also have aircraft.

RLM – abbreviation for Reichsluftfahrtministerium (Reich Air Ministry), 1933–1945 government department in charge of matters concerning civilian and military aviation in Germany.

SAR – abbreviation for the Search and Rescue service at sea and in the air.

Schräge Musik – pilot's jargon: schräg = angled, Musik = music; name given to the installations of upward-firing (65° to 80°) 20- or 30-mm cannon mounted in German twin-engine night fighters in WWII. They were used to attack British bombers from below, outside the crew's field of vision.

Shoulder-wing – is the name of an aircraft on which the wings are positioned below the pilot's line of sight, but above the body.

STOL – abbreviation for Short Take-off and Landing.

STOVL – abbreviation for Short Take-off and Vertical Landing.

TNT – abbreviation for trinitrotoluol, an explosive material that is the standard measure of strength of explosives (the TNT equivalent).

Transition – the crossover from vertical to horizontal flight and vice versa in aircraft that take-off and/or land vertically.

USAAC – United States Army Air Corps, name of the USAF 1926–1941.

USAAF – United States Army Air Force, name of the USAF 1941–1947.

USAF – United States Air Force, the air forces of the USA. As well as the USAF, the Navy, Army, Marine Corps, Coast Guard and National Guard had significant fleets of aeroplanes and helicopters.

VSTOL – abbreviation for Vertical Short Take-off and Landing.

VTOL – abbreviation for Vertical Take-off and Landing.

Warsaw Agreement – military alliance between Communist countries under the leaderdership of the Soviet Union (1955-1991); also called the Warsaw Pact in the West.

WHP – wave hp: the performance of a propeller or fuel turbine measured on the wave; the residual thrust is not taken into account.

Literature and websites

Angelucci, Enzo: The World Encyclopedia of Military Aircraft, 1981
Angelucci, Enzo, Paulo Matricardi and Pierluigi Pinto: Complete Book of World War II Combat Aircraft, 2001
Austen, Michael: Jet Airlines of the World, 1949-2001, 2001
Barker, Ralph: Epic of Flight: The RAF at War, 1981
Bowen, Ezra: Epic of Flight: Knights of the Air, 1980
Crosby, Francis: The World Encyclopedia of Fighters and Bombers, 2006
Endres, Günter and Mike Gething: Aircraft Recognition Guide (Jane's Recognition Guide), 2007
Gibbs, Lynne and Neil Morris: Mega Book of Aircraft (Mega books), 2004
Grant, R. G.: Flight: 100 Years of Aviation, 2007
Green, William: Modern Commercial Aircraft, 1998
Gunston, Bill: World Encyclopedia of Aircraft Manufacturers: From the Pioneers to the Present Day, 2005
Jackson, Robert: Encyclopedia of Aircraft: over 3000 Military and Civil Aircraft from the Wright Flyer to the Stealth Bomber, 2004
Jarrett, Phillip: Ultimate Aircraft, 2000
Miller, Russell: The Soviet Airforce, 1983
Munson, Kenneth: Bombers between the wars, 1919-39: Including Patrol and Transport Aircraft, 1970
Niccoli, Riccardo: History of Flight (from Technique to Adventure), 2007
Reynolds, Clark G.: Epic of Flight: The Carrier War, 1982
Rolfe, Douglas and Alexis Dawydoff: Airplanes of the World, 1982
Sanger, Ray: Blériot in Britain 1899-1927
Sharpe, Michael: Attack and Interceptor Jets, 1999

Walker, Bryce: Epic of Flight: Fighting Jets, 1983
Walker, Timothy and Scott Henderson: The First Jet Airliner: The Story of the De Havilland Comet, 2007
Winchester, Jim: Military Aircraft: 1914 to the Present Day, 2007

http://jnpassieux.chez-alice.fr/html/AirEspace.php
http://koi.legion.wplus.net/guide/air/index.shtml
http://wikipedia.org
http://www.af.mil
http://www.globalaircraft.org
http://www.airliners.net/aircraft-data/
http://www.airwar.ru
http://www.aviafrance.com
http://www.bredow-web.de
http://www.globalaircraft.org
http://www.heliport.de/heliport.html
http://www.jetfighters.dk
http://www.warbirdalley.com

Picture credits

AERO Vodochody a.U Letiste, Czech Republic: 21 b.
AeroAuctioneer, Neufra/Riedlingen: 103 b. l.
Airbus S.A.S., Cesson Sévigné, France: 5 8th picture from top, 15, 26 c., 27 t., 234/235, 236 b.
AirNikon, airliners.net: 21 t., 198 c.
Airport Brussels, Belgium: 99 b.
Airport Journals, Main, U.S.A.: 76 t.
AirTran Airways, airtran.com: 44 b. andishangar.com: 159 t., 200 c.
Archiv Fred Müller-Romminger, Bad Reichenhall: 151 t.
Archiv-Fliegerrevue, Berlin: 32 b., 36 t., 36 b., 60 t.
Olaf Bichel, Munich: 197 t., 197 b., 242 t.
Bildarchiv AirKraft, Mainz: 5 7th picture from top, 8, 9 l., 31 t., 33 b., 39 b., 40 t., 41 c., 47 b. l., 51 t., 52 b., 53 t., 55 b., 57 t., 58 t., 68 t., 69 t., 72 t., 85 b. l., 88 c., 88 b., 98 t., 115 t., 115 b., 118 t., 120 t., 127 b., 128 t., 128 b., 129 b., 149 t., 171 b., 187 c., 201 t., 207 t., 210 t., 213 t., 215 b., 216/217, 218, 220 t., 220 b., 223 b. r., 224 b., 225 t., 227 b., 233 b.
Detlef Billig, Berlin: 28 b., 30 b., 35 b., 48 b., 54 t., 68 t., 84 b., 88 t., 177 t. r.
boeing.com, U.S.A.: 45 b.
Bombardier Inc. Aircraft, Douglas, Canada: 46 b., 47 t., 49 b., 77 t., 77 b.
Boulton Paul Association, United Kingdom: 171 c.
Nico Braas, Almere-Buiten, Netherlands: 99 t., 111 b., 119 t., 124 t., 125 t., 140 c., 146 b., 148 t., 148 b., 177 b., 180 c., 186 b., 190 b., 200 c., 219 t., 220 c., 225 b., 243 t., 246 t., 247 t., 251 t.
Antonio Camarasa, airliners.net: 90 t.
Michael Carter, airliners.net: 123 t.
Dassault Falcon Jet Corp., South Hackensack, U.S.A.: 52 t.
Deutsches Wehrkundearchiv, Herford: 11 l., 11 t. r., 11 b., 28 t., 34 t., 34 c., 38 c., 38 b., 63 c., 63 b., 64 t., 64 b., 69 b., 73 b., 83 t., 95 b., 105 b., 106 t., 114 t., 114 b., 121 t., 121 b., 122 b., 127 t., 132 t., 133 t., 133 b., 136 t., 136 c., 140 t., 146 c., 147 t., 147 b., 150 t., 150 c., 154 t., 158 t., 158 b., 160 c., 160 b., 164 t., 165 b., 169 t., 169 c., 169 b., 170 b., 182 b., 187 t., 191 t., 196 b., 202 t., 209 b., 219 c., 219 b., 221 b., 225 c., 232 t.
Frank Doering, flugzeugbilder.de: 48 t.
Paul Dopson, airliners.net: 30 t.
Ralph Duenas, airlinespotters: 21 c.
Ron Dupas, 1000aircraftphotos.com: 140 b., 144 b., 146 t., 181 b., 194 t.
Dutch Airforce, Netherlands: 102 t.
EADS Deutschland GmbH, Munich: 60 b.
edcotescollection.com, photo: courtesy of Geoff Goodall: 105 c.
EL AL-Airlines,elal.co.il: 44 c.
Embraer S.A., São José dos Campos, Brazil: 61 t., 61 c., 61 b., 62 t., 62 b., 63 t.
Leonid Faerberg, airliners.net: 117 t.
Federal Aviation Administration Fairbanks ATCT, Alaska, U.S.A.: 152 b.
Richard Ferriere, airliners.net: 90 b.
Finist Air, Guipavas, France: 50 t.
Flap International, Brazil: 25 b. l.
Flughafen Dresden GmbH, Dresden: 20
Flugzeugbau Rolf Helmrich, Großpösna: 98 b.

Foto Galerie Koninklijke Marine, The Hague, Netherlands: 223 t.
Photographer unknown: 144 c.
Stephen Galea, jetpilot.dk: 13 l., 101 b., 143 t., 184 t., 188 b., 193 b., 198 b., 240 b.
Bob Garrard, airliners.net: 51 b., 82 t., 83 b.
Jordi Grife, airliners.net: 46 t.
U. Grüschow, Berlin: 133 c., 143 b., 212 b., 237 t.
Gulfstream Aerospace Corporation, Dallas/Texas, U.S.A.: 66 b., 67 t.
Gareth Hector, hyperscale.com: 187 b. Hans Rolink, Scheemda, Netherlands: 84 t.
Werner Horvath, airliners.net: 139 t., 173 t., 177 t. l., 179 b., 180 b., 186 t., 237 b.
Richard Hunt, airliners.net: 120 b.
Ilyushin Aircraft, Moscow, Russia: 227 t. l.
Interlake International Pilot Training, Manitoba, Canada: 86 t.
iwmcollectionsmorg.uk: 202 b. r.
JSADF, Japan: 232 b.
Junkers Bildarchiv, S+P Media AG, Munich: 73 t., 72 b., 105 t., 228 t.
Stefan Kessler, airliners.net: 106 t.
Eberhard Kirschner, Glattbrugg, Switzerland: 190 t., 199 t., 211 t., 212 t., 241 b. l., 245 b., 251 c.
Kogo, wikipedia.org: 107 t.
Manfred Kretzschmar, Berlin: 38 t.
W.T. Larkins, 1000aircraftphotos.com: 125 c.
D. Lausberg, jetphotos.de: 238 b., 241 t., 249 t., 250 b., 251 b.
Phil Lee of First Air, U.S.A.: 34 b.
Ruud Leeuw, ruudleeuw.com: 70 t.
Joachim Lippl, airliners.net: 109 b.
Brian Lockett, Goleta Air & Space Museum, U.S.A.: 226 t.
luftarchiv.de: 39 t.
Lufthansa-Archiv, Frankfurt: 14, 41 b., 42 t., 43 b., 49 c., 74 t., 75 b. l.
Chris Makerson, airliners.net: 123 b.
Rolf Manteufel, www.planeboys.de: 27 b.
Alfredo la Marca, airliners.net: 119 b. r.
Andy Martin, jetphotos.net: 49 t.
Jean Martorell, airliners.net: 119 b. l.
Frank Mink, airliners.net: 5 3rd picture from top, 96/97
Mitteldeutscher Rundfunk, Leipzig: 102 b.
Motivschmiede, Kassel: 9 r., 56 t., 74 b., 75 t., 79 t., 100 t., 125 t., 188 t.
Darren Mottram, airliners.net: 54 b. r.
NASA, Washington DC, U.S.A.: 13 r., 16, 17, 139 b., 226 b.
U. Noble, United Kingdom Flying Displays and Museum, United Kingdom: 144 t.
Grzesiek Okruszek, airliners.net: 110 t.
Old Rhinebeck Aerodrome, Rhinebeck/NY, U.S.A.: 100 c.
PAN-AM Airlines History, U.S.A.: 40 b., 41 t.
Den Pascoe, airliners.net: 126 t.
Yevgeny Pashin, airliners.net: 117 b.
Pegase.tv, La Haye Fouassière, France: 79 b.
Adrian Pingstone, airliners.net: 95 t., 164 b.
Gerhard Plomitzer, airliners.net: 33 t., 47 b. r., 53 b., 54 b. r., 67 b., 81 t., 94 t., 94 b., 95 c., 138 b., 142 c., 145 b., 151 b., 159 b., 170 t., 174 b., 175 b., 176 t., 176 b., 178 t., 178 c., 178 b., 179 t., 180 t., 183 b., 185 t., 185 b., 189 b., 192 t., 193 t., 195 b. l., 196 t., 199 t., 200 t., 205 t., 206 b., 209 t., 215 t., 223 b. l., 227 t. r., 230 t., 230 b., 239 t., 246 b., 250 t.

Polskie Zaklady Lodnice Sp.z.o.o., Mielec, Poland: 87 b. r.
Pressestelle Berliner Flughäfen: 12
Pressestelle Berliner Flughäfen, photo: G. Wicker: 5 2nd picture from top, 18/19
Pressestelle Berliner Flughäfen, photo: L. Schönfeld: 10 r., 43 t., 43 c., 50 b., 56 c., 70 b., 78 b. l., 80 b., 82 c., 122 t.
Fred Quackenbusch, airliners.net: 124 b.
Patrick Ranfranz, charleslindbergh.com, U.S.A.: 111 t.
Raytheon Company, Waltham, U.S.A.: 36 c.
Sergey Riabsev, airliners.net: 87 t.
Ian Robertson, airliners.net: 202 b. l.
Royal Air Force (RAF) Museum, United Kingdom: 132 b., 158 c.
Russian Aircraft Corporation MiG, Moscow, Russia: 189 t., 200 t.
Russian Aviation Museum, Moscow, Russia: 75 b. r., 91 t., 91 b., 104 b., 116 b., 149 c., 154 b., 156 b., 191 b., 198 t.
Saab AB, Photographer: Ingemar Thuresson, Sweden: 207 b.
saab-club.com: 157 b.
Jerry Search, airliners.net: 126 b.
Sukhoi Company (JSC), Moscow, Russia: 89 t., 89 b.
The Beijing Aviation Museum, China: 116 t.
Thorbjörn Brunander Sund, Danish Aviation Photo, airliners.net: 110 b.
Peter Tonna, airliners.net: 78 b. r.
Michael Traynor, Iona National Airways, Ireland: 50 c.
Tupolev Aviation, Moscow, Russia: 93 b.
UK Flying Displays and Museum, airmuseumsuk.org: 107 b.
United States Air Force (USAF), U.S.A.: 5 5th picture from top, 6th picture from top, 10 l., 129 b., 239 b., 130/131, 134 t., 134 b., 135 t., 135 b., 136 b., 137 t., 137 b., 138 t., 141 t., 141 b., 142 t., 142 b., 150 b., 152 t., 153 t., 153 b., 155 b., 156 t., 165 t., 166/167, 170 c., 171 t., 173 b., 174 t., 174 c., 181 t., 182 t., 183 t., 192 b., 194 b., 195 t., 203 t., 203 c., 203 b., 204 t., 204 b., 206 t., 206 c., 214 b., 222 t., 222 b., 224 t., 224 c., 228 b., 229 t., 229 b., 231 t., 231 b., 240 t., 241 b. r., 242 b., 243 b., 244 t., 244 b., 245 t., 247 b., 249 b.
U.S. Navy, Washington DC, U.S.A.: 145 t., 172 t., 184 b.
Norm Vargas, aerocon@earthlink.net: 80 o. vespa.dk: 108 t.
Christian Waser, Horw, Switzerland: 5 1st picture from top, 4th picture from top, 6/7, 22 t., 22 b., 23 t., 23 c., 23 b., 24 t., 24 b., 25 t., 25 b. r., 26 t., 26 b., 29 t. l., 29 t. r., 29 b., 31 b., 32 t., 35 t., 37 t., 37 b., 42 t., 44 t., 45 t., 48 c., 55 t., 56 b., 57 b., 58 c., 58 t., 59 t., 59 b., 65 t., 65 b., 66 t., 66 c., 70 c., 71 t., 71 b., 76 b., 78 t., 81 b., 82 b., 85 t., 85 b. r., 86 b., 87 b. l., 92 t., 92 c., 92 b., 93 t., 93 c., 94 c., 100 b., 101 t., 103 b. r., 104 t., 108 c., 108 b., 109 t., 111 c., 112/113, 149 b., 155 t., 156 c., 157 t., 160 t., 161 t., 161 b., 162 t., 162 b., 163 t., 163 b., 168 t., 168 b., 172 b.
Gordon S. Williams from the collection of W. T. Larkins, ronsarchive.com: 118 b.
Russell Williams, russellw.com: 103 t.
Andreas Zeitler, Munich: 175 t., 189 c., 201 b., 211 b., 221 t., 248 t.